LOST PLACES

Advance Praise

From one of the keenest observers of sign and symbols comes a collection of personal, meditative, graceful, philosophical, and puncturing essays that uncover the manifestations of the otherworldly that reside in the ordinary spaces of life. Nothing is as it might seem. These essays show us how to both beware and be attentive. From the trivial to the insurmountable, Cathryn Hankla rummages deep to unpack what is left after emotional and physical losses and relocations. She reaches outward to a vast variety of subjects in order to pull the world inward only to give it all back again. *Lost Places* is infused with poetry as only Cathryn Hankla can write it.

—Jenny Boully, author of *Betwixt-and-Between* and *The Body*

How do we define *home*? That central question, and the questing for answers, weaves through this collection (*or is it a memoir?*) that radiates like desert stars pouring over us "a river of endless sparkling water." And though this book explores the philosophical landscape with great insight, it never shies from journeying through the emotional and literal landscapes, the homes lost, the homes found. Books, too, serve as homes, as Hankla writes, "Sometimes…I'm most at home in books, writing or reading. I finish one, fold my tipi, and start another." This book ranges widely, delves deeply, and always comes up to the light of understanding. The language, the structure of each piece—all is brilliant. From a riff on buttons to nuanced juxtapositions that bounce into richer and richer associations, there for the reader to make. Each piece is underlain with love and loss and desire, a chocolate-covered coffee bean, the sweet and bitter just right to savor and make you want more.

—Jim Minick, author of *Fire Is Your Water* and *The Blueberry Years*

In essays erudite and deeply compassionate, Cathryn Hankla writes of the end of a love affair, but more importantly of the spaces left behind. Whether those spaces are pueblos or labyrinths, kivas or canyons, or our own psyches, Hankla reminds us that landscapes—fluid as gender and language and desire—hold memory. *Lost Places* is a fabric of memories diverse as wild orchids, moon boots, or the elliptical eyes of a snake, all a reminder that it is possible to reclaim the broken places and shoot them through with light.

—Karen McElmurray, author of *Surrendered Child*
and coeditor of *Walk Till the Dogs Get Mean*

A lot of fine memoirs and biographies cross my desk but none quite like Cathryn Hankla's amazing *Lost Places*. With her poet's eye and a scientist's keen instinct for inquiry, Hankla leads readers on a beautiful Magical Mystery Tour of worlds both seen and unseen, personally touching something elemental and eternal in us all—a longing for one's true home. By turns heartbreaking, illuminating, and fiercely brave, Hankla's *Lost Places* is a book to savor and be read slowly, dwelled with and inspired by—a stunning meditation on what it means to be a human shaped by nature and memory. "I am here to testify to the miraculous," she writes at one point, nicely summing up her own gem of a book.

—James Dodson, author of *Final Rounds* and *Faithful Travelers*

In her graceful, openhearted style, Cathryn Hankla invites us along on her life journey—her far-flung expeditions, spiritual quests, quiet moments of joy, longings, grievous losses, and optimism about tomorrow. This evocative memoir is a stimulating narrative of ideas as Hankla engages readers in questions about gender, race, history, nature, and the meanings of home. One finishes *Lost Places* wanting more, ready to get in her car for another next adventure with this lively, provocative companion.

—Valerie Miner, author of *The Low Road* and *Traveling with Spirits*

Engaging, funny, associative, and smart, Cathryn Hankla's *Lost Places* is the best book I know on the subject of home, in that it doesn't restrict its concerns to floorboards and beams, but opens its doors to animals, the body, God, sex, language, and something even rarer: the intimacy of entering a human mind at work.

—Paul Lisicky, author of *The Narrow Door* and *Unbuilt Projects*

MERCER UNIVERSITY PRESS

Endowed by

TOM WATSON BROWN
and
THE WATSON-BROWN FOUNDATION, INC.

LOST PLACES

On Losing and Finding Home

To Mary
Great writer
but more
than that
great person - I'm
so glad to be
in the same
place with
you !

CATHRYN HANKLA

Cathy Hankla

MERCER UNIVERSITY PRESS | *Macon, Georgia* | 2018

MUP/ P558

© 2018 Cathryn Hankla
Published by Mercer University Press
1501 Mercer University Drive
Macon, Georgia 31207

9 8 7 6 5 4 3 2 1

ISBN   978-0-88146-6485
Cataloging-in-Publication Data is available from the Library of Congress

Printed in Canada

Contents

1. The Final Frontier | 1

2. Cleaning Out the House | 13

3. My Life in Snakes | 27

4. Neighborhood of Desire | 41

5. Spirit House | 53

6. Dream House | 71

7. God's Eyebrow | 95

8. Place as Language | 107

9. Scarlet Tanager | 117

10. Natural Disasters | 131

11. Lost Places | 149

12. The Gorilla | 193

13. Invisible Cities | 203

14. Hole through which the Power Could Come | 221

15. The Indispensable Condition | 235

Chapter Notes and Sources | 259

In memory of my mother, Joyce Burnette Hankla (1918–2016),

one of the great readers of her time and my greatest supporter in life and art.

"An artist transforms."
　　　　—William Goyen, *Had I a Hundred Mouths*

Houses rise and fall, crumble, are extended,
Are removed, destroyed, restored, or in their place
Is an open field, or a factory, or a by-pass.
Old stone to new building, old timber to new fires,
Old fires to ashes, and ashes to the earth...
　　　　—T. S. Eliot, "East Coker," *Four Quartets*

"Same as it ever was..."
　　　　—Talking Heads, "Once in a Lifetime"

LOST PLACES

The Final Frontier

When first married, I wanted to move to the country, and following a brief period of house hunting we bought the house across the street overlooking my husband's old house. This can be debated, but of course it was a mistake, satisfying neither the urge to move nor the spirit of staying put. After ten years in that suburban house, I had to live in the countryside, in proximity to wildlife and the natural world of rocks, trees, and mountains in order for my inner life to find sanctuary. My urgency might have been a holdover dream from childhood: Don't fence me in, or at least stop looking at me. It might have stemmed from my many summers spent at a rustic YWCA camp where the only entertainments were nightly campfire songs and a frigid spring-fed swimming pool so achingly cold that it neutered the sexes. Perhaps I wanted relief from the state of metaxis, between-ness, neither this nor that-ness in which I found myself after divorce, which meant I was visibly a sexual person again but with no stated mooring. In marriage, my bisexuality, my queerness, while no secret to me or to my mate, had been obscured by a set of unchallenged assumptions others clutched and projected. Now, they would annoy me with a different set.

For me to relocate my interiority or myself, I needed space around me, more distance from other houses and lives. In fact, I did not want to be able to see a single house from my own. I knew I needed to go inward, and doing this required removal from anything that might impose, from everything that wasn't a presiding red oak or a tulip poplar, a wild orchid known as a pink lady slipper, a bobwhite wobbling along the forest fringe in a single feather headdress, giant slabs of Virginia bluestone, skittish deer herds, gaggles of turkeys, or bright and dull pairs of indigo buntings flitting back and forth across my country road.

I spent the days of my childhood mainly out of doors, wandering in every conceivable sort of weather, riding bikes, hiking in circles, digging holes, or poking around on the forest floor. My friends and I developed a precursor of contemporary outdoor gear for riding bikes in the cold. It's hard to imagine a world without so many forms of technical clothing, but my childhood predates even mass-produced running shoes. We wore Keds or Red Ball Jets with sawed-off jeans over heavy dance tights whose raised seams squeezed our toes into cones; two layers of turtlenecks topped by a sweatshirt; a stocking cap and riding gloves created by lopping off knitted digits or repurposing frayed gloves. Of course, we had never seen a bicycle helmet. Adults inside, children out. The larger world was ours.

My compatriots and I developed the art of getting lost from morning to dusk, with occasional little sisters and brothers tagging along, sticks and rocks our confidants. I think we looked long enough at tadpoles that we saw the big-headed, soft-bellied amphibians hatch from gooey eggs and become swimmers. As they grew legs and shrank tails, turning into frogs, we were standing there watching. Sometimes I took them home in buckets to follow their transformations more carefully. I needed to see how change was done in a mud puddle or a bucket. Maybe I developed skills for quelling boredom or for never being bored, the slow art of *turtling* through life while making room for imagination. Staring into space is a pleasant occupation that can lead anywhere.

In moving to the countryside in my thirties after divorce, I wanted to reclaim something from those prepubescent years before the world was wander-proofed, back when children were not so fussed over but instead left free to ramble and rumble, invention in the moment their sole field guide. Our band of Peter Pans set out to explore the neighborhood and the wild surrounds beyond backyard fences and sidewalks. What was I mastering while wandering? Nothing I could document for a focus group—and no one cared. No parent would have thought to monitor or direct my snaking bike routes or hikes in the woods. I followed no paths, stayed on no designated greenways, and, because I was a girl before Title IX, played no organized sports throughout most of my schooling. The skills we kids were practicing remained uncharted, off the developmental grid: some of us were cantankerous or sarcastic, sometimes downright ornery as we threw rocks to express internal tumult or cried over nothing, provoking the age-old taunt of *crybaby*; a precious few maintained earnest demeanors, others were vague and spacey, giggly or called stupid, and not one of us was mood-medicated—that would come later along with years of therapy—but for a brief time we embraced the motley presence of each other as inevitable in learning to be ourselves.

Most people seem to migrate, pull up stakes, and fold their tents without looking back. They follow careers, relationships, and sometimes the landscape itself. It's probably harder than it looks or than they admit, but for me, moves are difficult and perhaps against fate. While I hold a particular fascination for nomadic tipi life, I can measure my entire route from cradle to midlife on one map of one corner of one state. I am not talking here of bouts of traveling and place affinities, even significant ones, but about where one lives. My people are buried here—some in Rural Retreat, some in Bedford beneath Smith Mountain Lake, and the rest in the city of Roanoke—and this is where I live.

I still remember the tears shed when I was eleven and my parents announced that we were leaving my hometown and moving several counties over to another small town three winding hours away by car. I was in disbelief. Move? How? It wasn't that far away, they said, but I knew it would be monumental. I had everything arranged in my room, clothes folded in drawers and hanging in the closet. My world was round and wide enough: friends' houses, their telephone numbers committed to memory (37925—we only had to dial five numbers); our house and neighborhood; the pool where I spent summer days diving and swimming; my elementary school; woods at the top of the hill beyond the water tanks; my upstairs bedroom with low bookcases lining the wall; magic rocks of lurid color grown in a wide-mouth mason jar; a collection of trolls and troll clothes I'd cut from felt; and a dime store turtle in a scummy bowl.

My parents had moved several times around the state, as my father bought and sold portions of pharmacy businesses. My mother was pregnant with me, although unaware of it, the summer they'd moved to Richlands, an Appalachian, far southwestern Virginia coal town, and up to that point it was the longest they'd stayed anywhere. They'd bounced up and down the west coast from Washington state to southern California for a couple of years during World War II. Now it was the summer my dad was turning fifty and they were moving again, regardless of the upheaval they caused me. My sister had left three years earlier for high school, and she was headed for college. A box of children's books and games I packed from my shelves chased me down the staircase and landed on top of me in a heap. One world ended and another world began. *Warp speed, Scotty.*

In a month's time I was starting sixth grade as the new kid. It wasn't as bad as I'd imagined, but it was different enough. While I had wanted to land somewhere like Mars and star in *Lost in Space*, boys fought over my attentions with promises of tennis courts and backyard swimming pools. There were very few of either; this was another small town. I didn't like our ranch house or my new friends as much as the old two-story house and my old friends perpetually smeared with dirt and moss. I couldn't find any woods to wander; every seemingly wild place or field I could reach on foot or by bike was owned by an obvious someone and posted "Keep Out."

Driving anywhere from our old town we had traveled the Wilderness Road, a winding two-lane with occasional passing zones marked by dotted lines and mountaintop pull-offs where passengers were invariably carsick. If we broke the trip we stopped at a roadside café called the Gap Restaurant and ate in a knotty pine dining room where it seemed the only fare available was country ham on white bread. To children this tasted exotically of salt and required adult-sized teeth to sufficiently chew. When we took numerous shortcuts through what would eventually be our new town, we often smelled sewage wafting from the treatment plant, and as we drove through we held our noses, glad we did not have to stop. My mother would end up living there for thirty-five years.

We left the heart of Appalachia and its boom/bust *carpe diem* mentality filled with characters, loose cannons, and parents who often partied together and consequently did not always know where their every child might be at any given moment. In compensation for the move, I got a miniature poodle with pedigree papers. As a puppy she was incredibly sweet tempered, with curly apricot-sprinkled white hair, a roly-poly sheep of a pup. But after she grew, I didn't like her as much as I had liked the series of stray cats I'd trained to my whistle in my old backyard. Almost everything I'd left behind appeared a little uncivilized, a little feral with fewer constraints. I'd never had a dog before, and they were strange creatures to me, dependent and aggravating, especially the poodle because she defended her tender ears with her teeth and her purebred eyes dripped constantly from faulty ducts. Nearing puberty, visibly growing up, with the freedoms I'd taken for granted vanishing, I demanded a shoe contraption that I think was called space or moon boots, spring-loaded platform strap-on overshoes sort of like roller skates on steroids that you walked or jumped in, simulating the weightlessness of space—or spraining your ankles. Sometimes I wore my moon boots while practicing the clarinet, and the poodle howled along. I had wanted a saxophone.

Our new county was dry with a straight-laced façade of normalcy and our town was without obvious eccentrics, except for three mentally deficient brothers from a prominent local family who roamed the streets well groomed and dressed in nice-looking clothes. We saw the brothers everywhere, and especially in church on Sunday. One of them, the oldest and brightest who went by T., scared me by doing what he did to all females indiscriminately: he draped his arm around me and announced that I was his girlfriend. *Beam me up, Scotty.*

"Space: the final frontier. These are the voyages of the starship *Enterprise*. Its five-year mission: to explore strange new worlds, to seek out new life and new civilizations, to boldly go where no man has gone before." William Shatner's fat voice ran over the *Star Trek* credits, and now, each time I hear the theme music's opening bars pitching low to high like a musical siren, it brings back shivers of anticipation. I watched the first episode of the original series and most of the following seventy-eight during the next three seasons. While my mother and I often watched *Perry Mason* together, my dad and I were Trekkies, beginning September 8, 1966. By the time the last episode aired in 1969, it was the summer we moved, I was drinking Tang because the astronauts reportedly took it to the moon, and I was finally able to make it through the show without falling asleep; it had been moved to the last slot on Friday nights, too late for most of the kid audience and airing on a night when the elite adults who also favored the show were out to dinner. There it was laid to rest until syndication revived it (a quick resuscitation).

I adored all of the early aliens. There were the gruff and crafty Klingons who were always plotting apocalypse and drank something called Mind Lager; their gnarled externalized brainy foreheads made them look like a cross between beetles and rhinos with their horns sawed off. Then there were the Gorn, the Horta, the Romulans—so close in sound to the Romans, whose ancient legends often underpinned the show's themes—and, of course, the troubling Tribbles.

It was the twenty-third century, and I was there. It was thrilling to be there.

That first season, the show aired on Thursday nights from 8:30–9:30, a little late for me, but I was allowed to stay up. Dad was an impatient TV viewer of anything but news; seldom did a dramatic or variety show hold his attention. He started watching a program only to roam the house, but with *Star Trek* he mostly held to his chair. And he was almost assured that no one would be kissing, something he seemed unable to accept on television. He'd venture to the freezer for ice cream during a commercial, but I knew he would return. Our fandom was patriotic, as the show came at a time when America launched moon missions as an exercise in national honor. The "final frontier" took our collective minds off Southeast Asia and allowed us to safely project ourselves into space through a trio of main characters and spongy-looking space rocks. As it was also a time for activism, viewers including students from M.I.T. staged a protest march and letter-writing campaign to save the show. It worked, and then it didn't, but of course they were right about the show's merits.

The highest-ranking officers aboard the *U.S.S. Enterprise* were all—surprise—pale-faced men who expressed character traits ranging from the logical/rational mixed-race human/Vulcan Spock through the humanist/scientist McCoy, the chief medical officer, to the somewhat internally tortured, intemperate but inspiring-for-all-his-flawed-humanity ship's captain, James T. Kirk. Enthralled with these three, I wrote to Burbank California for 5x7 signed glossies, which I still have. Somewhere.

Now, I have to wonder if part of my dad's interest in the show was due to the way it paralleled his Navy experience on board a small carrier in the South Pacific in WWII. *Star Trek* involved speaking the language of crew, addressing challenges to the chain of command, following orders from a higher authority far removed from the critical circumstances of the moment. A member of King Neptune's society, which meant he had crossed the equatorial line, Dad must have felt he'd been at or near the last frontier, a floating target in the middle of the ocean on his "baby flattop" escort carrier. He could have felt he had visited the equivalent of another galaxy or that he had returned as some kind of alien due to his war experiences. Fire had rained down on his ship from kamikazes late in the war; men overboard had bobbed through the night as sharks attacked. Maybe something had piggybacked with him from one galaxy to another, but he was definitely a changed man. His struggles continued for decades, as he endured hospitalizations for episodes known as nervous breakdowns. On starship *Enterprise*, the same lieutenant's post that my dad had occupied on his ship, that of chief communications officer, belonged to Lt. Uhura, a Swahili female, whose name recalls the Aboriginal sacred red rock Uluru and the Swahili word *uhuru* (freedom). Black and white, we were tuning in to this show. In a nod to futuristic multiculturalism, the writers provided us with a few women and some diversity, combining our new issues, far-flung war and the civil rights movement, with our old issue, WWII. George Takei, the actor who played

Lt. Sulu, third officer and helmsman, had been sent to an internment camp as a child in California. If my father ever referred to him as a Jap I can't recall it, although it seems more than likely.

One white woman in the next tier down of ranking officers rounded out the ship's bridge, along with Mr. Chechov, who had few speaking parts. His presence was probably supposed to teach us cooperation with the Russians, who had helped liberate Europe but now starred with us as the opposing force in the Cold War; things near and far were volatile. In my new town, people of color and palefaces worked side by side in furniture, sewing, and ammunition factories, and worshipped in the same churches. In my old hometown, I don't remember any people of color unless they were covered in coal dust or heavily suntanned. People often stared at my olive-skinned, black-haired mother in the Piggly Wiggly grocery after we'd spent a week at the beach.

Due to geographical isolation, rugged topography that precluded large-scale farming operations, and religious objections, Appalachians' legacy of slave owning was small in proportion to that of the Shenandoah Valley and eastern portions of Virginia. Most mountaineers had little sympathy with the Southern cause and a hard time deciding, as did General Lee, which side to be on. Mainstream Protestant churches split in the 1840s over slave owning. Religion was used to object to and to justify slavery. Immediately after the majority of Virginia voted to secede from the Union in 1861, the northwestern counties denounced the decision, and West Virginia began its path to separate statehood, declaring that they would not send their sons to die so that the Shenandoah Valley could own slaves. Guerrilla warfare did not cease in the hills until 1865; some of it was organized, Snake Hunters and Moccasin Rangers representing the Union and Confederate sides, but there was also opportunistic raiding. The Underground Railroad depended on free blacks, Quakers, and other religious objectors, and though you'd never guess it from today's characterization of Appalachians as more prejudiced and bigoted than the rest of the country, quilts signaled the route to freedom in the mountains and hollers. White mountaineers, including women, were sued and lynched for aiding slaves. But nothing and nowhere is one way or the other. The history of the Appalachian town where I was born includes the horrific lynching of five railroad employees in 1893. Working for the railroad was one of the best jobs a black man could have during reconstruction; it paid well, conveyed status and mobility. Five black men were wrung from the train and lynched for little more reason than always the same: some white man accused them of something for which they were not given a minute in court to defend themselves. I never knew of this as a child, but knowing it now helps to explain why that town still remains more than 95 percent white.

As humans, we like to find someone to carry our freight of fear and loathing; we like to point to someone else's evil, too, and our efforts are always rewarded. We can always find someone worse or better. The curious racial slur Melungeon, indicative of a mélange or mixture of Native American, white European, and African, arose from the Cumberland Gap region. When I first heard this word I was a child in Tazewell County, and no matter how it was inflected it sounded so enticing that I wanted to be one: Call me Melungeon. If we do not self-appoint as messiahs, most of us have to recognize that we live with mixed sympathies that do not tear us from love itself, and that will have to do, for love is nothing if it isn't compassion, and compassion is meaningless if it doesn't change the way we feel about ourselves, everyone, and everything.

In one of my favorite campus jobs as a college student in the late 1970s, I projected a whole month of sci-fi films. In the various plots of these movies, something came from outer space, from out there. *The Incredible Shrinking Man* featured a miasmic dust cloud settling over an innocent husband on a boating outing who afterwards began to shrink, eventually forced to reside in his child's dollhouse. A giant woman, his 1950s-style wife, loomed over him. Shiver me timbers, those Rosie the Riveters must have been so threatening! In the original *Invasion of the Body Snatchers*, mysterious pods appeared alongside the warm-blooded, emotive humans, hatching duplicates of their exterior forms while robbing them of all affective dimensions if they fell asleep. In both of these classic films, the trouble did not start within the psyche of a person or even within the borders of a country but began with some malevolent visitation silent as a cloud that would steal our ability to feel if we did not remain vigilant.

The world of the sixties was shrinking and growing denser through connectivity, like the garbage we dropped into our new trash compactor contraptions. We weren't yet recycling anything, but we saved Green stamps, got our milk delivered in glass, habitually reused foil and paper bags, and returned Coke bottles to the store; it would be a few more years before I helped start an ecology club with the sole purpose of recycling newspapers. Awareness of planet earth as our home with limited resources, though, was on the rise, and we were supposed to find a way to live together with all of our many differences highlighted. While hippies went back to the land and started communes, the WWII generation remained in charge; they used contextualization as their mode of operations, which meant they were blind to the irremediable shifts that were upon them. Too much had been blown apart by two nuclear bombs, but, at the same time, it was not enough in relation to what's happened since for us civilians to have been thoroughly shell shocked back then. Our borders remained secure, but we were mighty paranoid. Very little about this has psychologically progressed.

Watching *Star Trek* taught me something about what it meant to live under the spell of metaphor. Most of the plots boiled down to an obsession with somehow proving humans were a superior species to all other life forms, a nineteenth century notion that might better have been left there. Screenwriter Gene Roddenberry claimed to have received the idea for the show in an alien transmission and first pitched it as "a western in space." As an adventure-plus-morality tale, it probably owed more to Homer's *Iliad* and Virgil's *Aeneid*, the latter written during times of upheaval at the end of the Roman Republic and weirdly evocative of the turmoil of 1960s America. There is a reason that Rev. Dr. Martin Luther King Jr. was a fan of the show.

Although our star travelers were supposedly explorers not invaders, men of science not conquest, many plots revolved around evasive battles, particularly with the pigheaded Klingons. The force shield did not always prevent the ship's damage in these situations—we witnessed a lot of rocking of the ship's set back and forth on its axis—yet the humans prevailed because of the pitfalls of our humanity. Our weakness was our strength; in other words, we had feelings to guide us to greatness. Captain Kirk proved a particular champion at the vulnerable business of being human. Some plots involved his capture by aliens who demanded access to his mind, and in these instances he fell unconscious and scrunched up his brow. Enduring bouts of severe homesickness, he could be tricked by projections of earthbound loved ones he'd abandoned to serve his mission. Occasionally, he was lured by the equivalent of Sirens on space rocks, beings that took the form of old lovers in order to twist his affections and undermine his judgment. In these situations Kirk might embrace or kiss various women, and my all-too-human father cleared his throat and looked away. But maybe more than diverted, or like Ulysses waylaid, Kirk was guided to the underworld, and this parallel existence created a projection into the galaxies, as above so below. Kirk and his team were habitually beaming down to the surface of unknown planets and then trying to beam back up unscathed.

An alternative world, a speculative opportunity for problem solving, the show, like the *Aeneid*, contained a number of parables about the contemporary city-state, which in our case was changing so radically that it seemed to be another world altogether, requiring new dimensions of self to navigate. A sacrosanct bit of humor between Kirk and Spock concerned Spock's inability to admit he had solved any particular problem through something other than logic, inadvertently engaging his human side. Kirk's superior but messier path provided for the preeminence of reason together with emotion; his humanity and ours depended on pragmatism plus compassion for definition.

Odysseus took ten years to wander home from war. Time sped up with modernity, for the *Enterprise* crew was granted only five years for its explorations. Occasionally the show addressed problems of relative time as the ship ratcheted beyond Warp-5 or 6 and vanished into an elastic streak to indicate that it had surpassed light speed, in defiance of Einstein's physics, which now appears more than possible. CERN scientists, despite their skeptics, have replicated the measure of neutrinos traveling sixty nanoseconds quicker than light. This broken barrier means that there is no absolute governing most of modern physics, and many anomalies will rush in to greet our former theoretical certainties, with the result being more uncertainty.

The ship's engine room quaked if Scotty had to somehow harness the power to accelerate up to Warp-10. But would it be fast enough to keep the crew from aging too rapidly to complete their mission? The farther we look into space, the further back in time we go. Yes, starlight = mostly dead stars. What we can see is dying. In more prosaic terms, I always have a week of trouble following our autumn fall back in time. How is it that the morning is lighter than before, the evening darker? Finally, I just have to let go of the problem and set the alarm. Meanwhile, the loved ones the ship's crew left behind on various planets including earth would grow old and die long before the explorers could return home. And maybe I would never go home again, to the tiny town of my birth. At the moment I left it, did it cease to exist? What narcissism is particle physics.

The novel I wrote based on the geography and social landscape of my hometown was a book of imagination constructed as a new thing, not a duplicate of reality. I heavily selected, left a lot out, reorganized, researched, imagined, and was not aware of many things: this makes fiction. We know that space is really time, and that to go anywhere, even into the *between* of traveling from place to place, is to be lost in a kind of spatial suspension that still does not escape the tick-tock of the clock. Or can time be stopped, erased? Can what was lost come roaring back to us, instantly overtaking the present? All the friends I left at age eleven when I moved from my hometown are forever children when I recall them, and even when I've seen them since, encountering them in grocery store aisles or meeting up for occasional meals, my mind flips back to their child faces and voices. It doesn't matter that I know they are in their fifties or that I've attended their weddings and met their children and that some of them are grandparents and well beyond the age of their parents as I remember them. It's because memories are chemical substances. Memories = things. These things I recall are physically lodged in me, chemicals firing, taking up space.

So where are we really?

Physicists report that the universe is expanding more rapidly than it was in the 1960s; it's actually been scaling up its speed of separation ever since the Big Bang, revving up with dark energy.

Physicists report also that there was no Big Bang, that the universe is infinitely old with no beginning and no end.

At the end of *The Incredible Shrinking Man*, the husband continues to contract at an alarming rate, fighting and losing battles with mice, then insects, until he's swept out of the house, down the basement drain along with water drops, and condenses into the night, suffused into the galaxy implied by a panorama of starry sky, swirling Milky Way. The voiceover tells us he merged with the cosmos, that the shrinking man ended by expanding infinitely, becoming one with molecular space.

In the energy/matter mix, 98% is dark material and energy, and to us it might as well be described as emptiness, says Stephen Hawking. It's the opposite of Ptolemy's universe in which there was no empty space and an unmoving earth lay at the center with other bodies whipping around in neat circles. The other 2% of the universe hits the spectrum in which we can

gather evidence, meaning more or less that we're living a 2% existence, training our telescopes and instruments and math on the other 98. It makes better and better sense that something must be trained on us, looking back from
the numinous water clouds, from the vapors surrounding all of those black
holes.

Captain's log: We contemplate outer space and galaxies to contact our ancient particle selves and the distant past of the planet itself, the components
of our biology and chemistry broken into combinatory probabilities.

    I remember *Star Trek* in order to remember my father and my younger
self. Meteors are said to carry human DNA chains and to have seeded our
planet with life. This might happen, might have happened, elsewhere. *Voy-
ager 1*, launched in 1977, is now more than 12 billion miles from Earth. A
frontier is a boundary of settlement, no matter how distant or how near or
how virtual, so, if the rest of the universe operates with anything like the
property rights of earth, to define space as the final frontier implies a conquest mission. And to move anywhere unknown, into untried space, means
to migrate, to lose and find a world and a self. There are no small moves,
only ever-expanding selves.

Cleaning Out the House

"All really inhabited space bears the essence of the notion of home."

—Gaston Bachelard, *The Poetics of Space*

The winter my aunt Glade, last scion of the family home, was seventy-five, she called to ask, "Should I take the apartment?"

"It's up to you," I said.

A small gasp elapsed from her after a beat or two. She'd been doing a lot of crying since her stroke, and it was often hard to interpret. In this instance, though, the meaning seemed a bit clearer. "How do you feel about it?" I asked.

"I don't know," she said, sniffling. "This house is too much to keep up with, and yet I hate to leave. I won't have the oak tree to look at or the yard—"

"Or leaves to rake or grass to mow or the cleaning to worry about," I cut in.

"That's it," she said. "But I have so many memories here. It's *home.*"

I wish I could have said with some authority that she would not forget or lose her sense of home by leaving, that home can be "a feeling and a way of being in one's life rather than any specific place," as Sarah Susanka writes, or, to turn it inside out in the language of the Greeks, home = *atopos*: a place that is no place. For me, home is that for which I'm perhaps always searching, which I have built and wrecked, found and lost again and again. But in my aunt's case, as in Dorothy's in *The Wizard of Oz*, the meaning was clear: "There is no place like home." The homeplace on Windsor Road was where my grandparents died, Will of a heart attack in the breezeway after Sunday dinner, and Opal years later in a hospital bed in the corner of the den where I reached up to give her a cup of pills with little child's hands. To keep the homeplace meant to keep them, their spirits, honored. This was where an extended family gathered for Christmas, and the site of much prepping, stuffing, basting, mixing, and cooking on Thanksgiving. Glade had often crept downstairs at 4 A.M. to slip a giant turkey into the oven. Multiple pies of freshly scooped pumpkin and pecans cracked from the shell adorned the dessert table. The dining room table was set with the best silver and hand-painted china along with a cornucopia centerpiece, pilgrim candles, Indian corn—the whole nine yards as only three unmarried sisters can produce with six busy serving hands. This house was also the place where my aunt Glade had fallen down the stairs with a laundry basket and broken her shoulder and elbow and bruised her fragile spine. This house was more of a long event than a thing of smooth red bricks with Tudor influences; it happened and kept happening. My aunt Glade felt an obligation to carry that space, to hold it open for the family.

After about a hundred more conversations like this with me and every-one else, and receiving no one's permission or discouragement, she decided to move, which meant cleaning out fifty years' accumulation from an original family of nine and an odd assortment of kinfolk and relative strangers who crashed the party from time to time, taking advantage of my grandfather, who was kind and employed year round as a carpenter-mechanic at the Vis-cose plant that manufactured rayon and lace.

Way back on Murray Avenue, when my mother and aunt were children trying to make sense of their elder half sisters' wailing behind closed bed-room doors from which crying babies periodically emerged, my grandparents needed more space and arranged to buy the house across the street. The widow struck a hard bargain: she would sell them her house but continue living there. The house conveyed with the widow, who controlled as much as she could by the authority of the grump, and my grandparents took care of her until she died. So much for long-term care insurance in the 1930s.

Before marrying my dad, my mother had lived briefly where my aunt now lived on Windsor Road, as had several half sisters. Cancer had whittled the three sisters who remained down to one in the last year, leaving a house with too many rooms, too many memories. I think I'd run screaming wear-ing only my favorite denim with the future in my sights. The prospect of freedom seemed to have the opposite effect on my aunt Glade. She had a household of stuff to keep, give away, or dispose of in some fashion, and all of these things exerted their gravity. Her new digs, though a relatively posh apartment, had only two bedrooms and a small adjacent storage space. For weeks she sorted and cried through room after room, closet after closet, moving closer to the full basement of shelves upon which layer after layer of dust and depression glass, odd hand-painted pieces of German china, chipped mugs, blue Ball jars, glass milk jugs, specimen bottles from her first job in a chemical lab, baskets, boxes of handmade decorations for all occasions, sacks of cookie cutters, my grandfather's rusted farm implements—some of the same ones that had led him to Indiana where his first wife died in a scarlet fever epidemic and then back to Virginia towing five little girls—and other less identifiable shapes and gadgets awaited.

From a cedar chest in the basement emerged a box containing cards of congratulations upon the birth of my sister. We unearthed yellowed newspapers declaring war and peace, a little chalkboard used in a one-room schoolhouse, perhaps where my grandmother had taught her five future stepchildren. We found rows of moldy readers for every grade level, the World Book from the sixties in which we would be forever racing to the moon, old cow bells, a triangle that could summon folks to dinner, and a literal horn lopped from a ram or a bull. I used to bust a gut trying to pucker a sound out of that shofar. And we also found a bugle, the one on which my aunt Glade had learned to play "Taps" as a Girl Scout.

So many things passed through our hands; we ran our eyes over so many purposeless items that I felt sick looking at them and ended up leaving behind the few things I could have taken that made any sense to me, like the cloth bag of colorful mismatched buttons I loved to play with as a child. *Button, button.* I wonder where that bag of beautiful, singular buttons went. Every wondrous lost shape and odd size of button shook together in that bag, some demanding skill to set in place and sew on straight, with four holes to hit on center and loop thread through. Buttons like planets. Funky dung-colored buttons. Quirky buttons (invisible quarks). Military-style embossed metal buttons, pearl buttons, bone buttons, plastic buttons. Rare gem or wooden buttons, buttons of bronze or opalescent shell. Triangle-shaped or square or button gumdrops. Those buttons, substances like no other, my alchemical *materia prima*, your nothing = my everything: humble, overlooked, underrated by zippers. Most of them clicked when you shook the bag; they made a pleasing sound less like marbles than like red and black checkers tapping across a hand-me-down board. You could organize them in color groups, by size, or by counting the number of their close-set or wide flounder eyes. Some of the largest buttons matched coats, but most were of a modest size meant for blouses or shirts, extra buttons that had come with the article, and a few leftovers from Grandmother's sewing; these precious buttons appeared rarely, like comets. I only knew her as an old woman confined to bed with Parkinson's shaking hands. A talented seamstress, she made suits and dresses for my college-bound mother and a going-away suit for her wedding day, and she had sewn as much for six other daughters.

These stories like buttons are not mine, but I don't want them to be lost. A splinter from the flooring of the house on Windsor Road once made me yelp. A microscopic piece of that house may still be inside of me along with the imprint of Grandmother Opal propped on pillows in her sick bed. She died in a corner that afterwards was occupied by a desk, and in a few days the same corner would enclose nothing but space itself. Much is lost beyond furniture and other effects when a house, a meaningful house, is emptied. And much is stored there, accessed only through recall. I chunk random information like binary code into my memory palace, my house of memory. Indelible *house*, I can still run around in you at five years old and bleat as a long splinter from the old oak floor gouges my foot. This happened between my twin aunts' beds. They scooped me up and placed me on the chenille spread, my bleeding foot flailing into the air; Marjorie held me while Margaret found the tweezers.

I've always had an affinity for abandoned, empty spaces and difficult, eccentric people. My father's emotional trials taught me to appreciate the abnormal. I admit I'm bored by uniformity, an irregular sort of person myself. Until I found a completely empty house for sale, I couldn't imagine living there. Most homebuyers prefer exactly the opposite, prey to elaborate staging that promises a clean, organized life dull as dirt. Houses containing furniture sell faster. Houses painted yellow outsell other colors, and then are quickly re-painted. Why do we prefer purchasing yellow houses but living in white or gray? This kind of daydreaming is best confined to fixer-upper buildings, because abandoned, odd people, although also ripe for filling with longing, can prove to be more challenging. And yet love believes it can rehabilitate even the most distant and disaffected; perhaps it can. I once thought it could. I hope to believe that again.

Ancient Egyptian rulers pressed their slaves to build pyramids, receiving architectural plans from aliens including precision stone-cutting instruments and exact maps—OK, maybe, maybe not. In any case, the pharaohs knew they'd spend more time dead than alive. They exerted a laser focus on where they were going instead of on where they were.

We build and buy houses, moving up or down economically as evidenced more by what we live in and where we choose to live than how we live or with whom. We accumulate stuff like we'll live forever, and then we have to shed. Most of us, like hermit crabs or snakes, shed smaller homes for larger ones, until age brings us more wisdom and we finally downsize and shrink our worldly accumulations.

Upon my meeting someone new, conversation tends to navigate from one established point of polite inquiry to the next. "Where do you live?" easily follows "What do you do?" We learn what we can without revealing much in return. The question of where one lives is considered safe terrain for complete strangers, yet a home is a version of oneself or at least an extension of oneself, a kind of self-portrait. We learn something essential by learning someone's address and, better yet, when we walk inside her house. "In classical Greece and Rome, *domus* meant 'house' in an expanded sense," Stewart Brand explains in *How Buildings Learn*. The *domus*, the household = the people together with their inseparable domestic space, a dynamic of inhabitants and habitat.

Everyone knows of a couple whose relationship did not survive the consequences of working on their house, a couple obsessed with finding, renovating, or building the perfect home, a partnership that dissolved before the last red throw pillow hit the off-white loveseat scaled to perfection for the space, just as the jetted spa tub brimmed with hot water, or as soon as the kitchen update revealed rather than resolved the emotional chinks. After my divorce, I was part of such a couple. This was not something I would have been willing to accept about my relationship at the time. We communicated so well, it seemed, and shared similar taste in décor. Were our complementary arm-wrestling styles too balanced, mine with few holds barred, and her evasions an expression of secrets too deep? I knew a couple that installed a peel-and-stick recreation room tile floor to match their alma mater's mascot and broke up within a month of its completion. Another couple bought that house; the husband had attended the same university. That rec room had "man cave" written all over it. For the second couple the house was a home, but not for the first. For the first it was what? What was it?

No substitute for the self, a house can still be a surrogate, experimental self, a personal cabinet of curiosities, an expression of one's tastes and travels, dreams, expectations—and neuroses. We also must consider the dark side, the hoarders buried alive. Who can ever forget the Collyer brothers, found in their New York apartment beneath toppled stacks of newspapers? A chaotic house leaves me confused, rattled, and has never attracted me to another person, yet I've been willing to overlook almost anything. When I noticed that my prospective husband had tossed a year's worth of mail onto his dining table, I rationalized the red flag. I was aware that as the stacks grew taller he grew ever more paralyzed to sort bulk mailings from bills. He closed the door on the leaning towers until a friend helped him clear the table before we married. I imagine the work was gridded and slow, an archeological dig. But stacks would reappear: I had to barricade my office from his mounting stuff and first clear the kitchen island before starting to cook. When I asked about the piles he replied, "I live for others." I'm still pondering what that means if someone else had to help him clean.

An obsession with cleanliness or order, adherence at any cost to the polished surface of things, can predict even more dire conflicts, can become more stifling than disorder when our soul mate decides that washing the car, bathing the dog, or manicuring the lawn—once again—is more pressing than spending an extra hour snuggling in bed. I've been here, too. So maybe this is what I want or need: less excessiveness, more in-betweenness when I thought I needed less.

In a Gothic tale by a Virginia author, "The Fall of the House of Usher," I note that Poe describes Roderick's head with the same discernible zigzagging fissure internal and external to the mansion itself with its "eye-like windows." The manse structure contains and echoes the inhabitants' psyches as well as their physiques. I do not believe in the separation of body and soul, or that a person can be described with any accuracy as a set of dichotomies such as mind/body, soul/body, at least not while the house is still breathing. Poe's narrator expresses a "sense of insufferable doom" when he first glimpses the house of his childhood friend, and we have to wonder who owns the pervading gloom the narrator perceives, whose "deep and dank tarn" does he explore, his own or that "of the melancholy House of Usher," a house whose heady mood extends its fog from the architecture into the surrounding landscape. This narrator is implicated and his narration complicated, complicit.

In the middle section of the *Divine Comedy*, Dante blindly navigates the fog. In the fog, I think, God waits for us. God sends us fog so we can touch blindness, unknowing darkness. And here I sit, sifting. I have two storage units filled with stuff from the family after my mother, too, gave up her house and then her condo to move into an assisted living facility. The darkness of storage units makes the stuff disappear until I roll up the garage door and the light comes on like a special refrigerator bulb illuminating stale food. The present takes all of my attention. This darkness is going to have to take care of itself. I lower the storage door, retreat.

Poe's unreliable narrator creates a narrative confrontation with one of the most profound and abiding puzzles of existence: our inability to perceive anything or anyone without the filter of our own consciousness, without our own enduring fog. We learn through this narrator that the act of observation alters the observer as much as the thing observed. Never named, Poe's narrator, inseparable from what he sees, plays character/emissary for the reader whose house of imagination co-creates the tale. In the end the narrator's brain reels, reporting the result of Roderick's extreme isolation: the house of Usher fragments like a meteorite at his feet.

Jonna calls to invite me to her house for dinner. "I've been cleaning," she says. "I haven't cleaned like this since he left," he being her husband now ex.

"That's been a long time," I note.

"Five years. I have to clean my house before I can move forward."

"Yes, you've been saying that for a while." Times goes fast when you are raising children. Her son is fifteen. Time to get the house back in order and remove the child proofing from the kitchen cabinets.

Yep, I think, overdue, past time. Last weekend when I called, she puffed into the phone, having been in the attic. She was reconstructing her wedding album, trying to piece it back together so she could shut the book. She found its pages strewn across the attic floor along with ten-year-old receipts, which were exactly what she needed to collect on a lifetime warranty for her insulated window shades. "It was all there," she said, marveling that her attic could contain anything helpful when she thought it was just junk, a rat's nest. "Everything's up there."

Fifteen years into the future she will be rustling in the attic again, searching for stacks of old-fashioned photographs to use at her son's wedding rehearsal dinner slide show. It will all be there.

Back in the 1990s, half a year past our joint yard sale, I take Jonna a pair of eucalyptus-scented green candles for prosperity and an assortment of incense to finish the cleansing of her space. She selects amber—a pungent, sensuous spice—jasmine for purity, and lavender for stress reduction. Murphy's oil soap leaves the scent of possibility anywhere there's a clean cabinet door. She reveals her freshly scrubbed bathroom tile and new arrangements for her son's bedroom and her own. No longer sleeping with her head in front of the window, she begins to dream again. We drink light beer with lime and talk about the man she's dating.

"He has no fatal flaws," Jonna says. We've both recently read a book about deal breakers like alcoholism and gambling addiction.

"That's hard to believe," I say. "Everyone I meet had a worse childhood than I did."

"He has some grammatical issues," she admits. "And he unscrews the salt shaker lid at the table. It's annoying." She reminds me that she first picked out her current partner for me, but then literally fell into his lap on a scuba trip. *C'est la vie.*

"Maybe I need to clean my house again," I say.

"Your house is always clean and organized."

"Then maybe I need to mess it up."

"No, you don't want to do that. Trust me, you don't." Embarrassed about her mess, Jonna has an established habit of appending the warning label "just don't go upstairs" to any invitation.

"Then what should I do?" I ask. I tell her I saw a personal ad with the header, "Please Be Normal."

"Did you answer?"

"I may be desperate," I say, "but I still have a conscience. Besides, I figure he's either got a giant ego or a monstrous case of projection. Someone dumped him."

"Probably just looking for a little wifey to do the carpooling and pick up the shirts," Jonna says.

"Why didn't I think of that?" I exclaim.

"It's too obvious for you." She means this as some kind of compliment.

Flash forward. *Warp speed* over sixteen years in which the scuba instructor leaves for California, marries and divorces in the Midwest, and returns to visit family in Virginia. Bingo, they reunite; his grammar and her maturity improved, they are closer than before, but there's a hitch: he's job hunting, and in order to follow his passion he must leave again within six months, this time for an island literally on the other side of the world, closer and farther.

☙

The motion-sensor light in my new carport flared on when I drove in. I could see my way inside. I had cleaned and reconditioned the decks, gotten some outside painting done, built flower gardens behind my house, and planted several seasons of rye grass for a future vegetable plot. In the past year I'd replaced the downstairs flooring and reroofed with forty-year architectural shingles. I'd tended my house through the ragtag end of divorce, bungled fresh starts, and general fumbling in the dark, but it was my first summer spent entirely at home since I'd bought the place, moving from a rental west of Lexington after taking a new job and then returning to the old one. I felt myself settling into the land, a rooting happening in the rough rocky ground with hardly any topsoil on Gravelly Ridge in the Catawba Valley.

My lambs' ears were either dying or simply not flourishing, so I dug them up and plopped them in some soothing potting soil. In a matter of a week or two the root system feathered into a multitude of white circuits. So many roots entwined the rocks at the bottom of the shallow clay pot that I had to sacrifice some of them in the transplanting. My velvety lambs' ears had had the whole backyard in which to expand, but they could not. Confined in a pot, they thrived. I replanted many stems in the yard, mixing compost into the soil, and the plants redoubled within a month.

When I moved out of the suburban house I'd shared for ten years with my husband, I expanded my possibilities and shrank my worldly goods. My sister and I packed up some boxes while I uttered witless, acerbic comments, trying not to cry. Finally, I just started bawling. I later apologized for the noise, but my sister said that was when things started getting better. Kind of like the release of cleansing ozone after a good thunderstorm or a pelting of comets from the Oort Cloud. *Never again*, I remember thinking as we carried the last box out the door. Did I mean that I wouldn't move again? Or marry again? Love again? Certainly I didn't mean I wouldn't try again, although I might have thought that at the time. Maybe I meant that a phase of my life had ended and never again would I throw blind trust at the future, or another person, or believe so unwaveringly in love's transformative powers. Neither would I ever have again the advantage of so much inexperience. *Songs of Innocence*. I sobbed as I turned the page.

Everyone I meet trails a shadow like an eclipsed moon casts a penumbra. Our shadows meet and merge or part, finding pinpricks of attraction laced with fear. So I'm not the only popped balloon at the party. Looking for home, it's hard to bypass what's familiar but unworkable, hard to recognize what's strange to us at first but potentially sound. My one blind date ended in the middle of the living room floor; he had moved there to get closer to me, he said. I sat on the loveseat looking slightly down to meet his eyes. Pre-cell phone and pre-GPS, he had gotten lost on his way to my house. Maybe all roads don't lead home. *Okay, just be*, I thought, as he looked up at me, gazing a bit too long into my eyes. At more than six feet, with a full head of endless dark curls and symmetrical features, this guy was by any measure a handsome hunk. But all he could talk about was his crazy ex-wife, his dead father, and his therapist. He was working on himself, he said, pumping his pecs at the gym. I started empathizing with his ex-wife who had left him for a woman. There was a significant pause after that revelation. I couldn't help my reaction; I wanted to leave him, too.

So cute, I thought, *and so doomed*. But worse, he didn't buy dinner, and I was bored. It was like listening to someone's random dream images, and this was someone I hardly knew. I didn't want to reciprocate with my own sad litany, confide that I regretted having no take-away child from ten years of marriage, so I kept playing music on the stereo. Unfortunately, the oldie mix I chose reminded me of other people, and by the time he took his handsome head out my door, I felt like crying or dancing, so I chose the latter, working it out solo to "Sexual Healing." No one was getting down tonight.

In a feng shui weekend workshop, I learned that my house in the woods was "Good for Money/ Not good for People." My little red house contained a whopping four rooms with the fatal combination of 5/2, "double earth," which I could only remedy with massive amounts of earth-reducing metal (barring wind chimes) and "wood," live greenery, meaning plants. After leaning golf clubs in the corners of the offending rooms—the two and three irons were much more useful there than on the links—and repositioning a coin collection and some brass bells, I thought I might sleep better. Instead, I was constantly on edge, wondering what would have happened if I'd never taken that workshop and whether I'd done enough to cancel "double earth." I dug a new large pond ten feet from the northeast back corner. I turned the water feature back on though it leaked. But I had several near misses with my car. Other drivers appeared to be aiming for me, head-on. I went for a checkup with the workshop leader/expert feng shui practitioner, who diag-nosed the problem as a slight miscalculation: I was to remove the golf clubs and brass bells from the rooms. Wrong, all wrong. My compass reading had betrayed me. I felt ready to return to intuition alone, without the ancient Chinese pseudo-science. Just follow my nose. Feng shui's "wind/water" folk wisdom was originally applied to burial grounds, to the orientation of the dead not the living. I might have been an inexperienced thriver, but I wanted at least to survive.

A conversation like a house you can live in, not a house of cards. A friend like a cabin in the woods you return to, a room that stays the right temperature—neither too hot nor too cold. Two voices interchange, playing both sides, cutting the deck toward the middle whenever possible. You fall, I fall with you. I give you silly Scottie dogs because they mean friendship. This begins with a plaque I find when my aunt is cleaning out her house: "Lots of things in life are junk, / Troubles never end, / But there's something never palls: A 'Really, Truly' Friend." Born in the year of the dog, faithful is how we wag. I receive a trio of Scottie candles, just because. Through the years, the porch light stays on.

"At least you have family; mine's mostly all dead," I say.

"They're going to die soon. Cancer. All kinds," you reply.

"At least you had the good sense to reproduce," I say.

"But you've saved more money. He might as well live in Idaho," you answer.

"And a prayer of grandchildren," I continue.

"I'm praying they use birth control. They're not coming for Christmas," you say.

"I'm sorry," I say.

"I'm a little relieved I won't have to go through all that again," you say.

"Oh yeah, the house cleaning. But you got the downstairs repainted. It looks great," I say.

"I finally unpacked my suitcase from Rwanda last night. Thanks for helping with the paint colors. Maybe if they don't come I'll have time for that—last night I was crying in the attic, again," you say.

"Why?" I ask.

"Looking for something. He has a hard time with holidays," you say.

"He's married now; it will be different," I say.

"There are bags stored up there. Why, why? Why do I keep all these gift bags and laundry bags and Kroger bags? And I have dozens of baskets. They could change their minds and show up," you say.

"Forget about the cleaning," I say. "Just be together."

"Do you think I'm depressed? I might be a hoarder," you say. "I'm avoiding being home."

"You're not avoiding anything important," I say.

"Those bags," you say. "I'm so afraid of being a bag lady, that's why I keep them."

"No, no," I say. "You keep them to hold all the gifts you give away."

The dark oak secretary with its leather-topped, fold-down writing desk I'd never paid much attention to except when looking for the phone book, the scissors, or the glue became an antique thing of value. Cherry, maple, and walnut chests of drawers in various sizes confounded me; side tables, trunks, and a battered sea chest; too many beds, antique cane chairs, and something called a Hollywood chaise that had been parked in the sunroom so long I'd stopped noticing it years ago until a relative removed it and revealed an empty space. The inevitable crewel-covered wingbacks would not be worth much at auction; I learned that upholstered furniture is about as valuable as Confederate money. If it is my task to determine what is clearly worth saving and what can be transformed, to sift through a universe of things, I do not know enough.

Marjorie wanted me to have the maple desk, received upon her retirement after forty years of teaching first grade at Forest Park School. She had stripped the institutional green paint, and it emerged a silken honey brown. I also ended up with my grandfather's rocker, in which he reportedly spent many a late evening reading with his black cat Baby curled in his lap; three Dürer animal prints I'd always admired; and a pair of framed antique Valentines my twin aunts had hung on either side of their shared vanity. For a while I hung the Valentines in my bedroom, but after moving thrice I lost track of them. Eventually, I let Grandfather's chair go into an auction. Grandmother's delicate bent wood chair came back to me when the friend who had stored it moved to Colorado. For a season, a little clear glass mortar and pestle refracted sunlight on my windowsill, but now it's a bookshelf dust catcher. Grandmother's wooden clock sits silently on a pantry shelf, metal hands perpetually pointing toward two o'clock. What could I claim from a house visited throughout my life, the one place that did not change?

It struck me in carrying furniture and crates of dishes out of that house how little I had noticed these beautifully kept things or cared to desire them, even though my name had been penciled on the bottom or penned on the back of quite a few items. The house had a feeling I cherished, a welcoming, settled energy and a kind way of enveloping you that my several homes had lacked, but all the things my aunts had cherished, even things they had made, held little value. I felt oppressed by their discarded things, the weight and awkward size of things in space. Their scattered possessions would not fit into my small house; these objects however beautiful belonged with *their* lives, in *their* house, and nowhere else. It was my relatives I wanted back and not their things, dear to them but now dry as grave markers, impersonal as their carved names to someone who had never known them.

The reminders I took seemed at first false and cruel, but then the things settled into my house and I was glad I had them, especially afghans they knitted, pillows they needle-pointed, quilts they stitched, and a bit of their hand-painted china, because the creative energy that made these things stays in them. And yet the tarnished silver under my bed makes me resist all bright lures, all illusions of permanence. Things left behind prove only that we die. Sharks love shiny things. Sharks bite. *It is better to die to the world than out of it* comes to mind, but I am not sure what the phrase means beyond its being memory's corrupted version of a Bible verse. Like my dear aunt Glade, the homeplace still exists in memory, although everything within it has changed, vanished, been replaced, and even the red brick of my matriarchal bloodline erased, washed white by new owners. I can drive by, but the house is not really the *house*.

There is no cause greater than truth, and there is no truth in which to rest. *If you want the truth don't rely on memory.* My sister gives me a dish towel with a map of all fifty states. It comes with a red heart button and an instruction: "Pin your heart where your Home is!" In the film *Little Fockers* Barbra Streisand tells Owen Wilson something similar right before he sticks his tongue in her mouth. And in this state of loss and receptivity, I am searching for something neither memory nor truth can provide: a home that does not depend on a house or a place or a time, a malleable option. Ice melts, substances change, tending one way this minute, and then, in the next, my love walks out the door. I am leaping ahead in my story, but eventually I will catch up.

When I don't know what else to do I clean my house. I start with the trash, the vacuuming, slide through the dusting as if I'm in a 1950s commercial wearing a belted shirtwaist dress, and finish by scrubbing the toilets with skin-stripping disinfectant, my hair remaining perfectly in place. Reluctantly, I reduce the number of toothbrushes to one. I polish the mirrors, wash sheets, mattress pad, and the shower curtain.

When my house looks as clean as it's ever going to get, I light some candles and lower myself into water steaming with lavender salts, a gift from someone I thought I could love. I never threw them out. No matter now; my nose gratefully accepts the bouquet. I breathe more deeply.

Drum music fills the house, my house, every corner of this house. I can feel the insistent rhythms in my heart as I pound them out, sweat them through my pores, empty my mind to the beat. I soak tired muscles and breathe in the sea-salty scented air still redolent from my purifying bath. I try to read and then shut the book, my eyes, sinking roots into this place I found by accident. *In the same way I will find you, whoever you are,* I think, the way I dropped into my family or indeed my profession: without enormous willpower or defense. *With nothing but your name on my lips and your eyes in my sights, I'll start over.* If it is true that the artist lives *nowhere*, I will be different. I will live here. House, body, and now the land: we are all one without a topic sentence or logical development. Extensions of each other, we are one and the same—same subject, object, and no verb unless it is *to be.*

A face floats now behind my eyes and I hear the words, "I will never leave," and the words, "I have to go."

All false and all true, I believe them. I sink until my tendril roots find earth and hold fast. This love is where I live.

My Life in Snakes

Copperheads are born live and emerge from a viscous pool of something akin to the primordial soup. I've seen copperhead afterbirth shimmering with alien hieroglyphics, black words scribbled in eight-inch snakes at the center of the goo. Until I saw this, I thought they came out of eggs.

My knees recall a watery buckle whenever I remember my encounters with snakes, their undulations across my path, their many permutations. Several years ago, in early summer I nearly stumbled upon an adolescent copperhead a foot long and as big around as a dime. It had moved into my storage shed, following the food chain. When I saw it, I did something without thinking.

Last week I was spit shining the Catawba Valley property, the red house, because it's on the market. I'd made a trip to the Catholic Historical Society and picked up a little statuette of St. Joseph; somebody said to bury him headfirst in the garden for the sale, so I did. Picking up the last remnants of shriveled oak leaves wedged between the heat pump and the house, I had one of those very human moments when you find yourself alone, surrounded by nature. There's a certain stillness I've come to recognize that means you are being watched. The human is object not subject; the gaze of nature turns back or the silence of nature is held in suspense as you stumble into it. Late autumn chilled the air, and just past my left foot a young copperhead lazed on a warm orangey-brown slab of flagstone, perfect cover for the snake, as rock and snake share the same mottled color. The snake's head tensed up, sensing in my direction. I glanced to check its pupils and confirmed that they were elliptical like a cat's. There was no mistaking this narrow fellow for a nonpoisonous variety.

The copperhead was very near, but I worked my way around it without scaring it off. Stealthy in my motions, I dashed inside for my largest kitchen knife, afraid the snake might slither too far if I trekked all the way to the shed for the hoe. The knife was one of those heavy cleaver jobs best wielded by professional chefs that amateurs keep in their kitchens for inspiration. My chef's knife had come with a German-honed set, and so far I'd only used the paring knife.

Leaving out the details, I used the big chopper on the copperhead, knowing they usually travel in pairs and hoping this one was still young enough to be dating around but old enough to have wandered far from its nest. Seeing it so close to the foundation gave me a shiver. I wish I could say that I regret having done it, but the last thing I need is some potential buyer getting spooked as he walks up the stairs to the back deck. I genuinely hate that I killed it without even a nod to the big picture of the life cycle of all us creatures here below, but I have to accept that I preferred the snake's death to the possible theft of a customer. This is probably a sign that it really is time for me to leave country living behind. When I first moved from the suburbs to the granary in Lexington, I was not capable of killing a mouse, let alone a snake. I carried all ladybugs and stinkbugs outside, leaving the spiders be and puzzling over the ants, large and small. Clearly, country living has not been the constant pastoral, the peaceable kingdom I once imagined. And I'm not necessarily more sanguine for having experienced its conditions. The first thing I saw when I moved to the countryside was a bunch of slaughtered hogs hanging on big hooks at the side of a barn. My new neighbors smiled and waved as I drove by in my Honda Civic.

The dictionary provides that our North American copperhead appears after "Copernicus" and before its capped variation, "Copperhead," which was a derisive appellation applied to anti-Lincoln "Peace Democrats," Northerners sympathetic to the South during the Civil War. The Knights of the Golden Circle was a Copperhead secret society. It's a term I'd never heard until I consulted Webster's to begin my elementary education beyond what practical experience had already taught me about a certain serpent: copperheads live in rocky areas and favor thick underbrush; they eat small warm-blooded mammals for the most part but will consume aquatic life and insects if pressed. How small are those mammals? I wondered. Most active in late afternoon and early evening, copperheads can grow to four feet in length but average two. I cling to averages. That last fact bothered me a good deal.

Now we hear that snakes originally walked around on numerous feet, that there was no slither to the snake primeval. *Snake* derives from a word that means to crawl. I can't help picturing snakes on all fours scuttling across the floor. It gives me a funny image of the fall of man in the Garden of Eden. Was it more like a centipede that tempted Eve? Not much of story. I prefer a walking dog or cat, familiar mammals with furry paws.

The coloration of copperheads approaches hazel with chestnut-brown markings. Bands taper across their spines like saddlebags or the hourglass. Shadows speckle their pinkish to white underbellies, and, yes, they do sport blunt copper-colored heads that taper like arrows on narrow necks. In addition to slit eyes, the arrow shape of their heads also signals poison.

The rubbery oblong eggs I later found in the rock pile along the driveway were those of the black snake, famous for climbing trees. I've watched one wrap around my nearest jack oak, spiraling gradually toward a nest to filch eggs or baby birds. A few times I tried to unwrap it from the trunk on its way up and managed to toss it into the brush with my walking stick, but the black snake always came right back, persistently after faint chirps high in the branches. I knew black snakes were good for eating rodents and for keeping away poisonous snakes, so I didn't disturb the passel of eggs I found sprinkled in the rocks.

Only after I'd tossed my shed intruder by its tail—out of reflex with one garden-gloved hand—did I learn another salient fact. I had done something quite foolish. As we sat around a table deep into dinner conversation much later in the summer, one of my companions reported that her husband had discovered a young copperhead in their house and been advised by the county extension agent to kill it swiftly, because these babies come equipped with a more lethal supply of venom than their parents. Like fine particle pollution from coal-fired power plants, the tiniest units of copperhead are the deadliest. Baby copperhead venom on steroids means the snakes' survival, and ignorance, perhaps, means my death. I levied some more wine from the carafe on the table, a stupidity tax, as I considered my luck at not having been bitten. My foolish left hand quivered in my lap upon my napkin. I had twirled that little sucker from under my feet without a second's hesitation. This is probably what ultimately led me to chop the autumnal copperhead in two with the chef's knife. I'm not really out for nature's blood. I believe in karma and try not to create the bad sort. I know enough to stop and think about what goes around.

After flinging that baby far away from me with one hand, I found my little copperhead again the following day, edging a kindling box in the shed, perched with anvil head up, sensing the air when I disturbed its lair for my garden tools. I determined then to reorganize the wood, destroy the snake's habitat or hunting ground instead of the snake. I spent the better part of a steamy summer afternoon dumping boxes of kindling into a plastic garbage can I situated behind the shed and firmly lidded. Something I've learned by experience is how attractive copperheads find wood, especially stacked lumber or firewood where mice nest. Everyone loves to hang out in the kitchen.

I've not seen that particular snake since, but I do not fail to stomp on the shed floor before grabbing or replacing a tool. I peer up into the rafters as well, because I've seen them sunning atop lumber piles, and I doubt they make fine distinctions.

"Well, well!" concluded Max O'Rell upon discovering that the snake he thought he was in bed with, in a rural town in Australia in 1894, was really his trusted walking stick. "Is it possible for a man to be such a fool!"

Since our first encounter, copperheads have had a tendency to make me look and feel stupid. As a consequence, I do not trust them to behave. Before I entered first grade, I could tell a snake from a worm and had seen a copperhead wriggling along the foyer floor. It confounded me, but not because I did not recognize it for what it was. My own reptile brain was hardwired for recoil even though I could not correctly pronounce the creature's name. I was left with another mumbled word that was almost as unwieldy in my mouth, since I had trouble with W's, too. After running outside, I announced to my mother, who was busy sunbathing, as people in the sixties felt no compunction in doing, that there was *a big worm* in the house. She urged me to just pick it up and throw it out the door.

I was not a squeamish child, but luckily my discernment—better then than now, apparently—did not allow me to follow her instruction. Instead, I bravely called my older sister out of her sacred room, away from her oil painting and teenage rumination, but by then the snake, or *nake*, as I said, had fled. Despite the amusement that usually followed my struggles with pronunciation, I'd named it a snake in my own language, but that only made me look like an idiot or a liar. Where was it now? And I was scared, too, because unlike my mother and sister I knew that what I had seen had been no simple *worm*, and I vigilantly kept watch for the viper to turn up under someone's feet. For weeks I checked my shoes before I tied them on.

I was closer with my "worm" than I knew at the time, at least closer to Norse legends of the Midgard Worm that girds the earth, tail in mouth, endlessly cycling through the yin-yang of oppositions. I think it was a long time before I saw another copperhead, with only harmless black snakes and their lost skins in between. Those freshly sloughed sheaths—glimmering on the grass, drying out on stone patios, lying decorously in flowerbeds, or carried down the attic stairs of my new house over the shoulder of the home inspector—have never failed to attract and hold my attention. Some of them have been intact and very long, giant transparent bean pods the texture of cellophane, something like a mask waiting for a dancer to peer back through its vacant eyeholes. You could pour the snake back into its old skin, I think. But, of course, you cannot. No more than you can turn back time or climb into your own lost skin of a life. I moved from suburbia and a marriage of more than ten years to a farm near Lexington and a different position. After two years, I moved back to my old job, but it was not the same life. I bought a small house in the Catawba Valley on some acres of trees. At the start, I had thought that in five years I'd be settled, remarried, have children, but twelve years of living alone would pass.

I found a dead black snake tangled in the green plastic netting of my pond; its skin had peeled in wriggling to escape. Seeing inside the split snake filled me with guilt. The protective netting keeping raccoons from scarfing up goldfish, and tortoises from drowning, had caught and held the snake. Obviously, there are greater forces at work than our individual intentions, good or bad. The backward motion of the panicked snake peeling itself reminds me of a recurring nightmare I had for years, in which I had to drive a speeding car with my view restricted to the rearview mirror. I had to try to anticipate what would happen from what was just behind. Twists and hair-raising turns lay ahead to which I was blind. It makes my stomach tense just to write this down. Eventually I'd wake up, wrecking the car. Posted on my marital refrigerator were several sage commentaries from baseball legends, including Satchel Page's "Don't look back. Something might be gaining on you."

Indeed. And there is nothing back there that's going to help me guess where this road goes next.

I've heard about black snakes that share living space with human households, plopping in a polite way onto cool kitchen linoleum after everyone has gone to bed. A friend of mine who rented a log cabin endured an infestation of black snakes in her walls that started in her underwear drawer. It was a rather long story that made her shiver to tell, which eventually led to a thousand dollars of damage to her truck when she moved out of her cabin in the middle of the night in a thunderstorm as snakes slithered from the walls and ceiling.

According to the Gnostics, we've snakes to thank for wresting knowledge from the gods, but if I am to restrict the limits of my life in snakes to firsthand accounts, I have only a few snakes left to tell about, aside from the six-foot timber rattler that buzzed across a hiking trail (no real story there); the several black snakes I've already mentioned that I unwrapped from summer tree limbs with my walking stick and tossed out of range of wren and barn swallow nests; the many black snake lodgers in the giant oak, inside its rotten trunk among gnarled roots, at the camp where I go each summer to teach; and certain others worth only short reports, merely glimpsed, stepped over and forgotten. One remains from a dream that haunts: a writhing copperhead in the driver's seat with an unknown man; eventually, it bit him on the back of the neck. The sight of a black snake scaling the wall of your house can do wonders for adrenaline, but it's probably not going to bite you unless you tangle with it, and even then you won't die of more than fright. Bear this in mind: a snake swimming toward you on any body of water bodes not well. Give it a wide berth if you can see more than a head or an open mouth, for if a snake floats it's probably poisonous, having gulped air into its lungs before crossing.

When I saw a copperhead in the renovated granary west of Lexington that I rented for a couple of years, I had no doubt about its identification, although I duly described the color and markings over the phone to my Indiana Jones-type friend in an attempt at denial.

"Yep, you've got yourself a full-grown copperhead," he replied. "I can get there in an hour or so. Just leave it alone and shut off the room."

Like I was going to stand there and poke it with a stick. I did what he suggested, but I had to reenter my bedroom to dress.

I'd been indulging myself in the inaugural outdoor shower of the year, one of the granary's many charming features, on an unusually warm Mother's Day afternoon. I came back into the bedroom and something stirred in the closet. All I saw at first was motion. I'm nearsighted and had left my glasses on the dresser before padding outside. Donning them, still wearing nothing but a towel, I saw the snake come into focus out of the dimness. There was no door on the closet, just a rod where I had not hung a curtain. The coiled copperhead, head up at the ready, successfully mimicked every image of a giant cobra I'd ever seen. I guess it had sensed my approach and was poised to defend its turf. I was its swami, my wet head wrapped in a towel. It looked large, thicker than the lower part of my arm just above the wrist. Before I had called my Indiana Jones, who lived near Charlottesville, I had called everyone I knew in Lexington only to get one answering machine after another. I figured they were all having dinner with their mothers while I was caught here with a snake. On some level, I suppose it served me right. Oh, Swami.

I rattled a few drawers looking for clothes, trying all the while to keep an eye on the viper. It slowly changed position, and I went to the closet to investigate in time to see it glide behind a stack of shoeboxes. True to form, it was just trying to escape.

I was glad it proved shy, but I was disgusted, too. "Great," I thought. "After Indiana Jones drives an hour to rescue me, the damn snake will be gone." The least it could do after making me feel so vulnerable was to validate my story. Foiled again by a vanishing serpent, I closed the bedroom door to be safe, but I didn't expect my visitor to return. The snake had no stake in my credibility. I amused myself by imagining the copperhead in my flip-flops or pumps. After all, it had shown an interest in my shoes.

Sleuthing for a slithery trail, I rounded the barn that was my house and found an array of loose boards stacked against the outside closet wall. Soon I located what I thought was the copperhead's entry point, a gap in the foundation near the ground.

While I awaited rescue, I made a quick trip to the grocery store for steaks. I wasn't going to drag my friend all this way over a mountain for nothing. The least I could do was throw something worthwhile on the grill.

Indiana pulled up in his truck equipped with a hoe, some bludgeoning logs, and his wild animal scat book. We started our safari in the closet; he pulled out my shoeboxes and uncovered the offending hole.

"Stuff some steel wool in that," he said.

As I gave him the tour of everywhere I had seen the snake, I strategically mentioned the steaks. Then I led him around to the side of the house, where I'd circled several times already, nosing around the lumber pile and searching for more entry points.

"Don't move," Indiana said. "Just back out slowly."

I backed out and stopped about ten feet from the stacked lumber, shoulders hunched, focus trained on the ground. Then I threw my glance toward the wood. Shoulder high, or where my head had bowed but a moment before, sprawled the copperhead, all three feet of it. Forget averages. My stomach lurched as I recalled the number of times I'd stood exactly on or near that spot in the last hour and a half. Yes, if it had been a snake.... Indiana informed me that, unlike other snakes, copperheads give no warning before striking. They hold their ground and lunge if cornered, but generally inject less venom than other poisonous varieties that give warning gestures.

I was breathing hard when I asked, "What do you think we should do?"

Indiana didn't hesitate. "Kill it. It knows its way inside now, and it'll keep hanging around."

I must have looked distressed or afraid.

"They mate, you know. Why don't you start the charcoal," he added with sympathy.

I did as I was told and never asked where he pitched the dead snake. He did say it was as tough as old shoe leather and hard to kill. I told everyone about his chivalry and derring-do. I kept thinking about Bruce Dern in the film *Tattoo*, with skin so completely obscured by patterns and designs that he ended up evoking a reptile's scaly art. But my Indiana was just a regular transplanted Yankee, with a penchant for trail wear, leather bomber jackets, and nature writing.

Unfortunately, he wasn't the only gentleman I had to recruit to kill a copperhead while I was living in the granary. Instead of being a genuine nature lover, the next one was enrolled at the university law school. I think I would have fared better with a medical student, who would at least have had an affinity for the caduceus. This law student had nothing more in mind than a few lazy weeks of R&R house sitting at the Big Farm House, not engaging in jungle warfare at the converted barn below. Law students and lawyers, in my experience, are generally tired or anxious most of the time. In their vigilance they fail to sleep enough at night. All of that left-brainiac stuff of building arguments against human nature makes them fall into a light coma the minute they sit down.

On a Sunday evening in hot July, I was sitting at the top of the stairs that led to my barn kitchen, sweating, with my portable phone pressed to my ear, chatting away long distance when I happened to gaze toward the stove. Or did something draw my attention? A few seconds later I saw a vibrating tongue and then a head emerge at floor level. No mistaking the slit eyes, the anvil head.

"Copperhead!" I announced into the phone. "There's a copperhead under my stove."

"You're shitting me," my city friend said.

"No, I gotta go," I said.

"What are you going to do?"

"I don't know. Damn, it just disappeared."

During the previous long winter months, I'd caught all manner of rodents: brown field mice with white feet; gray, smaller-eared house mice; and chubby, stubby-tailed, squint-eyed voles. I started by catching them in Havahart traps. Catch and release. But that sentiment didn't last through Thanksgiving.

After clearing out all other items from the cabinet beside the stove, I lined it with various death-dealing devices. Over glue traps or poison, I favored old-fashioned snap traps that worked more swiftly than gallows. I'd caught such a succession of mice and variations of mice under the kitchen counter that I'd pasted a picture of Mickey Mouse inside one of the doors, circled and canceled through his face with black marker. I had been practicing with small things, it's true, but I was not yet ready to kill a snake.

I eased open the door to my Cabinet of Doom and peered inside, but I did not find the copperhead. Due to the way the cabinet ran the length of the kitchen, and the kitchen connected to the bathroom just beyond, the snake could have been anywhere. Remodeling a granary into living space necessarily leaves some gaps of convenience, some loopholes through which civilization and the wild can find slippage, an exchange of sorts, back and forth. I would have preferred a pest-free living space, but the granary had its share of charms. I moved in with a sense of adventure. My cat had the same idea and vanished through a hole behind the water heater on our first afternoon in the place. When I stopped panicking and calling everyone I knew, I saw her, the consummate tuxedoed house cat, strutting down the driveway from the landlady's big house. I promptly called my landlady, who plugged the largest hole. Life had been proceeding in this fashion ever since, presenting hole after hole to be patched. I'd even seen it snow right through the wall, a magic weather trick.

I remembered what Indiana had said after killing the Mother's Day Special: "They follow the plumbing when they're thirsty." Did I say it was a very hot July?

I gathered up Boots the cat, remembering the copperheads don't climb lore, and situated her with her litter box in the loft where I also planned to retreat. It was almost dusk, and I didn't know what else to do. I waited, turning pages of a book. Just before ten, I heard a car crunching up the gravel drive and ran out to flag it down. It was the law student house sitter heading up to the main house after downing a few at a local watering hole. I told him about the snake and didn't stop yammering until he offered to come in and look around. Did I say he was reluctant?

"It could be anywhere by now," the law student said hopefully. "Probably went back outside." He suppressed a yawn.

But it hadn't. We soon found it pressed up against the back door of the tub and laundry room. At first, I was in favor of just opening the door, but I remembered what Indiana had advised about the other one. This was probably its mate, but perhaps not. There was no way to be sure.

"What do you want to do?" the law student asked, backing away.

I didn't blame him; my knees were water and my stomach felt like I'd just eaten a bushel of grass. *Death Valley Days* flashed through my mind, episodes that inevitably featured a bandanna tourniquet at some crucial point in the narrative, a knife scoring thigh or arm flesh, and our hero sucking and then spitting out rattlesnake venom to save a life. Forget about anti-venom. This was my home.

"Kill it," I said.

"But how?" the law student asked, now with more interest in the project.

"With a hoe or something?" I had not actually witnessed the other snake's execution, so I was guessing here. Didn't Farmer McGregor always swing a hoe after the rabbits?

"I've never killed anything before," my reluctant hero said, and then qualified his statement. "Deliberately, I mean."

"Me neither," I echoed, having already discounted the mice. I was the butcher of small rodents among women, yet I no longer stopped to count them.

If it had been anything else of a daunting nature, I would have stepped in at this point and volunteered, cheerfully relegating the law student to moral support. As a child I was read to incessantly from two books, *The Little Engine That Could* and *The Little Red Hen*. From these wise sources I've gleaned my personal philosophy of "I think I can do it myself." And most of the time, it works well enough. I can use a wrench, a drill, and two kinds of screwdrivers, truss and stuff a turkey, make a decent cherry pie from scratch, replace the inner workings of a toilet, shop for a car without male support, and I once drove a stick shift on little notice as my high school date puked Boone's Farm burgundy out the window, but I was not killing this snake.

Where was my nature writer/Indiana Jones or, for that matter, the Hell's Angel turned zoologist I later met with a dragon tattooed in his palm? The zoologist studied snake vocalizations by dissecting their throats. True. He was allergic to anti-venom and king cobras were his research subjects, but I'm positive he'd have had no qualms about killing this snake. For that matter, where was my Lady of the Lands, who had so skillfully wielded a cool poker to clobber a rat that had refused to die in one of my attic traps? The same woman, while dressed for a concert, had hoisted an entire road-killed deer into the trunk of her Mercedes so the tender loins wouldn't be wasted. Gentle reader, she was in France. I would have to make of this inebriated law student the one I required.

"I'm sure you can handle it," I said, as if dropping a file onto his desk at 5 P.M., offering him a preview of corporate law practice.

"I'll go get something," he replied.

I didn't expect him to return. I doubt I would have. Someone had whispered to me at an earlier point in the summer that she thought the law student was gay, as though I cared. Now, I desperately wanted him to go against whatever remained of that tired typecasting. To his credit, he came back down to the granary toting a hoe, an ax, and an orange snow shovel. They turned out to be good choices.

"I think you'd better do it fast," I said.

He did it slowly, and the snake bunched up like a bulging biceps brachii every time he tried to saw it with the dull ax blade. Eventually he managed to divide the copperhead into two stubborn halves while I held down its head with the hoe.

He carried it out the door in the snow shovel, one half after the other, apologizing for the iridescent mess of scales and pungent blood saturating the blue indoor-outdoor carpeting.

I just thanked him profusely, and after he'd gone I repeatedly scrubbed at the metallic blood. I swept up scores of glittering scales that adhered to my hands. It seemed I could not erase the stain with detergent and water, or even Boraxo powdered hand soap. Only time would wear the shimmer from my skin.

∽

Will my snake stories, like the World Serpent's endless circling—head swallowing tail—have no end? Or will I continue these encounters until I receive the message? What's with these snakes? *To live in harmony* seems an unlikely canard, after so much blood and fear. If snakes are following me, I have to wonder why.

Today I take a break from cleaning and walk outside to see how Ron's doing with the rockwork on the pond below the waterfall. I want it all finished before the first open house. Although he's a large man, a professional Greensman for the movies and as practiced as a Druid with rock moving, I'm a little worried he's handling too much alone. Virginia bluestone is much heavier than it looks; it's very dense stone. I remember that each of the eighty Stonehenge bluestones weighs up to four tons and probably had to travel 240 miles from Preseli Hills in Wales. It's enough to make you believe in aliens.

I'm trying to forget about snakes, about words and mysteries, when Ron says, "I'm sorry, but I killed a little snake in the pond. I didn't mean to, but I flicked it when I saw it. Reflex." Ron tells me it was a queen snake. Not poisonous at all. He pulls back a fold of rubber pond liner and I see it, bright green and still writhing. Ron tucks back the liner. "I'll get it later," he says.

Snake medicine is potent, linking us back through every culture to the first shamans, snake charmers and holy women, alternately despised and worshipped. Perhaps I need to take a dreamtime break like the Aborigines or retreat as the ancient Greeks did to their dream temples decorated with undulating snakes, guardians of sleep and healing. Maybe I need to consult an oracle.

My spoken language is tightly tied to the snake by my first encounter in the foyer of my childhood, when to speak its name through the shame of my imperfect speech meant the difference between complete and faulty communication, perhaps life and death. I didn't yet trust that speaking the truth requires passion, not perfection. There are still a lot of things left to learn and certain mysteries to ponder. Why does speaking truth so often lead to ridicule or silencing, even when the words are all pronounced correctly? Why do certain houses come with snakes?

Early in my ownership of the post-granary Catawba Valley house, long before I'd ever thought of selling it and moving into the city, I found another baby copperhead in my foyer late one spring, an echo of my childhood experience. I almost stepped on it, and surprisingly my ailing, elderly cat just avoided it if she sensed or saw it at all; even Henry let it alone after one sniff, neither cat nor dog alerting me to the intruder. Again, it was a woodpile that had attracted the invader, split logs conveniently stacked next to the sliding door. Sometimes I learn things only after constant repetition. Would I ever finally learn? I've let snakes go, aided in their deaths, and now I've cleaved one myself, but in every case they have returned, looped back with another variation, another chance for me to gain some ground, some wisdom. Maybe this story has no resolution. I know it carries no simple moral. Precious little is what I know. Will I ever learn to rest in the unknowing? My hair is hissing snakes, and I'm the only one who cannot see it.

I swept that copperhead out the door and gave it a good long toss off the shovel over the fence, into the woods. This time, at least, I cast out the snake with a shovel not my hand. Incremental progress, but progress nonetheless. The next few hours I spent in long sleeves, poking through the woodpile and gingerly removing each log until the steel frame cord holder was empty. I dragged the firewood frame far from the house, near the shed, before restacking the logs. Snakes moved into the shed, and I ordered a new sliding door. There was a gap in the old one that I could have filled with caulk, but I was into renovations in a big way, trying to achieve something that was all mine by rebuilding my little red house piece by piece. I had installed hardwood floors before moving in and replaced the faulty metal chimney that had a disintegrated liner, then the woodstove itself, graduating from a smoky appliance to one with a catalytic converter to save the environment. I replaced the kitchen appliances with Energy Star brands, added a heat pump and a backup furnace. Forty-year architectural shingles covered the roof; the overhead light fixtures were all upgraded with ceiling fan kits. I added a carport and finally a screened porch, new stairs and decking, a waterfall and pond. Soon I would be gone.

The man who installed the new sliding door told me it was far superior to the old lopsided door that had never opened smoothly. "Botched installation," he said, pointing out the rough and bent ridges of the original tracks. I had periodically re-greased them, but it never really helped.

The improved door was all metal, too heavy and snug to be lifted off its track by burglars, he said. I would no longer need the sawed-off broomstick I wedged into place every night, he assured me. Something about my country house on fifty acres of trees always brought forth keen interest from men, some of whom had wanted to move in with me after a few dates, while more than a few I'd hired to fix things had tried to sabotage something, maybe in hopes of returning.

"What about snakes?" I asked him.

"Snakes?" He reared up from the lock he was tamping and peered at me as if he'd finally noticed Medusa.

His tense shoulders said it all, all that I imagined he thought: if I was scared of snakes, maybe I and my copious bookcases belonged in a townhouse, not way out here in the sticks with wild turkeys and deer, owls, an eagle, raccoons, three kinds of woodpeckers, the occasional fox, and rare wobbling bobwhites, bobcats, and black bears. He didn't know I'd seen a mountain lion perched on an outcrop like a watchful old spirit guide one bitter winter night. And in the rocks and woodpiles, snakes, an assortment of mostly invisible beauties. Timber rattlers, copperheads, the hog-nose rooting for toads, cornsnakes, black racers and rat snakes keeping the perimeters clear, and water snakes down at the creek, swimming with their mouths unhinged, skimming the surface, each snake far more than a word to me, more than a name. Meaningful in a way I could not explain.

Sometimes on summer mornings mist wrapped Catawba mountain, or, in winter, its rough, jagged shape caught the light stark against a cloudless sky. Spring trees dressed its angles with clumps of impossible green. Soon the color would molt again, transform, shedding red and orange down its slopes to tumble across the valley toward my porch and into my eye. This view, this prospect of an earlier century's sort, with tree branches framing a distant mountainside, would probably belong to someone else by then. Moonlight, like daylight, would be theirs, too.

"Never mind," I said to the door installer.

"You had me going there with your snakes. I'd rather kill them than look at them myself."

His face relaxed as he bent back to his task of testing the lock against the strike plate. He finished fitting the door and caulked, but neither of us knew what was coming next, when something dangerous or wondrous would find a gap.

Neighborhood of Desire

Attired for church in a white suit and white gloves, the substantial black woman in the yard next door to us worked her way prayerfully around the house with the bright yellow siding. There between our houses performing her ritual, she closed her eyes tight and raised her hands high.

For Sale signs were planted in both of our front yards. Our house, a high Victorian with stained glass, a two-story bay, plenty of gingerbread, and bracketed cornices, had just sold to a newly wed couple from Florida, but the house next door had sat idling for a year, ever since the family renting it had been invited to vacate. Their sister, aunt, and landlord, who had bootstrapped her way from community college to the Ivies, held an academic position out of state. At that moment the full professor was standing in the yard with the Christian witch doctor.

The woman in white undertook solemn, emphatic work in praying over each corner of the property, north, south, east, and west. "Oh, Jesus, take the curse from this house," she implored in the side yard, her voice finding strength and rising. "Jesus, we're asking you to lift the curse off of this nice home. Oh gentle and supreme Jesus, in your name we pray." Now and again she raised her hands to the sky.

Stopping next in the front yard, she repeated the ritual, and then continued to the porch, into the house, and through each room. She finished with the upstairs back porch, while my partner, who will be known as A., stood pruning roses in our front yard, trying not to stare.

The owner of the house next door, the professor and conservative commentator whose scholarship examined US nationalism as an economic and racial divide, had obviously brought the Jesus woman to pray, although A. said the professor looked askance and rolled her eyes as she explained that her sister's family had hexed the house, declaring that no one would ever live there again. So far it had proven a heady curse. The professor had spent many thousands of dollars renovating the mess her family had made of the house inside and out; with her patience at an impasse, she needed the house sold.

We'd had our house blessed soon after moving in—by a gay defrocked Methodist and my Unitarian Universalist minister. I beat a drum room to room while the ministers prayed by turns, burned some sage, and sprinkled blessed water. A. and I were really not that skeptical of the Christian witch doctor's methods, but I thought it might take more than a single pass to lift the spell off the house next door. The family that had cursed the house might have been cursed themselves, as even their own family member had given up on them. My partner and I had felt our own hex nut loosen a bit when those tenants packed up and the house next door was gradually turned inside out by renovations.

Loads of abandoned appliances, trash, and a car were hauled from the backyard and every fixture and appliance replaced within. The old mattress stored on their upper back porch that had haunted me with nightmares of fire finally came down, thrown to the ground in one motion. Mangy carpet was ripped out, floors refinished, a new kitchen installed, and a new roof covered all. Even the roaches left behind, the ones that hadn't migrated over to our house when the tenants left, were exterminated, the yellow house tented and fogged. Flowers and shrubs took root in sculpted, mulched beds where before there had been nothing but weeds, shoots of onion grass taller than my hips, and several bent metal folding chairs immured in kudzu and Virginia creeper.

Our only disturbance since our next-door neighbors' departure, aside from the ladders and hammers of workmen, happened on a late summer night when the one brother not yet in jail brought his friends and vandalized the newly renovated house, poking the garden hose through the mail slot and throwing potted plants at the windows until some glass broke and woke the neighbors.

Our painted lady maintained her charm, even as we struggled daily against the 1890 design, which paved the way for many more arguments between us than I would have believed possible without a breakup. We desperately wanted our gamble on each other and this permanently transitional neighborhood to pay off. But the house and neighborhood were like a third party in our relationship, an emotional triangle, and we had space issues, place issues, issues that surfaced, and, like our two dogs—one assigned to the front yard, the other to the back—we were destined to meet in the side yard, in a full tilt barking display on either side of a locked gate.

For more than a year A. converted the front parlor into her painting studio. The parlor, though large enough, was totally inappropriate for oil painting. The walls had been drenched in a sort of milky Christmas green by the former owners, and we had not yet decided where to go with that; the horsehair plaster chunked out of the wall if she nailed in picture hangers for multiple works in progress. The walnut mirrored mantel, carved with vines and a smiling Green Man with matching acrid green ceramic tiles hand-fired by a German craftsman, had to be covered with a drop cloth and canvases stacked against its base. Delicate spindled shelves served as cubbies for brushes and odorless turpenoid. Another ornate mantel of oak dominated the dining room, where A. had ripped down the funereal wallpaper of navy blue sprinkled with tiny flowers soon after we unpacked. Intent on restoring anything with missing parts, I hired a wood turner to fill the gaps in the rows of mantel spindles. A rumor persisted of hidden treasure behind the living room mantel, stashed there from a convenience store robbery. All we actually found was a crumbling Roanoke newspaper from the 1930s. On one of the brittle bits of newspaper appeared the name of a local lawyer and future mayor, my ex-husband's father.

I felt like I was living in a paint can. My sinuses killed me, my head throbbed from the second I woke up, and I complained mightily, while A. was "just trying to make a living." I have to say this strife had never been the plan: she had rented a studio downtown and said she would work there before we moved in together. That was the deal. But then of course she had need of more space. "It is important never to forget how crazy painting is," James Elkins reminds us. "In order to produce the beautiful framed picture, the artist had to spend time shut up with oils and solvents, staring at glass or wooden surfaces smeared with pigments, trying to smear them onto other surfaces in turn." Elkins also lends some of his keen attention to sketching out the diametrical opposition between the work of painters and of those who work with words. While I agree that words will seldom be discovered smudged on a couch after I sit there fresh from my study or dolloped on a refinished hardwood floor in need of a can of Goo-Gone, I suggest that word-work carries with it distinct liabilities in domestic space. My clothes may not be stained, but my mind is surely messed up much of the time. I offer that writers—covering their ears and demanding quiet, or running away in search of isolation and three meals they don't have to make—are no easier to live with than those who chase paint.

"At least," A. would shout, "you can go to your office." She meant my office at the institution where I teach, which was then also housed in a nineteenth century building with a creek running beneath. All of the ceiling plaster had fallen in or cracked away over the years, replaced with wallboard grown furry with mold. My sagging office bookcases were sinking through the floor. When our department finally got a dedicated building, we left a suite of condemned offices that OSHA remediated.

As much as my partner and I struggled with each other, we struggled more with the habits of the neighborhood surrounding us. It was the same place that had impressed us as funky and chic after we attended a potluck held by one of A.'s friends who had long lived on the street and wanted us to join the club. Built-in friends, we enthused. Like Joe from Kansas, directly across the street, who had followed his ex-wife to Virginia to stay in his children's lives; Chris and Sarah in "Purple," on the corner, site of many potlucks; and Jim and Ann, converts to restoration, who were taking some of the most dilapidated houses and turning them into showplaces. How bad can it be, we had reasoned when considering the area's reputation for crime. It's only Roanoke, not Richmond, or for God's sake Los Angeles, where A. had lived for ten years holding her breath and clutching her paintbrushes.

Mention of our neighborhood never failed to produce in my academic colleagues a raised eyebrow among those few who ventured off campus, but I moved there for love. A. and I determined we wanted to live together, two women in search of someplace to make a home, where we could halfway fit in or at least not inspire any active hatred of the cross-burning kind. We were in danger of becoming lesbian lost causes. Both of us had married young and divorced once in the conventional sense, and in the long interval we'd cultivated little relational stability. We needed to reinvent ourselves as people who could be part of something larger, something like a couple who lived in a neighborhood. For our transgression of a life together in the state of Virginia (not for lovers like us in 2003), we chose a transitional neighborhood; we chose the most economically and ethically diverse street in town. At one end of our block shimmied a known crack house of prostitution owned by one of three notorious slumlords, who were all property investors on our short block, and at the other end stood a large eyesore of brick apartments housing mostly brown working families who had to vie with pimps and druggies.

A. had exclaimed that our house was the most beautiful house in Roanoke before she'd even seen inside. She took me across Elm Avenue one fateful night when we were still fresh in our house hunting, to the other side of Old Southwest, Roanoke's large historic district. Crossing Elm in those days was like crossing the railroad tracks to the wrong side of town. I had always perceived racism and lack of economic opportunity where others saw either trouble to avoid or alternatively cash to be made through property management. I didn't particularly want my understanding of structural inequality challenged with too much daily reality. Like all my friends of whatever stripe or color, I had mused on social problems while reading the newspaper and living elsewhere. This street would complete an education I didn't know I needed.

It took me a while to see our crazy quilt Victorian through A.'s painterly eyes. Our house came with stories, too. Bob, a former owner, had been responsible for renovating much of the house. We learned that an informal neighborhood committee had chosen the sixteen exterior hues represented in the legacy of stacked paint cans stored in the basement. "Bob, what colors do you like?" they had asked him when he couldn't decide on a palette. He didn't know, so the committee suggested the colors that Bob often wore: khaki, white, black, and several oscillating shades of magenta, red, orange, and yellow. The resulting multicolored columns around the porch were a little much to take in all at once, but since I loved A., and she loved the house, I didn't really have to love the house as much as she did. Luckily, when we first drove across Elm, the house was not for sale. The executive director of the Roanoke Symphony lived there and wasn't likely to move on. But a bit later we caught the house as it was just about to hit the multiple listing service. Primed from several months of fruitless search, we walked into the twenty-five-foot high foyer with an agent who had the scoop, and the For Sale sign never got hammered into the ground before we made an offer.

Even if the house had a Chinese red bathroom flanked by dark teal and brown bedrooms, the kitchen was large enough, quaint enough, with a black and white tile floor, and tasteful in comparison to the many aberrant décor schemes we had tried to imagine remedying without having to knock down the house. I finally would have a library with enough bookcases and more than 3,000 square feet of high ceilings, period details, hardwood, and stained glass, more than enough space for living and entertaining. As a bonus, a gardening shed in the back could serve as A.'s framing studio.

Just down the alley, a few houses away from ours, twelve cars regularly parked in a muddy yard. Polka music cranked up on the weekends, and when I went outside to hang out clothes, because our dryer was one of the first victims of an old house power surge, the volume made me wince. If I went out the front door I would hear rap or hip-hop. In the backyard off the alley someone rammed into our chain link gate so hard that the center pole bent and the lock broke off. From the front porch we observed a generously muscled man drop kicking a tiny kitten, and when A. could not help object-ing, loudly, he told us he could do what he wanted, "It's my cat." He was renting from the most notorious of the notorious. "Not for long," I shouted back, as the kitten skittered across the road and up our weeping cherry.

The Dick Tracy villain of a slumlord who owned that house liked to call us his "neighbors," but he lived across the bridge in a decidedly middle-class neighborhood while trolling the courts for no reference/no credit cash tenants, like the man who kicked his child's new kitten. Often this property investor provided tenants with scant working plumbing and no hot water for their rent, which he collected while riding around the city in antique cars holding his large, doughy hand out the window for wads of cash on the first of each month. Occasionally, he got his name in the paper for burying an anonymous baby found in a trashcan or contributing an inner-city lot for a community garden, shoring up his public image. The version of him we knew never answered the phone and didn't care if the green brick house had dog shit on the upstairs floors and a porch with no railing while toddlers lived inside. The green house across from ours was his first rental house, he had proudly told me, purchased for only $1,000, and he had invested little more than that in the forty years since. "You overpaid," he informed me.

Early on we learned that entertaining on our wraparound front porch could be challenging. During our inaugural lesbian fete, a couple of locals had commenced down the sidewalk with the woman twenty feet ahead of the man, in a call and response of "Get off my dick!" as the man returned, "You bitch!" While our party looked at each other in stunned silence, the chorus of "Get off my dick" followed by "You bitch" continued until the couple had promenaded the entire block. At the end of the housewarming party our guests drove away to their mainly white, middle-class or better neighborhoods where good educations and jobs were not scarce quantities and obscenities screamed on the sidewalk weren't quotidian. We shrugged it off and absorbed "Get off my dick!" into our mock-fighting vocabularies. After all, as we liked to joke with Joe from Wichita, we were not in Kansas anymore.

Our neighborhood hadn't always been a catchall for lost souls, bohos, hos, and the underserved; our house had been built by one of the original investors of the railroad in Roanoke, William Williamson, who had lived in our house until his death in the late 1930s; he was responsible not only for the original 1890 house but also for the addition of 1917 when the sleeping porches were converted to a kitchen and an extra upstairs bedroom and bath. The oldest main corridor in the city, Williamson Rd., was named for the man who built our house.

One morning as we sat across from each other at the stainless steel cook's table, where we drank our coffee and solved the world's ills in the room farthest from the street, I read aloud a short article from the newspaper about an attempted robbery at nearby Sparky's convenience store. The name was published, but I will omit it: "_____ of the 500 block of Day Ave. is accused—"

"That's our neighbor!" A. interrupted.

"Which one?"

"The teenager next door. The long-faced one."

He had introduced himself to us when we were walking the dogs to the park. "Hi, I'm your neighbor. I live next door." He smiled at us, strolling with his girl. On that one summer evening it was a calm world, but I also remembered the same teen wailing in the middle of the street during an August full moon, threatening to kill himself after his girlfriend dumped him. "Just love me, just love me," he kept almost singing at the top of his voice. And in the next breath, lower in his range, it was "Hate that bitch." While he stumbled around, his mother watched from their front yard. She had already lost one son to jail. She was crying for her youngest to come inside when the intervention team handcuffed him and carted him away. His public breakdown marked the culmination of an active week for social and emergency services on our block. We had watched a young child escorted from the upstairs apartment of the infamous green rental across the street where fighting pit bulls were being bred. Someone else had beaten us to 911 and informed Social Services about the condition of the apartment where the toddler lived. The dogs snarled and barked with regularity through the broken banisters of the upstairs balcony, but we had never seen them exercised on a leash. Our favorite property owner had skirted every action against him over the years concerning that house and thirty others; "Everything's legal" being his most sacred mantra. If you have ever extolled the evils of gentrification, consider this: there are conditions under which no one should ever have to live and places no one should ever have to call "home." Section 8 subsidies amounted to cash in the pockets of landlords without conscience. After we watched the child carried out, A. dialed up the property investor as she had many times before. "I thought you'd want to know what's happening at your property." She left another message.

Earlier that same week, the family dog next door had been removed and put down by Animal Control. Their chained stray, which we fed and tried to water through the fence, was finally taken away when it broke free and fatally chomped a little yipping dog at the pink house down the street. Everyone was out for blood over that one. The white folks in the pink house were yelling the N word, while their children cried over their precious Pomeranian.

The two little children being raised in the house next door, the teen boy's nephews, scattered their grade school papers in the gutters, casting perfect homework scores for urban anthropologists like me to pick up and try to imagine how I could save these kids from their circumstances, adopt them into the possibility of a college education, which would of course solve everything, as it had for their great-aunt, the Ivy-educated professor. If I had children, no doubt I would have done as all of my friends had and sent them to the best schools I could afford, while supporting public education in theory. Actually, public education even with the turmoil of the 1960s and '70s had been good enough for me, but times appeared to have changed. The children would never speak to us when we tried to address them. We were the strangers who lived next door. The professor's sister, their grandmother, was raising them; she drank and suffered from manic depression, the professor later told us. Unlike her grandchildren, she would chat with us through the chain link separating our backyards. That's how we learned the poor dog's name was Poochie.

"They said he used a hammer," I paraphrased the short article about the teen's crime. "They recognized him at the store and the police have already picked him up."

"Poor boy."

It was just sad, all of this. An infection of sadness we tried to avert.

A. and I sighed heavily before raising a joint eyebrow and singing together our little ironic chorus from *Mr. Rogers' Neighborhood*. His warm and fuzzy sweater had seen better days; gallows humor got us through, but admittedly it was growing a bit stale. We were still trying for beautiful days, still trying to be good neighbors.

Embellishment of fact into fiction became unnecessary in the three years we lived in our beautiful house of many colors. There wasn't much left to say about it, and we didn't know what to do except to continue what we were doing while we drew up an exit strategy. We showed up gloved, with buckets and trash bags aplenty, for neighborhood cleanup days, helping to remove the accumulated tons of litter and plain old nasty garbage that kept blooming in the alleys, yards, and gutters around us, just beyond our black iron hoop-and-spear fencing in front and our tall, battered chain link in back. Needless to say, not one of the property investors ever showed up to help. We thought about that, especially when we were picking up soiled diapers.

I left out the details when speaking with my family. All the things I left out added up to a horror tale that eighty-plus-year-olds didn't need to add to their worries. There was the day I saw a thin young man breaking the glass of the back apartment window of John's house to the right of us. There was the lunch spoiled by a rat skittering across our kitchen, tattered tail vanishing beneath the cabinets on its way to the basement just as I raised a sandwich to my lips. I put down the sandwich and screamed. There was the time an officer tackled a man in the side yard mere seconds after I had pulled laundry from the line and carried it inside the mudroom. I saw a blur of motion and peered out the window through the chain link to see a policeman pinning beneath him a panting fellow with a gun in his hand. Some nights I came home from evening classes to find no parking space in front of the house because customers were idling there waiting for hookers. And there was the afternoon I saw a pickup truck slow down just enough for one of our favorite girls to expel a dubious substance from her mouth. She was probably the same girl whom my partner had trailed to Highland Park, calling the police along the way.

"Citizen's arrest?" A. asked the dispatcher, not in jest, wanting someone, even herself, to arrest the man who'd picked up the girl for sex.

"Go home," the dispatcher insisted.

We were both losing our minds a little at a time. Day by day it got harder to tell whether the dysfunction was issuing from within or without.

I feel bad writing this down, and yet I must, because it was relentless and much louder and more intrusive than a representation on canvas or in print can ever convey. I thought I could live in the middle of lives out of control and keep my cool, my theory intact. It was a giant strain on my resources of spirit. All I really wanted was to turn my head away. What my reaction amounted to was the fruit of the privileged, sheltered life I had enjoyed, and yet I deserved as much peace as any other person. Both of us had survived childhood traumas, and the neighborhood dredged it all back up, triggering PTSD, no exaggeration. We were annoyed to distraction by the spillover from lives in survival mode, the chaos that surrounded us. It made us feel more distraught than we had ever felt in dealing with each other. Frustrated, we fought more over less, while in saner moments we sent up morning prayers for the folks next door. The constant noise of the street depressed and freighted us with anger of all kinds, the sort we heard in streams of obscenities when we went outside and the kind we felt when our peace was impinged. All we had wanted was a home together, not this onslaught. "Get off my dick!" indeed. It became clearer and clearer that it was time for me to locate little St. Joe in whatever storage-unit box he was hidden and bury him again.

Yet every time A. painted the backyard scene beyond our kitchen window, cut roses in blue vases in the foreground with climbing roses abloom and garden beyond, the painting was guaranteed to sell. Everyone wanted these light-filled still lives; they fought over them. No soundtrack of cursing—instead a captured moment of iconic beauty in bloom, suspended in time, like the slanted fierce afternoon light swathing facades of multicolored houses on our block, the pink and the acrid green, the gray, and the mint julep all glowing together. Pink azalea bushes framed our front porch, fennel high as your hip teemed in our south-facing garden, and in all seasons of the year pink and yellow roses continued blooming, even through the winters. Our chocolate point Siamese queen, Ms. Jones, came to us out of the mess and muck of the alley, crooked tail to prove her lineage, slant eyes of teal splashed with ocean. Children tossed balls in front yards wearing Indian headdresses, children of every color who studied in public school together. In a certain cast of light, our crazy street sometimes looked for an hour or for an evening the way an American neighborhood was supposed to be, giving us a little demonstration of the enduring promise of democracy.

❧

Around small points of potential, even isolated moments of bliss, our neighborhood tilt-a-whirled. The owners of Lewis Reserve, or "Purple," became parents, adopting the child from India they had awaited for several years. Now Sarah stood outside with her three-year-old on a warm fall morning, shoveling up the dirt and weeds that grew along the curb. Everyone passing by got a wave. She was used to dodging Johns mistaking her purpose. Truckers routinely cruised their eighteen-wheelers through our neighborhood illegally, and sometimes Sarah stepped out and snapped their pictures: surprise!

One evening a stranger knocked at Evan's front door just down the street. Evan had invested in the neighborhood, become president of the association, taken citizen police training, and gotten involved. His parents had moved to the neighborhood from Northern Virginia and started renovating a house a couple of streets over. Flipping on his porch light, Evan opened his front door to an unfamiliar white face streaked with red. The handle of the stabbing implement protruded from the man's sinus cavity, and from its length looked to be a chef's knife. With blood pouring down his face, the man asked for help. Evan sat him on the stoop, made the emergency call, and waited with him for the paramedics. The newspaper reported that the knife had almost severed the man's upper spine. Luckily, doctors were able to extract the blade from his face without further injury. The man's live-in partner had stabbed him, and afterwards they continued sharing quarters.

All of these lives in proximity, all of these people trying to live together without pressing charges, filled with rage and love, stabbing each other with desire. The gay mixed-race couples, the ex-cons with diabetic wives, the Latino fathers and mothers toting laundry baskets up and down the alley from the big brick apartments on the corner to the laundromat a block away, their children trailing in neat rows.

When we sold the most beautiful house in Roanoke, neither of us was particularly sad to leave—another project beckoned—but our bond was ever deepened, in ways that lingered for good, by the annealing pressures of the neighborhood. In our minds, it would always be *our neighborhood*, and in time both of us would return.

Spirit House

One night when my father was stationed near San Diego during WWII, he borrowed a car from his landlord in National City and crossed the border into Mexico, escorting my mother to Rosarita Beach for dinner. They had a fine time, but on the way back, in the middle of nowhere south of the border, a tire blew out. With no spare, no Spanish, and an eleven o'clock curfew looming, Dad made a plan. The only light in the distance glinted from a shack up on the hillside above the curving road. He didn't have any choice; he had to go for help. Mom locked herself inside the car. If he did not make it back to base on time, he'd lose his privileges or be counted AWOL.

Unable to see past the car windows, wondering what she would do alone on the roadside in Mexico if he never returned, Mom waited. After some time, out of the darkness, Dad appeared with two men he had found drinking beer on a lighted porch who volunteered a spare. They rolled the used tire toward the car and changed the flat. Dad barely made it back to base on time.

Mom's home-front stories are filled with occasions like this when she received help from perfect strangers across various borders of ethnicity, language, or country. During the experience of being flung cross-country far from immediate family, she developed her faith. Whenever I need help and no one can really help me, Mother says she will pray. Like my mother, I try to practice the art of lifting up whatever's too heavy to hold and letting it go. I picture a lead balloon floating into the stratosphere. Sometimes I remember to do this right away before things get too freighted with worry, ingrained with impossibility, but most times I forget. I stew and hold my head and wake up gasping in the night. I feel locked in a broken-down car on a dark stretch of road in rural Mexico. I sit in the darkness waiting alone, but no one has gone for help.

In Southeast Asian cultures—in Burma, Cambodia, Laos, and Thailand—it's typical to associate altars with sacred trees and also with houses and businesses. Families mount miniature house shrines, built on pillars, inside and out in auspicious spots to shelter any restless spirits and ensure protection; they burn votive candles to appease spirits. In return, the spirits provide luck for businesses and homes, or at least fend off wrath. Spirit Houses catch and keep any unruly spirits from troubling the living and honor protective spirits lingering there. In ancient Roman tradition, the *lares familiars* stayed with the house or place instead of going with the family if they moved, and thus the *lararium*, the shrine to the *lar*, had to be tended by the current inhabitants in order to keep it satisfied and willing to aid. If one ignored the *lar* by not tending the *lararium*, one might be tempting fate, especially if the statue representing the house guardian turned its back.

I wander down to the river for the first time this week. A waterfall gushes over the dam from the pond, falling back into a spring tributary that empties into the river rushing by. A rope spaced with floats stretches across the water, marking the swimming hole just where the river bends. A walking bridge spans the spring tributary to the riverbank and wooden steps lead down to the water, which is usually clear and swift just here and said to be cleaner than most Virginia streams. I've come to the Cowpasture River each summer for more than two decades, having taken a chance on an invitation from out of the blue. Like the nearby Bullpasture and Calfpasture, this river is named not for dairy cows but for bison (buffalo) or elk, translated from the Indian *Walatoola* as "winding river" or "figure drawn on the ground as the waking bull buffalo urinates," which of course conjures quite an interesting picture. By tubing parts of the Cowpasture, I've confirmed its winding route; all of my associations with this place continue to take unexpected twists and turns. I sit down on the wooden steps and watch the light ripple on the water.

My annual pilgrimage began with a phone call from Charlotte in the middle of winter, or maybe it began before that with Trudy's tarot reading, which presented me with an image: I am in a green pasture holding my writing notebook with students sitting around me. When I didn't quite get it, Trudy said, "a summer camp for adults," was the best description she could give me. These were the very words offered by Charlotte when she invited me to lead the writing workshop in Bath County. Sight unseen, "I'm in," I said, experiencing a frisson that raised the hair on the back of my neck.

My actual class sits inside in a circle of mismatched, musty chairs with broken rungs and ripped, tattered seats, talking about the words, the sentences, the characters and plots, the tensions in all the choices writers make. Charlotte and I have worked with participants who are drawn here, each on her own path for her own reasons, as we continue to shape the workshop into something worthwhile, a shifting community of writers more attached to this place than to us. Our circle is not by any means exclusive, but mainly women attend, ranging in age from twenty-something to eighty-something. They don't mind hot days without air conditioning in a rambling old lodge and associated structures dotting the grounds, cool nights under blankets, shared bathrooms, or a week's separation from family in order to get back to themselves and back to stitching words. We subscribe to the best writing advice there has ever been: butt in chair. We repeat it as our mantra. Every day, we are served three delicious family-style meals that feature fresh garden vegetables and herbs. Frankie, the owner, grew up here in the main house, and her father owned a summer camp; her homemade biscuits and rolls are larruping good. Our organized activities extend only to one-on-one conferences, workshops, and nightly participant readings. It's a low-key creative community, an anchor of a place where people know and accept each other as part of the scenery. I return here, my year hinging near the end of each July, gathering energy from the soft-forested hills, the river, and a rare green heron nesting around the bend.

On my way down to find the water's edge, I covered old ground. In less than half an hour, the lunch bell would ring. I passed the weathered hay barn, slowing to look through its open mouth. Behind the barn, giant chunks of the old oak tree jutted like monoliths. The massive tree had to be taken down and chopped into pieces the previous winter to satisfy the insurance company.

The main house with its hodgepodge of additions was first a hunting lodge, then a family home, and dates back to the mid-eighteenth century. A large dining room bridges to the new kitchen from the old parts of the house. Every house this old was probably at sometime also a stagecoach stop. That sacred oak stood for parts of three centuries, and aside from shading the front yard and protecting the main house it sheltered dozens of black snakes in the gnarled recesses of its roots. On an interior ring, the tree bears a blackened gash from an old lightning strike or rotting disease that subsequent growth covered, sealing the hollow core with new rings and no bad medicine. How many more years would that tree, scarred and healed, have stood strong?

Just as I tried to see how much of the trunk and how many limbs I could count from the wood laid to rest in amputated segments, a shadow crossed my line of sight. I looked up squarely into the gliding shape of a raptor, like a perfect paper cutout. Chunky of tail and chubby of outline, it had a white head that reminded me of an eagle's, but this raptor was too small, with pinions neither wide enough nor wingtips distinctly fingered like an eagle's, nor was it soaring high enough. It might have been a red-shouldered hawk, as those are common enough there, but I couldn't be sure. It was probably a buteo or a buzzard hawk, with its stocky body and squat fan of a tail. Maybe some form of falcon, or are falcons smaller and leaner? Could it have been something as rare as a Cooper's hawk? A birder would enjoy educating my untrained eye. The sun emerged from behind a cloud and I could not look any longer, only blink. This genius flying contraption, what I'm calling simply *hawk,* edged closer to the ground with each half circle; its dusky projection crossed in front of my feet, darkening gravel, stretching a distorted gargantuan shadow hawk for an instant to bar my path.

I look up again and shade my eyes from the nearly vertical sun; my body casts no twin at true noon as the clock reads one, and in the distance some eager child rings the hand bell for lunch. The only shadow belongs to the moving hawk, and it is arcing again, crossing overhead. An uneasy feeling of being watched triggers my patting of pockets. Inventory: no keys, no money, no ID, but I don't need them. Even if I forget who I am, nice people here will remind me. I'm at this river to remember. I rise and head back toward lunch.

Driving a country road when I lived in Rockbridge County, I saw a hawk swish through the air over my car and snatch a squirrel from the edge of a hay field. It struggled with its squirming prey to the top of a smallish tree that bowed with the additional weight. I stopped the car to gawk but then drove on, my stomach flip-flopping.

I question this hawk's shadowing me, as it seldom flaps wings, drifts tighter circles, catches thermals and glides silently up then persistently toward earth again. I ascend the gravel path with the hawk expanding circles to include me, following my footsteps away from the river. Clearly, this hunter-bird searches, waiting to strike. The shiver that knowledge sends through me is real, but I trust the natural world more than this. I know that hawks generally eat rodents, reptiles, and even grasshoppers and are not confused enough to swoop down on solitary humans. I can almost see its feather pattern, one arc-shaped tip layered against another as it drifts along with me, familiar as my missing shadow. I used to dream of flying but those dreams have stopped.

ॐ

At seventeen, I trekked cross-country on a renovated school bus with cracked brown leather bench seats, no seatbelts, and rusty aluminum windows. I had bounced to and from public school on the same sort of bus for half my life, except that those yellow buses had been in better condition. We christened our steed "The Blue Goose" in honor of the quick coat of Carolina blue that covered flaking yellow and rust patches. Forget air conditioning; the only ventilation came from muscling the metal windows open from the top. Phil, our high school psychology teacher, had no doubt read Tom Wolfe's *The Electric Kool-aid Acid Test* and Kerouac's *On the Road* and was inspired to create his own gang of merry pranksters. He added a propane cook stove, a tiny food prep area, and a camping toilet in the back of the bus.

A skydiver and ski patroller, our leader was the type of guy up for anything, and he assembled a tribe consisting of his wife, their two small daughters, about twelve teenagers from his classes, and another young male teacher to chaperone—a rooster-guarding-the-henhouse assignment that only fooled a few parents. This was decidedly not the sort of trip any public school teen would nowadays be allowed to take, and no teacher could organize such a venture and expect to stay employed. We scraped together a couple hundred dollars each for gas and communal rations and headed down the road toward a month of bedroll sleeping in improvised and occasional real campgrounds, mostly on the ground. Some nights we rolled beneath our Goose for shelter in some eighteen-wheeler parking lot where our bus attracted amused commentary from professional long-haulers. *Breaker-breaker, we've got a bunch of crazy kids in a blue bus, over.* We did have a CB radio strapped to the dash that rattled along with us.

Phil had not done the kind of advanced planning and logistics one might expect—it goes without saying that GPS did not then exist—and sometimes the bus didn't move as fast or as far as predicted. We were not above borrowing gas now and then with a siphoning hose and the cover of darkness. For a few days on the return trip we were waylaid in Tuba City, where an invisible line separated Reservation sun time from non-Reservation daylight savings time, and we were forever in the wrong zone waiting for a bus part.

Our first night on the road heading south we drove through a heckling rainstorm somewhere outside of Nashville, and our collection of green army-issue duffle bags roped to the roof rack were thoroughly soaked. These were the days, my friends, before Gore-Tex and lightweight raingear, before

many things I cannot now live without. Imagine sending your teenager off
without a phone for a month on a cross-country camping trip traveling on a
retired school bus. The fact of this journey alone may furnish enough retrospective proof that in 1975 parents were much more relaxed, gullible, or at
least much happier to see their offspring disappear without a trace. No cell
phones! No Internet! No Skype! We launched west into the wilderness, set
free to roam. My mother still wonders at her judgment, but it is my theory
that after living through WWII, my parents were not as neurotic about the
world as current versions of parents and grandparents roughly my age, who
typically have lived through nothing more extreme than graduating college
without dying from alcohol poisoning.

The second night along our journey, my revelations began. It started
with nothing more spectacular than unrolling my foam pad and plunking
down my sleeping bag in some ugly parking lot; I crawled inside the plaid
flannel-lined bag and then, oh then, looked up. We had parked the Goose in
north Texas and the sky poured over me like a river of endless sparkling water. I could not stop counting stars, riding the wash of them with my eyes.
The sky would swallow me up; it was as if we, the sky and I, were merging. I
could see everything, including the smeary Milky Way, which was unlike
any bright cluster of unnamed stars or planets before or after. And in that
moment I was transported, connected, changed. Like my version of Black
Elk at the top of the highest mountain, "I understood more than I saw; for I
was seeing in a sacred manner the shape of all things in the spirit, and the
shape of all shapes as they must live together like one being." The sky took,
broke, and rebuilt me. I fell into the sky: the sky that I had only glimpsed
before, framed by mountains, framed by trees, presented in thin slices like
specimens on slides, in sheltered prospects, only in small bites. Was this
even the same sky that had always covered me? Hard to believe the sky could
expand to envelop me under its curved dome. The world finally blew its
breath into me, and it was more than my lungs involuntarily deeming I
would live. I decided to breathe on my own. I was home. I took it all in, and
it took me.

And then we docked at White Sands, New Mexico. Sunset in a moonscape of sand, mounds deposited by desert winds. I climbed the sand hills
and slid down them, photographed, and chewed on the grit of them after
rolling down. Sometimes the earth's configurations can be enough to blow
all your fuses, re-amp, and start you again with sand in your pants.

In El Paso we drifted over the border to Juárez, crossing a bridge prominently inscribed "Roanoke Iron and Bridge Works": a little reminder of my mother's hometown where I now abide. Just on the other side of the border, a youth vigorously approached our band of explorers. "Hey Mister, I'll give you my sister...." He wanted our Kodak Instamatic, the sort of cheap camera sold off the shelf in drug stores. The girl looked to be around ten. And just at that moment a Seals and Croft song wafted over the street through the feedback fuzz of loud speakers: "We May Never Pass this Way Again." If no one would take the pleasure of his sister, the boy offered to take our picture with the camera, rubbing two fingers against thumb for dinero.

Jonna, Teri, and I wandered around later that same day, wondering where they'd parked the bus; it had been moved from the place we got off. We sampled the shops, walked and walked, thinking we were supposed to meet up. By the end of the day some of our number, mostly the boys, had fallen prey to tequila and were literally crawling through the campground. I went to bed early, unfazed and merely bloated, as someone had tipped me off not to eat the street food. I'd eaten an untoasted Pop-Tart slathered with peanut butter for dinner.

At Four Corners the western map concretized into a game of four square, and I skipped into one state after another, laughing at the speed of my transition from New Mexico to Colorado, Utah to Arizona. Whether or not the monument is actually in the right physical place matters not. The state leaping is conceptual. I knew exactly where I was in space and time, one pinpoint dropped like a record needle onto a map. When I was a teenager locked in my bedroom by choice, alone or with a friend, I often passed the time by playing records, especially my favorite songs. It was necessary to pick up the arm and drop the needle over and over again into the right groove to find Joe Cocker's "With a Little Help from My Friends," Paul McCartney singing "The Long and Winding Road" at the top of his range, or Joni Mitchell singing anything. I found a groove thing on this trip west that furnished some operating instructions for computing true interior distances as well as exterior distances on the map of the contiguous forty-eight. Part of my new understanding was that when I said *sky* I had formerly meant something different from the expansive sky I saw in Texas. And the meaning of *mountain*, likewise, changed after I gazed upon the Rockies. My original *mountain* was much greener, older, and softer. Improbably blue in the distance, my first *mountains* still zigzag along, belonging to the Blue Ridge or Appalachian chains.

Mesa Verde jolted me into an encounter with deeper American history, before seventeenth century colonization and the age of exploration (exploitation). I climbed down into a kiva on a replica leather-lashed wooden ladder, and when my feet dropped to the earth I was like an antenna into the past. Already a refugee from three years of Virginia history in public school, I had not realized until that moment of contact with the kiva floor anything about what it meant to be purposefully misinformed. History's omissions, erasures, gaps. Our inherited civilization existed in another, completely realized form in this place long before the Pilgrims or the Jamestown settlement. Obvious now. Back then not so much. I had learned that Virginia once stretched west, encompassing Kentucky, then part of Fincastle County, which meant Virginia also contained the eastern parts of the Buffalo Trace migratory route. I had much to learn. As the sky above me expanded, transformed with a wider view, now the roots grew beneath me, too. The land's meaning was changing.

With more grounding, I was right-sizing myself. My state, so central to every shred of history I knew, birthplace of presidents, was shrinking along with me, as what I thought I knew collapsed and then opened out into what I sought, walls collapsing into open territory. I was on my own Lewis and Clark expedition. I wrote letters to my friend, Jay, took daily notes, and sketched the new land's features, flora and fauna, as they appeared to me. I tried to read Virginia Woolf's *The Voyage Out* on the bus and soon found it too poetic for bouncing along. Our first Arkansas thunderstorm lit up the landscape with such intensity I could see colors at night. Stinging ants crowded my foam sleeping pad, I reported in my letters, and El Capitan was like the inevitable gray peak rising at the start of old Hercules movies. I imagined myself at its craggy summit, arms outstretched. Pack-rat Jay, whose mother and mine played bridge together, saved my letters for nearly forty years! Rereading my own words, I am taken aback by how little I've changed since that summer, how much I sound just like myself.

I did not write to Jay about the multitude of bats streaming out of Carlsbad Caverns as we warmed the bleachers at sundown, but I remember their startling noise beating the air, as loud as helicopters, but really like nothing manmade; my heart raced with the moving currents surrounding me. Enlivened day by day along my new path, energized by sleeping under the night sky, I embraced armadillos, ants, bats, and all. Traveling the western landscape claimed and tuned a part of me to its channel. Sky and stars claimed me first, enveloped me as I fell up, and then stark desert mesas, rushing rivers, snow-encrusted Rocky peaks, sandstorms scuffing us in the night, our rented tents collapsing in stinging whips of wind, scorpions nestled in my shoes, every particle of space. Traveling in the west made me understand something about the unseen reciprocity between the land and us, and what it means for us to be out of whack, out of synch, out of touch, to take too much or too little, to lose footing through an unbalanced exchange. "We are not restoring the planet; she is restoring us," writes Paula Gunn Allen. We continually have need of stepping out of doors into sunlight, moonlight, and falling into place. Camped near the Grand Canyon, I saw four shooting stars and a UFO in half an hour. The whole of this crazy journey felt akin to the different light I'd never quite been able to account for in my mother's eyes whenever she said the word *California* in discussing the war years.

Into Pacific waters in Oceanside, California, I ran, where waves rolled in over a mix of cold black and green pebbles scrunching the soles of my feet. The boy I had broken up with before the trip, an Ethan Hawke double, started looking quite the dude on a surfboard, with tousled hair naturally sun-streaked. That summer I dipped into the Pacific and the Atlantic oceans within a month's time. We toured the San Diego zoo and Disneyland, but the fake sparkle wasn't alluring. Floating down Utah's Virgin River, hiking sandstone bluffs, and photographing high desert flowers, I found my magic kingdom. Not to mention Bryce Canyon: What kind of wonder-world was this, with jutting spires and sandcastle upside-down cakes, dripped by whose hand? In Crested Butte, Colorado, our Blue Goose paraded in their traditional July fourth on the fifth celebration, and our nubile beauty scandalized the locals at the unisex bathhouse.

When I returned home to my Jefferson-blue bedroom, my mattress was too soft. I unrolled the well-used foam pad on my bedroom floor and slept there for another week.

My parents' good friends, Tally and Wendell, lived on Claytor Lake. Marked with a hand-painted pointer of a sign, the rocky, pitted Burma Road led to their place. Whenever I traveled the Burma Road in Tally's wood-paneled Jeep I was bouncing to a secret world. At the top of the hill before you could see the log home at the end of the drive, a grassy spot thrived with a birdbath and a birdhouse. They'd also planted a couple of oddly vertical topiary firs that in retrospect remind me of Italian trees. Their renovated and winterized cabin perched atop an outcrop above the green lake, a tree house closer to sky than water. To get to the water we had to walk down an ankle-twister of a path to a dock where our feet often collected splinters. Wendell hoisted his motorboat with an electric winch his father had installed years before; this contraption held my attention whenever he pushed the button, or allowed me to, and metal cords wound or unwound, ferrying the boat toward or away from the water. I learned to water ski and, sometimes, I swam out of their cove into the nearly opaque lake with the dock shrinking behind me until I was breathless. I was a strong swimmer and worked several summers as a lifeguard and swimming teacher, but that distance was still a challenge. I give myself a lot of credit for continuing to dive in the lake and swim after seeing a huge snapping turtle—wider than my extended arms—glide beneath the dock near the ladder we regularly climbed without the benefit of water shoes. I thought of that turtle's beak on my tender toes every time I climbed the ladder, and the turtle kept growing larger. Soon the turtle of my imagination had swallowed the lake. The lake was a green turtle shell. Every idyll has its monster. Despite the gargantuan lurking turtle, those summer lake visits remain one of the spirit houses I touch and retouch.

I've visited many places, tendering them as possible talismans; some places surprise me with their constancy, others with their transience. I don't know why certain places stick or why I have stuck to certain places, but it must be more than accidental that I still work and live in a small sphere and have a record of long relationships with people, things, and places, any of which can change form and still endure. "Place is space that has the capacity to be remembered and to evoke what is most precious," writes Sheldrake. I have certainly found that to be true. Spiritual homes are points of contact with the earth that we use as recharging stations, plugging in for the feeling of well-being we find there. Among my spiritual homes will ever be the varied western landscape, especially from New Mexico through the Colorado plateau and the canyons of southern Utah; as soon as I went west as a teenager I knew I would go back. Added to that is my native eastern mountain watershed environs, a kid's tree house hammered with bent nails and boards that half fit along with a wind-blown walk on a strip of South Carolina beach with pelican patrols and dolphins bouncing in and out of the surf, one banging its tail high, splashing. And then, lodged long in memory, there is a bright green moist, mossy place where I played when I was less than ten years old, a private fairyland in the woods. I stretched out for hours of silent imaginings, touching spongy moss, caressing little live-wired green sprouts that broke the velvet surface, almost levitating with the infusion of negative ions, dipped in that ocean of green energy. The moss carpet grew in a rabbit thicket. I'd crawl inside alone or with a friend and sit well protected from any weather. I tried out the Lord's Prayer there, feeling the need arise for some ritual and forgetting the words halfway through. I didn't really need formal prayer then and still have no ease with it. Those words were too solemn, shopworn. I'd have rather spoken with the rabbits. Even PBJ tasted like food of the gods in that thicket, a hymn to childhood those sandwiches sang.

My spirit houses, more than a list of places, also encompass my walking a divergent spiritual path that intertwines with the Protestant forms into which I was born. My Jesus is a radical who blew apart institutions with social protest and healing actions like chasing money changers from the temple, chastising gangs of men cradling ready stones in their fists, and raising the dead. My Jesus interrupted the natural cycle at its core belief that people and things will die. Maybe not, he said. There's a different way to live that doesn't accept death as truth. "Why do you look for the living among the dead?" (Luke 24:5, NIV)

In college, I started searching through traditions in earnest when I read a string of spiritual autobiographies, including St. Augustine's *Confessions*, St. Teresa of Avila's autobiography, John G. Neihardt's *Black Elk Speaks*, and Simone Weil's aphoristic journal entries collected in *Gravity and Grace*. In the same semester I also read *Autobiography of a Yogi* and *The Cloud of Unknowing*. As I tried to focus only on the word *God* as instructed by the anonymous medieval mystic author of *The Cloud*, I was given nothing but a word, a sonic blip, a strangely round and finally meaningless tone with a few unfortunate English rhymes that kept popping to mind (cod, sod, mod, odd). I brimmed with admiration and bafflement as I constantly attempted to divert my thoughts back only to *God*, in a word, lost in perseverations of *God, God, God*. Of course, that was the point, to empty oneself of everything but.

Emptying to be filled, a living paradox. Get used to paradoxes if you want to know God.

Much earlier in elementary school I had selected odd subjects on which to report, subjects that could not be copied whole cloth from the World Book. I indulged in a lengthy study of Iceland in the fourth grade when it was time to research a country. Carefully constructing a flag from felt, I applied droplets of strategic glue to an embedded red cross on white on blue. I wrote across seas to the chamber of commerce at Reykjavik. They sent me a number of leaflets and bland recipes including "Braised Turnips" and "Reindeer Stew." Poor Rudolph! I learned about *hydroponic* vegetables, a new word I adored. I received these facts with a certain ecstasy while my classmates held forth on Italy, Germany, and Japan. In sixth grade my research project was on the Shakers. I can't remember how I found this arcane religious sect, strange material for a little Appalachian girl...or maybe not. Plain but beautiful furniture was part of Shaker aesthetic, and their ascetic nature forbade converts, marriage, or children. Their ecstatic way of worship, "touched by the spirit," was perhaps the most familiar part of Shaker tradition to me, as I had heard a lot of stories about tent revival hoedowns and even sneaked into one as a child to see the high drama of Pentecostal-style witnessing, speaking in tongues, snake handling, and "falling out," which meant you were felled by the spirit. Someone touched your forehead and you fell down.

Searching for my place in traditional Christianity, in my mid-twenties I read various seminal texts from a variety of Protestant religions. I started with the sermons of John Wesley because I had been raised a Methodist, and then I read the meditations of George Fox, thinking I might be a Quaker at heart, as I sought and believed in inner light rather than doctrinal affirmations. Still, I had the idea that I wanted to belong to some established way of worship. My then-husband was of the liberal American Baptist tradition; he didn't go to church. I tried a Friends' meeting and felt ill at ease with the silent waiting and then with the blurting. Did one really have to be so humorless to be blessed? I tried Sufi dancing. Again, it was awkward and felt more like a contra dance than a service. Plus, the men were strange willowy creatures.

In my thirties I joined a spiritual healing circle led by an excommunicated priest who nonetheless had the power. I never found out what he had done to earn the church's wrath; he had spent a lot of time in

South America on missions. An obvious drunk, red nose and broken blood vessels on his cheeks, he still directed the group without narcissistically becoming the center of attention. I've come more and more to appreciate anyone who is adept and mentally healthy enough to accomplish this. At each weekly meeting he introduced an hour's worth of topical conversation followed by pushing back the circle of chairs for standing prayer. Our group was populated by struggling gay men, a man who had been deliberately infected with AIDS by his ER nurse wife, some scattered university professors, at least one lawyer, an architect, and a woman who had lost her son to a drunk driving accident one holiday night.

The circle could be powerful, and within it I finally experienced falling out for myself. It was like bathing under warm water and being gently floated to the ground as hands caught and lowered me when I fell back from the touch of the (ex) priest, like REM sleep without dreaming. In this semiconscious state I could hear those around me, but I could not fully respond or move. It was like being paralyzed in a dream, but pleasantly so. Some people stayed in this state only momentarily, some for half an hour or more, lying on the floor undisturbed. We entered deeply meditative states, which is probably what triggers any healing that takes place.

The healing circle community migrated and reformed around a Louise Hay-inspired minister who was newly ordained. Her nonprofit still exists as a place for new age healing arts. I took a class there in energy healing, which is something like therapeutic touch without the physical weight of hands. It took me twenty years to return to that practice in learning Reiki, another form of energy work.

Certain color combinations provide me solace. Blue and green form a slippage from sky to water and water to earth, a blend and balance: blue water/green fields; green water/blue air: swimming pools, waterfalls, rivers, oceans, great blue heavens/grass, moss, mountain laurel (which is related to sassafras and cinnamon), fir as in evergreen. The combination of blue/green soothes, furnishes relief from anxiety.

I light a candle and place it on a hand-built altar, a pitched-roof steeple over a house of sorts, over four walls representing the earth, a square to the circle, a family to the timeless realm of cycles and scriptures. All of us must find a spirit house where we fit as much as we must find nurturance from a *domus,* from house, from place, and from what collective community can mean. In turn, each of us must be a house for others, a place where others are not turned away.

Jay Shafer's tiny houses aren't much bigger than ritual spirit houses, where the rest of us might light a votive. Shafer turned his obsession for living small into a lifestyle, a business, and a trend that keeps evolving. I already had Shafer's self-published *The Small House Book* on my shelf when Alec Wilkinson's article, "Let's Get Small: The Rise of the Tiny-House Movement," appeared in *The New Yorker*. At the time, I was frustrated to see the article, as I wanted to believe that tiny houses were an unusual area of knowledge I was cultivating, like my obsession with tipis and tiny RVs. During the years it has taken to write this book, the tiny house has risen in popularity until it has its own HGTV shows, living proof that trends are fast and writing slow, the opposite of viral.

What would freedom look like? Maybe it would take shape as a tiny house built to sacred proportions on a horse trailer frame, weighing less than 4,700 pounds, able to move from place to place or be more permanently installed if one wished, a self-contained one-person hive with its own camp toilet and solar-generated electricity. You might build it yourself for fifteen thousand dollars or have the Tumbleweed Tiny House Company build it for twice that, but it's not legal to live in a space so cramped. You can camp in it, but in most places it doesn't qualify as housing for building, zoning, or tax purposes, and at the other end of the spectrum, even in some campgrounds, your structure will be considered too tall for an RV. You're not even allowed to park it on your own property unless you also own a regular-sized house and pretend, as Shafer did for a while, that you are camping in your own backyard. Shafer secretly rented out his big house while living in his first 8 x 12 Tumbleweed.

What would freedom look like? For most of us it wouldn't contain a mortgage, but if you are employed there are tax incentives for carrying one, especially if you are single with no dependents. No mortgage company will qualify you for a tiny loan to build a tiny house on wheels, because aside from its not meeting code in most places, it's considered a trailer not a permanent home. Structures surround us in which we have to operate—so many codes, zones, and multi-layers of regulations. Many of the same considerations drive the economic engine of the country with laws written to sustain the status quo. The construction industry is so huge that one has to wonder if it might be nearly impossible to step off the wheel, not to mention the grid. Some electric companies will charge you for not hooking up; some localities will fine you for unmonitored pooping. But the picture is brightening: in Madison, Wisconsin, a tiny house village built for the homeless has opened. Hurray. Detroit has followed suit as well as a small but growing list of other places.

Jay Shafer's life changed. He got married; with wife and child his requirements shifted. Even though Shafer's current domicile is not as large as most people think they need, one dream busted another, even for an evangelist of living small.

On the road in Mexico, New Year's Eve 2007, I booked a driver online who would transport us from León airport to San Miguel de Allende, roughly an hour and a half away. A. and I had made this journey twice before, once with a group of Roanoke artists and again for a writing workshop. Both times we had used the airport in Querétaro that was a little closer than León to San Miguel and booked a reliable driver from the airport, but the general idea remained the same. Our flight to León arrived on time and our driver greeted us with a sign bearing my name. It was around 10:30 P.M., and we were thinking we'd see in the New Year in San Miguel, probably among fellow Americans at some bar or other, as the town has been a vigorous expat destination since the end of Vietnam. We loaded our bags into the cab and sat back exhausted as the car left the terminal and entered the dark countryside.

Outside the window there wasn't much I could see; there were no streetlights past the airport hub and no houses close to the highway. I was dozing when the driver pulled into a gas station; it seemed a bit odd that he'd not bothered to fill up the car before fetching us. Some minutes later we were heading over dark winding roads again, but before we could relax into our seats our driver pulled to the shoulder without comment, opened his door, stepped ahead of the car into the headlight glare, and proceeded to relieve himself. We could see the furious arc of urine. Peeing like a racehorse, as the expression goes. Peeing like an Icelandic five-gaited horse that looks like a very broad pony or like its angry trainer. We were praying he wouldn't turn toward us. I had involuntary flashbacks to a nearly fatal horseback-riding outing in Iceland some years earlier. The stable owner/guide had led the way across the fields over winding paths toward the craggy coast where colorful, entertaining puffins awaited my viewing. As soon as he left sight of his wife and several small children, he climbed down from his horse and took a whiz right in front of me, in some primitive assertion. I turned my head away, but yes, clearly this Icelandic caveman was equipped to put out a campfire with his own water, thank you Freud. A long dismal, rainy afternoon ensued in which my barn-sour horse tried generally and specifical-ly to kill me, first by pitching me onto a Volcanic, black sand beach, and then, following that maneuver, by kneeling strategically to crush my pros-trate body. "Roll, roll," my comrade shouted. I did, and the irate horse turned and ran back almost all the way to the barn. I couldn't walk for a few days afterward, but the puffins were indeed roosting along the well-earned cliffs, and I snapped a few pictures of them while wondering if I would live to tell the story of their bright plumage. As I watched the puffins I was aware that the incoming tide was filling the channel we'd waded across. Rid-ing back from the beach, we had to swim our horses. My stubborn horse, caught and returned by our guide and even more irate than before, was strapped to the guide's horse with my leg caught between two fat girths and stirrups. The friction was memorable, and now, in Mexico, the memory was even less comforting.

As we waited somewhere on the road to San Miguel towards midnight, A. was raising an eyebrow that said "drug cartel" and poking me in the side in the backseat of the car. Still, I was not that worried, perhaps because as I child I had survived many a ranting car ride. Or maybe I was just too tired. For me, flying always induces numbness along with a dearth of emergency emotions. I thought if pissing were the end of our driver's antics, we'd arrive at our hotel soon enough. This all happened well before our country's most recent economic crash and before the worst violence heated up across the southern border. Our driver returned to the wheel, steered the car back into traffic, twisted and turned for some miles, and then drifted to another stop: police barricade. Was it some kind of New Year's Eve traffic stop? The driv-er exchanged a few words with two policemen, who requested his papers and then shone their large heavy flashlights into the backseat for several endless moments as we blinked. After this, the driver rolled up his window and our car trundled back along the road into the darkness, never meeting another vehicle.

A. believed it was a close call. I hadn't often seen her rattled, but it happened twice in Mexico. When we'd visited the year before, also on New

Year's Eve, she'd suffered altitude sickness, which felt to her like a sudden, squeezing heart attack. After I had investigated the local hospital options, she recovered on her own within an hour. We traced her problem back to the Texas-size tub of carbonated soda she'd drunk in the Houston airport. My dream of an annual New Year's vacation in Mexico might have been flickering. On this trip, our last across that border, A. could not be persuaded to leave the hotel room for much more than food, stoically painting from photos she had taken the year before.

I was usually the hypervigilant half of our duo and the physically weaker one, waking in the night with sudden stomachaches when trains rocked over the rails or startling awake from bad dreams in champion bouts of worry. For some reason, in this instance I made little of the fact that we were in central Mexico with an unknown quantity of a driver who could take us anywhere he wanted, and I had obviously forgotten that police were not necessarily good but often procured bribes from tourists. They could easily have marched us over to an ATM and cleaned us out before our vacation began. The fact that they did not means something, but in truth, at the time I was just annoyed that our driver had stopped so frequently, which meant we were not going to make it to our hotel by midnight and thus probably not to my favorite bar, Tapas and 'Tini. The New Year was turning, the mirror ball had dropped in Times Square, and we were way too long on a dark rural stretch of Mexican road trying to reach San Miguel de Allende.

When we arrived at our hotel at the sign of the bull, the driver demanded twice the agreed-upon fare. Crossing the Styx with no coins to spare, I was too tired to argue, so I told him no way, forget it. Again, A. thought I was taking a risk. To me, it was just another annoyance. Any recklessness on my part was only a function of exhaustion. I refused to pay him more, as he would produce no round-trip receipt for us to use on our return. I was cranky and hungry, and it was late. We stumbled to our room, no Embassy Suite, dragging our bags along the narrow outside corridor paved with rough stones. A. collapsed on the bed. All I wanted was to go out and find my 'tini. I cannot remember now whether or not we did, only that we felt relatively safe in Mexico, a pitcher of potable water waiting for us in our room, thirsty as we were from having traveled a dark and winding road.

Dream House

For most of my life, I have repurposed commercial properties in my imagination. Abandoned warehouses, overbuilt shopping malls, failed grocery chains, office parks, or storefronts: what would it be like to live there? I've enjoyed speculating about how these buildings meant for manufacturing, retail, or warehousing could best be divided into domestic space. Where should a kitchen go in relation to the bedrooms? Do windows need to be opened along the brick west wall? And what about skylights or light tubes? Where would the bookcases fit, and where should living room furniture be oriented for views? If this is a normal use of imagination for a grade school child, then I was normal. I'm not sure what started this line of thought in me, but it was probably a silent game I played to pass the time on car trips as we drove past different kinds of structures, often too recklessly with my fatalistic father at the helm. "When your number's up, your number's up," he would chant.

Home as a concept involves transformation. My relationship to it—carrier pigeon's instinct to return—has never quite felt satisfied and stays enlivened by dreaming of what might be. My lack of a settled feeling or definition dovetails with a passage from Philip Sheldrake in which he reminds us of Michel de Certeau's suggestion that we are all on "a kind of perpetual pilgrimage that somehow parallels the mystical tradition. We experience dissatisfaction with final destinations or completed places and are driven ever onwards in a movement of perpetual departure." Amen, brother. Preach it. Sometimes I think I'm most at home in books, writing or reading. I finish one, fold my tipi, and start another.

For a while I believed my spatial ruminations must mean something vocational, a bent toward architecture. I did enjoy building igloos in the snow and digging pit houses in the woods in the warmer months, but ensuing years of education proved I had aptitudes and sensibilities headed in other directions. Still, my avocation for imagining conversions of commercial into domestic space inevitably, if unconsciously, led me to our rehabbed space, the downtown loft occupying the sixth floor of a former office building erected in 1905 and amended in 1917 from three stories to eight. The process of creating this space in an abandoned structure, like self-creation, proved anything but dreamy. I fought against its complexity of layered contracts, argued against its grandiosity given our modest means, without even considering the crucial expenditures of time and emotion. Even if *time, an abstraction, isn't made of anything*, and neither are emotions, both of them prove to be the most substantial materials in the end: time and *im*materials.

Relationships often don't survive building projects easily, of this I was aware, but I wasn't worried. I knew I had to sign off on the project or A. would never forgive me, and it was time to leave our troubled neighborhood behind. Therefore, I inscribed the second line on the contract, my name under hers, and began the process that would construct a dream house for an artist and a writer, one with studio and display needs and the other in need of an office and library. In order to fund our loft, we had to let go of several other living spaces, which involved orchestrating the sale of three houses owned between us. And, more difficult than the rest of the process, we had to relearn collaboration, how to build a collective dream. "Finding a house that fits is like finding a soul mate," my friend May-Lily said wisely, and much later. I thought A. and I had arrived.

Barbie probably interrogated her dream house, although I remember moving her around in it from room to room, dropping her through the open roof with rapt attention while her face with its pert expression remained unchanged. I parked her convertible nearby and sailed her into her car, top down, for driving dates around the den floor. My Barbie donned a tiny pair of cat-eye movie star sunglasses when she ventured out, balanced on her miniscule nose and ear bumps, but I was focused not so much on her bizarre shape and accessorized outfits as I was on attempting to fit myself inside that roofless house and that convertible by imagining myself in her shoes. I was moved more by space and speed, preferring Lincoln Logs, Tinker Toys, LEGO bricks, and a toy car that fell apart when you slammed it into walls. If you pieced it back together, it would break apart again.

The fact of no roof on Barbie's dream home was practical for playing house, but the incompleteness of her shelter worried me. What about wind and rain and that fearsome huffing and puffing? I opened a large picture book and made her a roof.

Self-satisfaction, not sleep and certainly not dreaming, is the enemy of consciousness, and without consciousness there is no art in living. As I'm writ-

ing this I'm wondering what I mean. The sentence is like a dream: it ema-
nated from me and simultaneously came from elsewhere, as I did at some
point, filtering down through DNA strands to planet blue, planet three.
From the hospital I was taken home in a snowstorm to a red brick house
with a primitive coal furnace tended by someone other than my father due to
its potential for smoke and hazard. A local Beelzebub came with the rental
deal. Soon after my arrival, now a family of four, we bought the house
around the corner with three upstairs bedrooms and an oil furnace. My first
move happened before I turned one, but true to form I didn't go far. A. and
I would be moving five blocks east, to urban Roanoke.

At its best, a home is, as Sarah Susanka writes, "a lens through which the
inhabitants of the house can experience more of who they really are and who
they are becoming." Creating a home, a conscious act of self-creation, contains inherent tensions because it is necessarily collaborative, co-creative. We
collaborate with existing structures in trying to fit our lives and possessions
inside without incurring the cost of too much modification, or we collaborate with architects and builders on the perfect space for ourselves and other
family members with divergent needs and wants. The room in our loft that
we remain most proud of is the kitchen, the room where each of us got part
of what we wanted but not all. I insisted on upper cabinets and A. insisted
on stainless steel counters. We agreed on the espresso-stained cherry cabinets, the island on wheels, the appliances and layout. It is the room where
we made order together, cooked and cleaned up, shared food and conversed
for hours. In the kitchen we successfully combined our aesthetics of surface
and function.

   For months in prelude to our building project, A. and I would convene
at the stainless steel cook's table in the kitchen of our 1890 Victorian, poring
over half-baked floor plans. I'd haul out my graph paper and try to redraw
areas that were going awry. The architect's plans, unwieldy when unrolled,
flopped over the table. We sat across from each other, using our coffee mugs
as paperweights, consequently with one of us always looking at the plans
upside down. As much as we stared and stared, inspecting the scale drawings, we were more lost than we realized. I sketched and erased and balled
up the graph paper time and again. The language of flat lines hardly rendered the four-dimensional space where our condo would take shape. The

emptiness of our demoed floor, flooded with light, called to me more than the blueprints.

When we first bought into the project, our floor still contained all of the old wall divisions, doors with flaking gold-stenciled professional names arched in old style, brass switch plates, slab marble bathroom walls, a wedged window for an exhaust fan to ventilate an old-style blueprint drafting business, and even a drinking fountain. My library was once a lawyer's office. In early photographs there's a sign for an insurance company in one of our east windows; among my mother's papers I would find a policy from Equitable Life of Iowa, issued from the office of Louis N. Hock, whose office was on our floor in 1942. A little scar like a tear marks A.'s face from some dusty venetian blinds that fell on her as we explored.

All of these layers, including cast-iron pipes, wires, and plaster, were removed and the space demolished to reveal steel columns and concrete floors, with only the old double-hung windows salvaged. Though deemed unsafe by contemporary standards, these had to be retained to satisfy the terms of the historic tax credits. We tried to recycle other original elements but found numerous impediments to reuse, including a difference of measurement between old door frames and new, which made rehanging old doors too costly, the labor involved in resurfacing stained marble and removing lead paint, and the necessity of matching dimmer switch plates, not to mention the cynicism of our builders. We were stubborn, though, and the Carrara marble stripped from our baths was stored on a lower floor while we pondered. Eventually, though, it was mysteriously carted off when our attention was elsewhere. They furred out the perimeter walls with six inches of insulation to create a more energy-efficient shell, but the footprint of the floor retains its original trapezoid shape that fitted the building to its corner lot. Ten-foot ceilings jag up and down with the bulkheads of an unanticipated ceiling plan, but in the end the various ceiling heights help define the space. The twin elevators, prone to random ghost openings, stage arrivals of empty cars. On our polished concrete floors, areas of darker concrete mark original doorways and walls. We live with an inadvertent historic imprint beneath our feet. Our view extends to rough, worn fingers of the Blue Ridge Mountains that cup this valley. I remember standing on the roof with our developer and other original owners early in the project, looking out past whimsical man-in-the-moon French copper work in all directions, thinking our building was in the center of the valley, that we were standing at the very heart.

Inflation, deflation, my lungs' rhythm, and a true measure of anything, everything, even this: pride in the project inspiring envy, leading to heartache, a quick boom-bust cycle. Must time always move forward?

In my parents' house, I dreamed a series of flying dreams. Each dream opened and shut the same way. I'd wake in my room at the top of the stairs and swoop down the staircase to fly out into the night through the front door, our house a red brick head, its door a mouth, above it two eyes, the right winking window my sister's room with curtains drawn. The left eye, blinking or not, was my parents' bedroom. My room overlooked the backyard where I could see into the sooty limbs of a giant oak tree. In waking life, I ran fiercely into its trunk, chased in a game of Blind Man's Bluff, and bounced off the tree, my face streaming hot tears and blood as I woke up on the ground seeing stars. Eventually, after many years, my jarred molar would react.

In my dreams, I skimmed down the stairs, the second half of a fast piano scale, and flew out the front door of our house, gaining altitude into the night sky, a caped super power with hawk vision trained on the landscape below. Some nights I practiced my bat radar. In each dream adventure I would spy a troubled situation and glide down to help, but it's mostly the flying itself I remember from these serial dreams when I was between the ages of seven and ten, and how it felt to be weightless, with cool rushing air lifting my perfectly lithe body, the athletically toned limbs and core of a child who roamed the home planet on a banana seat butterfly-handled bike, or traversed by jumping, swimming, running, prowling into storm drains on all fours, mucking along for hours from one end of the public works to the other, until the grate above her head gave rise to infinite sky.

At the end of every flying dream, no matter the episode's plot, I had to turn the door knob on the front door of our house, which thankfully was never locked in my dreams, then walk, not fly, each note ascending the stairs, and tuck myself back into bed next to my bookcase, next to my desk, next to my turtle's bowl. No one ever knew where I had been, or the extent of my powers for good. In fact, Mother had forbidden me to get up in the night without calling for help because of the proximity of the staircase to the bathroom door. I enjoyed calling "Mom, Mom" in the middle of the night when I wanted water. The limits of consciousness, the rules of waking, affected my dream life not at all. I think one time after a flying dream I woke up downstairs on the couch, so it's possible that I occasionally walked in my sleep when I thought I was flying. But I was flying...there were plenty of things I wanted to escape even then.

Many things that I had witnessed in our house did not appear in these dreams, but were reflected in a post-Halloween nightmare in which my family members changed from their benign forms and peeled off day facemasks to reveal their actual, horror-show night faces, transforming into their true selves, monsters in the living room. Long after we left the house, the town, and the events contained there had lost some of their childhood giganticism, I could better remember the structure of my flying dreams than the specific events that triggered them. In that house, I figured out something was wrong with my dad. I know several people whose fathers were nonexistent, crazier than mine, or simply hateful for no reason. At least we had PTSD by way of WWII as explanation.

Most of the night sky was invisible in the mountain town where we were tucked. Stars and planets appeared vivid due to low light pollution, but there was only a narrow band of visible sky framed by jagged mountains, never a Milky Way. I did not know what I did not know. This is still the case, but maybe, eventually, when it has all become a story told and retold, one new detail will surface to forever change the meaning after we thought we knew everything we could ever know.

By purchasing a house in the Catawba Valley, I had extended my dream of country living from the granary I'd rented on a farm west of Lexington to a little red house and eighteen forested acres. Over the next several years, my acreage grew to fifty when some of the rocky adjoining ridge came up for sale. Subtly, my physical molecules took on a new arrangement through my daily writing practice, which provided me with a ground wire. The past, both recent and more removed, no longer threatened to swamp me, and through much solitude and venturing into a range of new relationships I paddled along, powered by my own frog kicks. I dug two fishponds in the small backyard and installed a natural-looking waterfall. Overnight, real frogs migrated from the creek below to populate the newly constructed shores in the woods. How did they know? They leapt from their old life into my new ponds while I slept.

I had decided to buy the red house for two practical reasons: a view of a mountain and a wall of bookcases in the den. Before I left the red house I had written four new books and most of a fifth. With a deck turned toward McAfee Knob, at 3,200 feet the highest regional peak, my location should have marked a culmination, but it was a bit remote. Several run-ins with animals, wild and domestic, including a totaled car and a dead Black Angus, confirmed this. There were several equally messy human relationships.

After making a home in the Catawba Valley for twelve years, altering the house bit by bit, refurbishing the inside, and at last adding a screened porch and redesigning the deck and exterior stairs, I could leave. By the time the double screened doors were hung on the new porch, I had already moved to start a new experiment in living with A., on an actively questionable street. There is something about finishing a house to one's satisfaction that tends to empty it out again. Of course the next owner would immediately tear the screened porch off my perfect retreat and replace it with a two-story addition.

During the three years A. and I lived in our Victorian downtown, I did not have two weeks in a row without summoning a workman to paint or repair siding, fix roof leaks, or shore up the complicated guttering. The Victorian house contained a library, but the shelves had been spaced for music CDs. The built-in bookshelves that had solidified my decision to buy the little red house had to be reconstructed in the Victorian, along with a closet wide enough for hangers. I still owned the little red house and visited to mow and perform a host of chores, but mostly it stood empty except for the wildlife that encroached the minute I drove down the driveway to take the twisting road over the mountain. In my dog's absence, the sullen raccoon turned giddy in its patrols of the fence line. And soon the masked bandito broke into the storage shed and applied its teeth to an antique chest.

In retrospect, I was never truly alone out there in the sticks. I shared my house with Boots the cat and the famous dog-patriot Patrick Henry, and the wildlife adopted me. Deer crossed my driveway on their way down to the creek from the ridge; flocks of grubbing turkeys bunched the hillside behind my house, sufficiently camouflaged by leaf litter and canopied hardwood; an eagle scanned for field mice. Snakes found my shed convenient for wintering and lazing through summer days, and, like the raccoons that chewed their way inside, stubborn woodborers buzzed within boards. I learned to replace the riddled planks myself with a crowbar, hammer, ladder, some paint, and a saw. The borer bees had a party on the underside of the new decking, coring neat holes with their sander butts; they tunneled to lay eggs in weathered fence slats. Woodpeckers heard the buzzing and pecked for larvae, leaving gashes of splintered wood. The main house resisted fairly well while my dog lived there surveying the perimeters, but it was clear that, in our absence, the wild would press in. I had to sell. The loft project's expense completed that thought.

After I killed a copperhead near the back door of the red house, the first offer came from a family that had been greeted by a giant black snake curled in the driveway. They thought the snake auspicious. It may have been the same one I'd seen coiled around the oak tree, spiraling toward hatchlings. If not the very snake, it had at least issued from the nest of eggs I'd discovered among the rocks. A memory of something the home inspector had removed from the attic when I was in the process of closing on the house came back to me: fluttering over his shoulder was the recently shed skin of a black snake, a nearly transparent but specifically patterned sheath not yet dry enough to break. No human being could ever make such a perfectly fitted garment without seam or zipper and wriggle out of such delicate material while leaving intact most of its shape. Our shed selves are broken chrysalises, the paths behind us strewn.

If building a house were as easy as straight-pinning Simplicity patterns to cloth and cutting on the bias, the difficulty of sewing notwithstanding, or roughing out plans on napkins, then I would be an architect. There's the stone house I dreamed of when I was married and tried to capture in a waking sketch. It wasn't so different from the actual house where we lived as it might have been, but the image of a stone house replaced the cedar-sided suburban ranch and revived my dreams of a solid foundation. I kept adding to my sketch. After the divorce I found the notebook again. Out fell the imperfectly rendered image of something perfect in my dream: the stone dream house. I wanted solidity. Divorce taught me more about fragility. Free, I was more than fragile: I was like a bird with nest disturbed, eggs scattered. I wanted to run home, but there was no home to run to.

More sketches: the octagonal beach house on stilts, not to scale, on the back of an envelope. Why did I keep that wobbly image so long and what had prompted my drawing it? I'd sketched it long before seeing or studying the *bagua*, feng shui's eight-sided grid of interior design for better health, wealth, career, and relationships, and before I'd heard about Orson Fowler's octagon-shaped house craze that gripped America in the mid-nineteenth century. My tiny pencil lines worked across envelope seams turned up from time to time when I opened the yellowing sketchbook. The pages documented a six-week drawing course, but unfortunately, as much as I'd enjoyed it, my daily drawing practice had ceased at the end of the summer term when I began teaching again. Stuffed between many blank sheets was the scrap of business envelope, which I might have thrown out numerous times, and wavering over the envelope's seams, my beach house of smeared graphite stood on disproportionately spindly supports. A railed widow's walk finished the top; windows on opposite walls looked to the distant horizon where sky met water. Both bodies of water bore neat labels: *inlet, ocean.* Onto that octagon on stilts attached a smaller equally elevated octagon, suggesting a main house connected to a bedroom.

At Monticello, Thomas Jefferson built a north octagonal room and dome. The elongated dome with rear windows half clear and half mirrored was Jefferson's twist on the Temple of Vesta in the Roman Forum, even though all temples to Vesta are reportedly round. Something about eight sides obviously impressed me, along with Jefferson's seven-day clock—with its weights dropping through two holes in the foyer floor—large wooden window bins meant for holding massive ice blocks for passive air conditioning, and the passageways, kitchen, storage, and laundry rooms beneath lengthy porticos where Jefferson cleverly hid the domestic industry of the house that was performed by his slaves, some of whom were close relations. Much has been made of the fact that Jefferson inherited his slaves, but more importantly: he did not free them.

Virginia's school children of the 1960s were routinely indoctrinated with the genius of the founding fathers, who largely hailed from our state. That being said, Jefferson did not invent much of anything save a plow good for hillside cultivation, but he was an innovator of domestic space, incorporating a host of modern conveniences into his homes, including "double acting doors, lifts for conveying wine from the basement, self-winding clocks, weather vanes with indoor dials," and functioning indoor privies for the winter months. I learned these facts of convenience from a chapter in *Notable American Houses*, edited by Marshall Davidson. Omitted from the discussion are Jefferson's relations with Sally Hemings. Not notable, I suppose.

Despite these technical innovations, the plans of Jefferson's houses maintain and reinforce the prevailing social structures of his time, suggesting that he expected those structures to extend into the future, even as his political placement allowed him uncommon influence on the question of slavery. He was an architect of more than homes and gardens. Whether he personally subverted while publicly upholding these social structures is a question of heart more than fact. At best Jefferson was ambivalent, which is not in his defense. He was less ambivalent about the fledgling constitution and sought as president to undermine its power, leaving the nation in debt and without a standing army when he left office. Perverted power cannot be redeemed by private feeling, which time and time again brings us to the romanticized justification of Jefferson's relationship with Hemings: notations of her white blood, her blood relation to the family, or their mutual love are no more than whitewashing. She was owned by him.

On my first visit to Charlottesville and Monticello, I was in the seventh grade. I knew nothing of historical revisions of the Jeffersonian myth. I remember staring down at the graves below the back hillside garden. Our tour guide gave no explanation other than "This is the slave graveyard." On my more recent tours of Monticello, the script has changed. And that's the difficulty with the house on the little mountain and its construction of Jefferson. "This is an American thing: to wish longingly for a romanticized ancestral home," Mat Johnson writes in his satirical novel *Pym*, which appropriates and appraises an unwieldy work by another revered Virginia figure, Edgar Allan Poe. "This is a black American thing: to wish to be in the majority within a nation you could call your own, to wish for the complete power of that state behind you." Only gradually has the hypocrisy of Jefferson's whole biography been exhumed. His university stands, his hallowed Grounds, sexual assaults real and imagined, a black student bleeding from the head, thrown to the sidewalk at the Irish pub. As I walked through Monticello on my first tour, the guides broadcasted nothing but respect and awe, and I had no awareness that my identification with the narrative of Jefferson's brilliance was inherently flawed, impossible, that even the university he founded was still inaccessible to me, as the last public university in the nation to admit women. I didn't know I was barred from attendance when on the same tour we, boys and girls, walked along the tiered lawn of UVA and saw the Poe room, where a young man was honored to be living. I looked into the little room with a fireplace at its end and imagined myself there in the rocking chair, a college student reading a book like the disheveled, perhaps hungover male student in tattered bathrobe whom we had disturbed.

≈

Poplar Forest, Jefferson's octagonal country villa, served as his retreat from public life and was probably the house where he and Sally Hemings found fuller expression of their true selves in their relationship. Of course Sally served him there, before and after the passing of his wife, who no doubt also served him. Without the pressure of public life, Jefferson's country villa would never have been started or finished; it was nothing less than his dream house away from the spotlight. And in this house there was a secret hidden in plain sight.

Begun during Jefferson's presidency in 1806, Poplar Forest with its bone-white columns, like much of our public architecture of the Federalist period, was inspired by Palladio's villas and rendered in Roman revival style. If it had really been Roman, those columns would have been painted more brightly. Witold Rybczynski finds Palladio's American influence remarkable: "That a handful of houses in an obscure corner of the Venetian Republic should have made their presence felt hundreds of years later and halfway across the globe is extraordinary." Poplar Forest was held privately for years and underwent several façade renovations that obscured the strict geometrics of its original plan; its ongoing restoration only began in the 1980s. Thus, on my several forced marches through Virginia historic landmarks courtesy of the public school system, I was never subjected to a word about Jefferson's second home, which was farther west and much closer to where I lived than Charlottesville.

As I drive the long narrow road to Poplar Forest for my first visit, I can feel the necessity of its location, its removal, and I am trying to reconcile what it concealed. The house is as secreted as my little red house in the Catawba Valley, set off the road and invisible to passersby, only accessible by invitation. I know how important removal proved to the re-construction of myself. Although I expected it at the time, I'm now surprised that family, friends, and lovers were willing to make the trip to visit me. Jefferson's second home was probably inspired by The Octagon House in DC (1798–1800). The eight exterior walls of Poplar Forest required custom obtuse-angled bricks to turn the corners, made on site by artisan and slave labor. Sometimes it overwhelms me to write sentences containing the word "slave" and then simply keep writing more words. It's not just a word but means to be in exile, to suffer, to die, to survive somehow, to leave your blood mixed in the bricks of every historic place.

A twenty-by-twenty-foot dining room at the center of the house, lit by a long rectangular skylight, radiates sunlight into the surrounding octagonal rooms. I stand in a thick shaft of light angling into this cube room after high noon. From here I can look in four directions of the compass, through double glass doors ushering additional natural light from adjacent rooms. Were I invited to dine, I'd pull up my chair to an octagonal table under the skylight, a specific theatre set in which we break the fourth wall of history, served by others who can never dine with us.

Architecture, gardening, and reading were Jefferson's passions; there's a strategically placed small library at the back of the Poplar Forest house, a transitional space to the lawn. And he "made hundreds of drawings, ranging from rather wobbly freehand sketches to measured drawings...drew plats, maps, city plans, garden designs, and furniture, as well as sections, elevations, and floor plans for numerous buildings." He inherited precision drawing tools from his cartographer father, who had surveyed Poplar Forest plantation long before Jefferson inherited the 4800-acre plantation from his father-in-law, and he brought other fine drawing instruments from London, finally favoring pencils and graph paper purchased in France, where he spent five years as US ambassador. Jefferson used his favorite French papers so sparingly that a few blank sheets still remain. How I would love to have a sheet of that paper! No matter how much we renovate Jefferson, I want to fill those surviving pages with his confessional chapters, truth telling written in his hand. I want to understand how this man could say what he did and do what he did, compartmentalizing so much psyche and intellect, dividing so much consciousness from action, private emotion from public life. I want to know how we walk tiered lawns of his university without stumbling.

The worst thing about rehabs is that they are never really over; revisions and change-orders keep on coming, and the energy required to sustain the process grows heavy with strain. One is reminded of the original meaning of stories: each level of a building tells a different aspect of the whole structure. When you renovate a building you start at the top and work your way down, learning as you go.

Four years after we moved into our loft, the builders, after some negotiations, reappeared to pack all of our furniture into corners at the far ends of our condo in order to plaster smooth the ceilings and regrind the concrete floors. It was the dynamic laws of practical karma at work, as our city is a small one. The contractor's potential customers, our friends, had asked us about the rough surfaces of our ceilings and floors, and word travels. We were removed to an apartment village south of town where my mold allergy erupted and my sense of taste eroded until I could recognize nothing on my palate except the sweetness of red grapes. Before this phase ended, workers dragged our furniture from one end of the condo to the other no fewer than six times, and everything we owned was covered in plaster dust.

Rolling back to the very beginning of construction, we thought our challenges were no bigger than mentally projecting our living space from two-dimensional drawings, and the layperson imagines that even this part is easy. I remember giving an architect a few scribbled ideas for a two-story addition on my little red house in Catawba. He returned with meticulous elevations that proved my sketch quite inadequate, for I had forgotten about the large white oaks that framed my house. Poring over condo blueprints, A. and I were handicapped by inexperience, by things we could not see. Sometimes the dynamics between us blinded us to what we were trying to build. It was exhausting for us to include another person's vision along with the practical constraints of time and materials in every decision. The space, though capacious, felt too small for both of us to control, and no one outside of our dyad seemed particularly helpful. To make wise use of professional counsel, you have to know which questions to ask.

The studio expanded and the library shrank, with no line inserted for the cost of bookcases. I thought we might withdraw from the project, but the bank was holding a large amount of our cash in a certificate of deposit, and in addition to the moneys lost we'd be open to lawsuit if we didn't close. Pressing on, we tried our best to navigate against odds we did not know were stacked. We were aware of overt misogyny and the special accelerant to that fire due to our being a couple of queer ladies, but five years after moving in we were still engaging in forensic discussions about what had happened, as in WTF.

Our building was renovated in consideration of DHR (Department of Historic Resources) state and federal tax credits for the developer, energy efficiency credits for the builder, and LEED certification. This meant we'd not have to pay the full tax bill to the city for ten years, which sounded good. We didn't know that our project was designed to rebrand the contractor's company for timely "green" design or that the contractor hired by the developer would in turn employ the developer as a consultant once the project was complete. As for LEED awards, we assumed they were vetted by a government agency but subsequently learned that LEED is a self-reporting process, a membership organization. Nevertheless, the governor of Virginia and a senator celebrated the designation, our building being the first such energy-efficient repurposed building in Western Virginia. If not for the general economic downturn in 2008, this might have added up to something for our development team.

Throughout the construction phases, A. and I continued to focus on our little set of plans, thinking about the proportions of living to workspace for studio, home gallery, and study, worrying over total costs and an upper figure we could not exceed. I was in number-crunching mode. Although skeptical of those who sold us on the project, I went along, alternately buoyed and shamed by my partner's unwavering insistence, her stubborn attachment to the idea, and her abundance of energy in working through each hurdle. In the balance of faith and grit, I'll usually take the latter. It's hard now to recapture and convey the fervor of redevelopment and economic imagineering in 2005–2006. So many projects speckled the landscape; we could throw a few rocks and hit several around us. A. and I attended a Downtown Roanoke, Inc.-sponsored luncheon with Richard Florida and felt privileged to be part of his wave of "creatives" moving back into the center of mid-sized cities, which in previous decades had been abandoned for suburbia and suburban malls. We did take note that while the main theme of Florida's blueprint could be summed up as "follow the gays," the hosting Roanoke officials applied careful editing in their summation of his conclusions, nonetheless jumping aboard the "Cool Cities Initiative." And of course we later realized that Florida's creative class applied to intellectuals, visual artists, and writers but was more fawningly meant to identify a well-educated rising young professional class of techies who worked from their computers and phones. These "creatives" did not need pesky studio or display space or a traditional office with real books; they were well suited to the amenity-rich warrens being carved in abandoned warehouses and department stores.

My partner had compiled several different loose-leaf pattern books over the years containing ideas for furniture and fixtures, kitchen and bath designs, but I went into our project blind to such details. How many different styles of fixtures, cabinet hardware, and doorknobs could there possibly be? In elementary school I anticipated my turn at building a whole Indian village out of glued sugar cubes after admiring the sugary Western fort my sister and a friend made for class. I tried to fashion something on a smaller scale out of toothpicks and Popsicle sticks that leaned out of plumb. I still retain a fascination with school glue. By contrast, A.'s father was an actual homebuilder, her great-uncle the first developer of Mill Mountain, and she had spent time around the contracting business. She'd also rented a live/work studio in L.A. in an industrial building next door to a salmon packing plant. With our loft she was imagining a re-creation of an urban artistic community, not just the creation of our private living space. For sure, she sought to repair the world from the sixth floor. For six years she had served on a nonprofit board that tried to lure an Art-Space project to Roanoke. I had no such credentials or experiences and no particular vision in mind beyond my background in scribbled napkins and the proclamation that I liked modern spaces filled with art and books.

When our first home together, the Victorian, proved unworkable because of its layout of parlors, a maze of rooms opening into other rooms, and the encroaching slumlords and their tenants, we toured most of the available buildings. In the end we chose to limit our investment to one floor in someone else's project. We drew our contemporary industrial aesthetic in unequal parts from magazines, our hearts, and our heads, but I had seen a few converted urban spaces: in Barcelona, a top floor walk-up carved out of a historic building; in Dallas, a converted storefront, with the warm feel of old wooden floors together with an industrial kitchen; and on lower Manhattan's Canal Street, a loft so large it contained a dance studio, family bedrooms, a kitchen, and a print-making studio almost the size of the dance floor. This apartment hung in jeopardy like many others in New York, with the owner attempting to push out the rent-controlled renovators who wanted compensation for their many improvements.

But all I deeply wanted in our loft were big closets and enough bookcases. If you add in ample storage, I agree with Cicero: "If you have a garden and a library, you have everything you need." With our balcony of potted tomatoes and flowers, we didn't have to leave off the garden. In every house I must have my books situated; books are the mind of a house and need a certain dignity. At the time we moved into our loft, it was a sore point that my bookcases were not yet built; it unnerved me to see my collection boxed in the small room where the shelves were supposed to be. After some months I got the shelves built, and I loved my library space, but too soon I was stacking books on their sides: you can never have too many books. I wish Thomas Jefferson had always agreed with me on this, but alas there is evidence that he did not. To Thomas Law in refusal of the plea to add a volume to his library, he wrote, "Dear Sir, I am now entered on my 69th year. the tables of mortality tell me I have 7. years to live. my bibliomany has possessed me of perhaps 20,000. volumes. of these there are probably 1000. which I would read, of choice, before I should the historical, genealogical, chronological, & geographical Atlas of M. Le Sage. but it is also probable I shall decamp before I get through 50. of them. why then add an unit to the 19,950. which I shall never read?" (23 April 1811).

My dear Jefferson, some archeologists believe that the pyramids were built not as tombs but as libraries, storehouses for ancient knowledge handed down from the sky people to the inhabitants of the earth. I think our homes should lend themselves to similar speculations.

At one point in the design/build process, A. erected a model of our proposed kitchen and discovered that it was where the living room should have been and no one had bothered to tell us. That she had to discover this on her own by duct-taping together unwieldy slabs of cardboard still rankles both of us. "When you build a thing you cannot merely build that thing in isolation, but must also repair the world around it, and within it, so that the larger world at that one place becomes more coherent." I read this in *A Pattern Language*, which is something like the Bible of building. Unfortunately, the immediate world around us was becoming more and more incoherent, encoded and secretive as construction progressed from asbestos removal and core work to framing and finish trim, and all the while we future residents of the building, kept apart by the developer like angry exes, were nonetheless becoming more interconnected through systems, from the HOA to the enclosed loop HVAC system that would require our ongoing participation in reading meters and figuring pro-rata shares.

In any case, how could the two of us, A. and I, repair something as pervasive as the effects of patronizing greed and skullduggery, remake the world into a more transparent and respectful place in this one spot? Until we asked an interior designer friend to help us, we were very much adrift with ceiling plans, duct plans, and lighting plans—and then he was kicked off the island by the contractor and developer. All of the architects and designers were thrown overboard from the pirate ship, which left us with the short end of the design/build stick, and only a co-opted developer between us and a pair of project manager brothers, one of whom, we later learned, was simultaneously building his own house on the mountain. With no design professionals on the scene, it was sort of like the banishment of poets from Plato's *Republic*: "lovers of sights and sounds" be gone from the city-soul, but here the comparison must skid to a stop; I cannot in any way picture our project managers as philosopher-kings.

Outside of Chicago in Oak Park, Frank Lloyd Wright's house and studio and the surrounding neighborhood impress visitors with the totality of his vision, from generous roof overhangs to custom furniture, an entirely constructed environment down to artisan stained glass and crafted clothing hooks. I seriously doubt that Wright ever resorted to duct-taping curbside cardboard. When I took the tour, it was with a hushed tone coupled with the suspicion that these interiors were always more like museums than living spaces. Wright took undue pride in his signature leaky roofs, while the owner of "Fallingwater," his triumph in Pennsylvania, nicknamed the house "rising mildew."

Borrowing design elements from nature is not unique to Wright. In Barcelona, I followed the trail of the Catalan architect Antoni Gaudi whose sandcastle-like cathedral Sagrada Familia is the apotheosis of his professional and spiritual journey. His Casa Milà apartments curve along the street, while within the building arcing benches echo curved walls. Touring Gaudi's hillside Park Güell, I heard flute music drifting like smoke from a pagoda and ran my hands over dragon statuary covered in *trencadis*, mosaics of broken ceramic with which he also covered the bright chimney stacks I stood among on the roof. Gaudi's tensions and shapes were inspired by nature, his ellipses and curves drawn from aquatic life. Working mostly from 3-D models instead of drawings, he employed legions of artisans to mold elaborate curvilinear ironwork. Master carpenters and carvers and wood turners along with stained glass and furniture craftsmen built to his specifications, tamping and tapping. Whatever billowed from his imagination, they fixed into sensory form. A solitary, devout old man, "God's Architect" nearly went unrecognized in his shabby clothes when he was run over by a tram, and he died before completing Sagrada Familia. His grandest project was a temple to God not a personal mansion, but still, it left him penniless.

Our developer's palace, which occupies the top two floors of our building, was sold back to the bank on the courthouse steps in a matter of minutes less than four years after he moved into the building, and nearly simultaneously the newspaper reported that our contractor was being sued for non-completion of a government project. A highly publicized employee fraud prosecution followed. But the castle, the monstrosity of questionable taste occupying the two floors above our heads, was its own form of imperialist pleasure dome, rendered in the chivalric style kindly called "old world." I often picture our developer's face in place of Orson Welles's in *Citizen Kane*, as he drifts into memories of rosebud.

A Pattern Language: Compression of pattern can make a space "better," "cheaper," and the "meanings in it…denser," turning a building into "a poem." Most assuredly, our developer's faux ancestral castle presents a full-blown case of the opposite. Archeologists might conclude of these folks something along the lines of what Pueblo Indian architectural historian Rina Swentzell said about the ancient dwellers of Chaco Canyon: "These were men who embraced a social-politic-religious hierarchy and envisioned control and power over place, resources, and people." Thus, we may chart the local abandoned condo by its hideous decorations of gargantuan warehouse furniture, giant king and queen chaise lounges, tasseled reproduction rugs and overstuffed brocaded sofas, fake potted palms for a tropical or Mediterranean flavor, hanging tapestries of uncertain heraldry, and a grand hall studded with *fleur-de-lis* sconces containing energy-saver light bulbs and nary a particle of natural light. In my three weeks of touring Loire Valley chateaux, I admit I found nothing quite like it. I suppose we should have been grateful there was no set of armor stationed in our building's lobby to guard the reproduction tapestry that our developer claimed as his personal coat of arms. A pair of dog and lion penises bracketed the seal that bore the oft-used French motto, *Honi soit qui mal y pense*, translated variously as "evil be to him who evil thinks," which is also featured prominently on the coat of arms of the United Kingdom. Over objections, our lobby tapestry was finally swapped for A.'s painting of a natural scene.

The only time we saw the developer's penthouse, we were with a realtor after the foreclosure; during our developer's reign we'd never been invited up—so much for the "condo family," as he often referred to the building's inhabitants. We wanted to be able to recruit buyers to the building and figured we'd best see what was up there. As we turned the corner, we stepped into the bathroom suite and the realtor flicked on a light that illuminated a shower the size of a lap pool. "Party shower," she gamely rehearsed. As we moved through bedrooms and hallways, we noted the consistently textured walls; buckets upon buckets of plaster had not been spared, even on the ceilings, in a treatment we might loosely call Venetian, though one member of our condo family aptly referred to it as late Olive Garden. Dark as the catacombs, the seventh-floor foyer was our last stop on the tour, since we had entered the cavern from its top floor and worked our way down. We stumbled around feeling for light switches. The furniture here, as everywhere, dwarfed us; inordinately tall lamps perched above our heads on high tables. When we had first surveyed the building in selection of our space, we settled on floor six when the light kept increasing by some geometric proportion with our ascent from floor to floor. The top two floors were already claimed and would in any case cost more. It now seemed impossible that they had managed to make a mausoleum of floors seven and eight. Heavy drapes concealed and pooled below each of the many windows meant to provide long views of distant mountains.

The realtor located a light switch in the foyer, and when a lamp came on we blinked in a space decorated to bring a grand palazzo to mind, perhaps vaguely. I looked back into the condo through heavy, arched doors roughly modeled on those of a wine cave, which reminded me of the unfortunate Fortunato in Edgar Allan Poe's "The Cask of Amontillado." A lush with an appetite for fine wine, Fortunato inadvertently insults Montresor, whose umbrage extends to a madman's plot to wall up Fortunato at the far end of his family's vast catacombs, where he is left to wither among bones from the last century. As the two men descend into the passageways on a false mission concerning some special cases Montresor has purchased, Fortunato gulps more and more wine proffered by his assassin, as we are fed delusions of faults that render the victim deserving of fatal punishment. Fortunato manages to insult Montresor again by mistaking him for a brother of the Freemasons. We recognize how much that must sting our narrator, as his family coat of arms bears the motto, "No one assails me with impunity." All the while Montresor continues to dupe Fortunato farther into the vault, "to smile in his face," hiding his murderous design behind a disguise of grins, cluing us in at one point that he smiles only to imagine Fortunato's death. Besotted Fortunato begins his hollering way too late for rescue, so late in fact that his murderer easily drowns out his cries with his own as he chains him immobile and immures him, proving to be a deft mason after all.

I walked to the seventh-floor windows to look down upon pedestrians crossing the walking bridge that connects a historically African American neighborhood to downtown. The refurbished Martin Luther King Memorial Bridge had been dedicated since our moving into the building. The bridge plaza contains a bronze statue of Dr. King along with stations of benches that offer recorded speeches with the push of a button. When we first moved in, I photographed the exterior of our building from the top of the MLK bridge for a Christmas card of our twinkling tree in the large front window while "I have a dream" resounded into the night.

The elevator at last arrived. As we stepped inside, the realtor turned to us and asked in a cheery tone, "Is your house anything like this?"

A library of well over 6,000 volumes—where would these books have been collected in early America if not for Monticello? Jefferson's books formed the basis of the Library of Congress, despite some objections to the contagion of their "infidel" ideas. Distressed that the Capitol library of 3,000 books had perished in a fire set by British forces in the war of 1812, Jefferson offered to sell his entire personal library to Congress; he had always planned to leave his books to the public. In 1815 his library of 6,707 books within their bookcases made its slow journey to Washington, shipped by horse-drawn wagon. As soon as he received the promised payment of $23,950, Jefferson settled some debts and began buying more books. "My repugnance to the writing table becomes daily and hourly more deadly and insurmountable," he wrote to John Adams. "In place of this has come on a canine appetite for reading" (1818). As Jefferson aged, he left off reading newspapers in favor of reading fiction and the classics. The classics, as Italo Calvino points out, are books we are never just reading but always rereading, whether for the first or tenth time. Jefferson read in six languages, including Greek and Latin: "I had rather be shut up in a very modest cottage, with my books, my family and a few old friends, dining on simple bacon, and letting the world roll on as it liked, than to occupy the most splendid post which any human power can give." At the time he wrote this letter (February 7, 1788) to Alexander Donald he was stationed in Paris, not to return home until the next year.

Jefferson wrote to James Madison that "a library book lasts as long as a house, for hundreds of years" (1821). He wrote this letter in the same year that his personal life was being reported in the news; on that he made no comment. He still owned slaves when he died, including some of the six children he fathered with Sally Hemings, although he had lobbied successfully to outlaw the Atlantic slave trade. Perhaps perfect houses will always exist only as ideas and sketches, as notes and plans rather than bricks and mortar, and certainly no house built of slave bricks can ever be a dream house.

The museum/house we see at Monticello is nothing like the work in progress, the unfinished labor of fifty-six years that Jefferson lived with for most of his life, having begun sketches in 1767 and started clearing the site for construction the following year. The restorers of his other home, Poplar Forest, have made some attempt to offer us not just finished spaces filled with period furniture but also unfinished layers to observe. By the time Monticello was finished in 1823, it was already decaying, with its owner/builder's economic circumstances much reduced. A Bostonian visitor to Monticello remarked in 1815 that the leather chairs were losing their stuffing and a glass panel was replaced with wood. The original glass was too large to be made locally, having been shipped from Bohemia, and by then Jefferson could not afford a replacement.

Jefferson had only been married ten years when his wife died, but while she was alive one of their children fell through to the basement because their living space was a construction site. "We are now living in a brick kiln, for my house, in its present state, is nothing better," Jefferson wrote to his friend George Wythe in 1794. Revisions to the house and grounds continued until his death; as his mind changed, so did his plans. We tour house museums vainly, hoping to discover how people lived. When Jefferson died an octogenarian, his grandson inherited the Poplar Forest dream house and sold it within two years. He paid off some debts with the proceeds and promptly moved to Tallahassee.

A house providing everything you ever dreamed is doomed, and if you had it you would stagnate. It would leave you wanting. Perfect shelter = perfect fiction. The hat trick we are trying for is a psychic fitting of soul to self, thought to action, a place with a heart. Perhaps dream houses are made mostly for books and of books, like the *Child's Garden of Verses* I turned into a roof for Barbie's Dream House. We live in a world in which dreams do not materialize so much as dissolve as soon as we gain the knowledge to make them real. "Knowledge of the world means dissolving the solidity of the world," Calvino writes of Ovid's *Metamorphoses*. As the dream appears, the prior world must dissolve like sugar in hot tea. Here is the church and here is the steeple. I open the doors of my thumbs to show you all the wiggling people inside the church of my hands. Then the church is gone, my fingers disposed to other tasks. The world becomes our knowledge and erases into our ideas as they manifest, as an artist erases guidelines from an inked drawing or paints over an underpainting. Luckily, we can move through the dissolves, the world of ideas and material, with books or virtual books, objects that may change form in our lifetimes but still deliver essentially the same experience to us, retaining their possibilities and effect. Neuroscientists confirm that our brains can't tell the difference between imagined and lived experiences. Want empathy? Read fiction. Books special to us can create an experience that we inhabit and a relationship by which we measure ourselves through the years. We can return and return to the pages of the same book, and it may provide us with new insights that shift as we do, even as we indulge our sense of nostalgia in rereading a beloved book. Our readings may be sharpened or dulled by other readings; rereading is revision of self in text. Our books contain us in unfinished, evolving form.

In her nineties, my mother still reads three books a week, mostly for plot, for story, for escape, but even reading has begun to point to her body's decline: achy, stiff vertebra require more pills and stretches; books are often too heavy to hold with arthritic hands and her eyes often too blurry to decipher the words. She starts a book only to declare that she's read it before. Occasionally she'll reread a book, but not because she's forgotten how it turns out. More than recreation, it is the breath of imaginative life breathed into her: reading has been and is her life. Books shelter us, I think as I play with a paper pop-up book of Poplar Forest after taking the tour. But more than this, my 3-D life is built from writing, made out of words. I learned this much from my mother: when you want freedom from difficulties, when you want time to rush forward, do not wish your life away. Live in it and make it your home day by day.

"I have your Dream House," the caller said. Years after all of my Barbies had been passed down to younger cousins, and they had discarded the dolls after shearing them bald, a stranger called to tell me she had them. It was sort of like a hostage situation for something you no longer wanted. The woman told me in no uncertain terms that my name was written on the Barbie case. Gumshoe, she had matched my name to the phone book. I believed her because my child self had often practiced inscribing my name on things in blue ballpoint. I still have a first baseman's glove with my name printed on the leather. All the same, she could not convince me to take the old doll collection. "Antique," she called them, and "original."

"Enjoy," I said and rung off.

Confounded, she called me again in a few days to ask, "Are you sure you don't want them back?"

I remembered everything about the original Barbie in her zebra-striped swimsuit tottering on impossibly high pumps around her patent leather house. "Stop calling," I said. "It's *your* Dream House now."

God's Eyebrow

"This World Is Not My Home"
—song by Jim Reeves

"The horses run around, their feet stay on the ground...I fell and sprained my eyebrow on the pavement, the pavement." These are lyrics from a crazy song I learned at Camp Iva near Bluefield, Virginia, around 1966. The experience was my introduction to surrealism, back when going to summer camp actually meant something close to sleeping in a tent for three weeks without flush toilets; when poison ivy and hell-froze-over-and-left-this-spring-fed-swimming pool in the woods were for our edification. The folk song dates to around 1900 with many variations in the verses, though usually including "peering through the knothole in grandpa's wooden leg.... Oh, who will wind the clocks while I'm away, away?" Parents, don't let your children be badasses or bad swimmers. If a camper couldn't at least dog paddle across the pool at Camp Iva, she got a "sinker," a large metal washer for a lovely necklace. We rose united in song in the Quonset hut mess hall when the camp director known as Feet tied it on: "Around her neck, we tie the green ribbon. We tie it on her neck 'cause she couldn't swim across, 'cross the pool, 'cross the pool...." No archery, no soccer with rising talent or young writers camp, not even the exultant bore of band camp, stumbling through marching formations in stifling heat. All of that would come later. Day by day the green ribbon shrank, as we, gasping, learned to dip our faces, turn our heads, breathe and kick in that incredibly frigid pool surrounded by soft green hills. We sang a corresponding song when Feet cut the ribbon off in another ritual once the camper managed to swim across. Without exception, everyone learned to swim; no one balked or threatened when confronted with these inarguably shaming methods. We chewed sassafras root to make native toothbrushes, wrote on Indian paper with sharpened sticks, and sang odd songs around the nightly campfire. "Go get the ax, there's a fly on baby's mustache...a boy's best friend is his mother, his mother."

Mother's plucked eyebrow enthralls me. One is a salt and pepper bushel of wiry dimensions, and the other, the one that enthralls me, sprouts a few stubborn bristles growing at different rates and angles. A flesh-toned mole acquires prominence because of the weed-eaten grass of the right eyebrow.

Anchored in the choppy waters of Marsaxlokk Bay, on the island of Malta, a bunch of fishing trawlers, *luzzis*, bear Egyptian gods' eyes composed of black dots, stylized pupils, with thick curves of painted eyebrow above them. Tourists snap photos of the eyes painted on bright blue and yellow bows. I trained my camera on schools of minnows chasing through the aqua shallows, swelling and deflating, in swiftly morphing patterns. God's eyes are unchanging, ever watchful.

"Mrs. Eyebrow," one of my college students called me in 1991; I never bothered to pluck with any gusto, and the blondest student lent commentary. Give me some respect here, I wanted to say, but I've learned it's best to ignore things like this, like the time a high school boy in my class asked on a dare about my bra size. Is this why my nearly blind mother in her nineties cannot leave her eyebrows alone? Someone must have shamed her body hair a long time ago. Not all women can be smooth-skinned and blonde, not all men with the fashionable amount of fur. What would it take for us to feel at home in these bodies, these imperfections? When I was in fourth grade I chose my boyfriend because his arms were hairier than mine. Some preemies have downy hair, lanugo, covering their shoulder blades and backs. We are animals. Get used to it. I'm lucky to still have eyebrows.

Mother, a pirate, lying on the living room couch where children seldom roamed much less sat—I wasn't used to seeing her prone; usually, she was industrious with homemaking chores unless sunbathing with a book propped on her lap. A white gauze patch covered one eye. She had had a mole removed from her eyebrow. I had noticed the dark speck of flesh—a dark eraser sprouted and splayed the brows around it—but I didn't know its fate until it had already met the scalpel. Now it looked like she had lost her eye, and she promised me there were a number of stitches. The doctor's bulky bandage and tape straps extended around her nose, down her cheek, and over her forehead. Ahoy. It was a lot of to-do over a dark dot.

I asked if it hurt. "Not much," she said. "But I'm taking a nap."

I asked if I could see the stitches when she woke up. "When I change the bandage," she said. I was squeamish about needles but loved the concept of first aid, or maybe it was the kit I loved, the organized compartments of bandages and ointments.

↩

A dark dime marks the back of my upper left thigh. When I was a child the proportions made it appear to be worth more, closer to a quarter-sized polka dot on my skinny leg. At the swimming pool people sometimes stared at the brown spot of concentrated melanin, but it was always behind me as I ran, and growing up I didn't much care. I was dragged to the pediatrician at least twice a year, and during each routine visit my mother asked about the removal of my birthmark. My pediatrician remained blasé.

A classmate at the college swimming pool told me, mincing no words, that I was going to die of cancer. My spotted leg was propped up on a railing as I lazily surveyed the pool for my work-study job as a lifeguard. "It's a birthmark," I said. The young woman assured me that I could still die. I was nineteen with a plastic whistle hanging between my breasts. I knew she was probably from a family that had everything extracted post-haste, every blemish, tonsil, adenoid, nose bump, dimple, every sign of less-than-perfect life. Good luck keeping up with that.

Sealing the deal, she said, "My father is a doctor." I knew this was supposed to be authoritative. I grew up with a lot of doctors' kids and they were sometimes paranoid, exposed to bad news and hushed tones on a regular basis. But all that sickness made them richer than regular kids. My dad was a medicine man, a pharmacist; he dispensed pills, although when he first passed the state board he also mixed, compounded, and did some prescribing of controlled substances. He knew the chemical origins of most drugs and their botanical bases, even, I imagined, back to the rain forest, whence he told me aspirin derived from the bark of a certain tree. Some of his customers paid him in farm animals, once a black lamb. We lived in town, so this was a tactical problem: no barn, lamb in basement, grazing backyard. Mother remembers my father in the prescription department gently daubing to remove cinders from the eyes of miners who called him "Doc." They couldn't afford a real doctor. Word got out and he had more cinders to remove.

When the law changed so that only doctors could legally prescribe medications in this country, drug companies began to make their billions. My father complained that doctors didn't study pharmacology long enough to know what they were doing and ended up depending on drug reps who were only interested in selling them on the newest, most expensive drugs. I remember his saying this, but I didn't understand it at the time. His complaints continued for decades. I only heard about the change in law much later when I met someone who was writing a history of drug stores.

My father died in 1999, at the start of a sunspot cycle.

I take a load of recycling to the trash alley, which constitutes ritual devotion to what seems like a substantially good idea until I look into the bin marked in fading stencil "Paper Recycling Only" and spy a white kitchen bag of trash on top of some cardboard boxes. This kind of disregard gets my dander up. I pull out the offender and re-file the white bag in the "Bagged Trash" bin before dumping my newspapers and office paper assortment, bulk mailings, etc., into the paper-only bin. Feeling virtuous for a minute, I catch sight of something near my shoe: folded, crumpled wings wadded up like dark brown paper or a small black umbrella around a fuzzy face, teeth smashed to mouse status. Bats have been dropping from a virus called white nose syndrome, but this one's nose is a taut black button. I reach into the paper bin and extract two pieces of cardboard, scoop up the little brown bat, drop his body in with the bagged trash. I am strangely moved. A bit saddened. Maybe I'm the sort of person who can become emotional over anything, but something tells me this is a death worth mourning.

Attacking the hair on his back, my father tried to shave with uncertain swipes while twisting to look in the mirror. He must not have wanted to look all animal in his swim trunks at the South Carolina shore. Although blue-eyed, he had thick chest and arm hair. His vanities included occasional use of QT tanning solution that tinted his skin orange, wearing expensive leather shoes, well-cut suits, and matching socks to his shirts no matter the color, even bright yellow. He took a lot of showers when he was not hunched and tortured, raving ill. He picked a dark-eyed beauty in my mother, olive-skinned with absolutely coal-black hair. People often said this of my mother's hair when she was a child, and it made her cry. She thought they were saying she had "cold, black hair." Most people said my parents made a handsome pair. Although my father was short, he was taller than his father or brother and probably less than an inch taller than Mother, who was 5'4" and a smidge on a righteous day. My parents were sweethearts from the time they were sixteen and seventeen, or maybe it was fifteen and sixteen; my father lied about his age, says Mother. They both went to college early at a time when public school students could test out of grades and half grades, which is how they met so young at a college dance.

A pair of American goldfinches perches in forsythia as if they've grown there. It's not easy to see them as birds because they could be exotic flowers blooming from the bush, as the narrow shoots give sway beneath their small bit of winged weight. The male is magnificent, the color of the sun in a coloring book, and his mate duller, her yellow tending toward green, partially camouflaged by foliage. I am reminded of Botticelli's Venus emerging from the sea and that not everything in nature makes much sense. Just then a branch shakes when the male takes flight, flits over to a bristly stand of thigh-high purple-headed thistle. He sings atop the thistle flower, lending his complementary bloom.

"You want to see?" I lean in. There's a shining design under the magnifying lens. "Here, look at the other one," the eye doc says, backing away from the machine again. "She's a nine out of ten." I stare at the golden, glowing arcs of Mother's cataracts. Almost perfect these are: each eye holds a pot of gold. We have another version of the discussion we had with the knee-replacement doc. Mom is dedicated to avoiding all unnecessary interventions. She wants to be left intact. "At my age, what difference does it make," she says. Even though her insurance would pay, she doesn't think the expense is justified. "I can still see to read," she insists. With Mom nearing centenarian, "Come back in a year," the doc says.

I'm walking in downtown Roanoke on a narrow one-way street, having just spent a happy coffee hour with Joe, talking about his family, mine, his children, my cat, our different but equal frustrations. We part with a hug; a car passes me. Someone shouts back, "You look sexy in that shirt!" Ordinarily, I'd be peeved, but it's neither a redneck nor a seventy-five-year-old man. It's a high school girl engaging in some gesture of feminine solidarity. There's a reason I'm particularly pleased by this rudeness. My partner saw herself interviewed on local TV and did not approve of the configuration of her shirt front, so a few days later I found myself complimenting her new shapeliness and she confessed that she'd made a trip to Victoria's Secret. Upon hearing that, I hopped in my car rather instantly. It was Saturday at the mall, the store stuffed with sniggering teenaged boys and wide-eyed husbands. I wove a path through the leering menfolk and corresponding wives, sisters, and girlfriends rifling sale bins to the checkout counter, where I discreetly asked for a bra fitting.

"Let's do it right here," the clerk suggested. I nodded. She whipped out a measuring tape and draped it around me strategically, pronouncing various numbers I had apparently been leaving to chance for years.

So when the rude high school girl rolls down the window to shout, I give her the thumbs up, the Queen's wave, my fifth decade salute.

Is it worse for women to be too tall or too hairy? At model height, my aunt Glade hunched her whole life. When a woman raises her arms in summer to reveal hairy pits set against a pastel yellow sundress, I become squeamish. So I am a bad feminist, but tell me, where did she grow up? My revulsion is laced with envy and respect. Not in the South, I think. Not around here. My father would have said, "A barn." She'll never be a college administrator, I think. Not great for fund-raising. Maybe she'll have to settle for being an oracle, an artist, a hippie, or, in time, a crone.

Mother recently confessed that she's stopped shaving beneath her arms and also stopped shaving her legs. "I can't see to shave." Her legs are nearly hairless now anyway. She tells me this while I am helping her pull a spandex camisole over her head. The shelf bra of the camisole catches on her chest above her flattened smudges of breast. As we work it down into place, I see sprays of long gray hair stubbornly hanging on beneath what Mother calls her "little scrawny arms." Neither does she wear bras most of the time. "Oh well," Mother says, letting go of one more thing.

In my teens and twenties I had several tall friends. I never really understood how short I was by comparison until I'd see a photo, a group shot in which I looked stunted, standing as tall as possible. The tall girls looked better in their outfits no matter what they wore. I still remember the hour, the minute my father turned to me without prelude and announced that he had just realized he was short. "Cathy," he said, "I'm a short man." He was seventy-five at the time. He waited for my reaction. "Yes," I said, "I know." Every part of him fell silent, stunned. Even I already knew.

My feet have always been small; even in army boots they look dainty. Up until the fifth grade I thought they would grow, but instead they decidedly stopped short. My grandfather shook his head, looking down at my feet. "You've got to have a firm foundation." Maybe he had seen what happened with livestock back on the farm he couldn't wait to leave, or with mongrels whose puppy paws indicated the eventual size of the dog. Maybe he knew what to expect from me. My grandmother Bonnie, whom everyone called by her first name, never reached five feet in shoes. All of us grandchildren passed her one by one, pressing our backs to hers, and then we were gone. I passed her quickly because she was already shrinking, age eighty when I was ten. She wrapped her silver hair into a bun and pinned a circular hairpiece over her bald spot. I used to deliver a paper bag when Mother and I shopped for her. One day I looked inside to find a pack of tall brown Virginia Slims and a pint of bourbon. On my twenty-fifth birthday we buried Bonnie in Rural Retreat, Virginia, in the cemetery on a hill above the town where Dr. Pepper is also buried, always the coldest place on earth.

I'm going through every drawer in Mother's assisted living bed/sitting room because she has been robbed. We're checking as the facility manager has instructed, in case we have misplaced the hinged gold bracelet. While I perform this duty, I know we haven't simply lost it. Just last week I shied away from taking it home when Mother urged me to; now I'm kicking myself. In the center drawer of her dressing table I find a stash of half a dozen different pairs of tweezers. "Don't get them mixed up," Mother says. "Leave those where I can find them." When I ask her if she wants to throw some of them away, she says no.

This morning I looked in the mirror in better natural light than usual and saw that my mustache was growing in. In my fifties it's decidedly harder to see, and I wonder how on earth my mother manages to continue to tweeze in her nineties. Her bad eyesight has something to do with the brush fire she has made of her right eyebrow: a scorched forest with regenerating understory. Or maybe it's the arthritis in her hands that has compromised her hand-eye coordination. Her fingers twist like bonsai.

I check the side drawer of the dressing table, and from the very back I extract a scrap of white cotton fabric that looks like an old handkerchief until I unfold it, shake it loose, and find the shape of a smocked baby dress that's been shortened with scissors to a tiny tunic.

"What's this?" I ask. She says it was either mine or my sister's. "What do you want to do with it?"

"Leave it," she says.

I stuff it back in the drawer next to one of my dad's old tee shirts that I've already asked about. Mother insists on keeping it there.

A week goes by before I walk up to the Roanoke city police station to file a report. The woman at the window is very helpful in taking down the details. She also tells me that, a few years ago on the nursing side of the same facility I have chosen with great care for my mother, they had a male nurse or aide who was abusing the patients; I wish I didn't know this. He's in prison, "put away," she tells me. The assisted living facility is running its own investigation, reviewing hours of surveillance tape to see who went in and out of Mother's room. Since it seems like an inside job, I doubt these tapes will yield more than the obvious schedule of baths, room cleaning, and meals. Someone who takes care of my mother is a thief. This is troubling.

My father implied that I was too selfish to have children. It stung, but I didn't defend myself because what I had to say would have indicted him more. His periodic illnesses zapped me of strength and will. Mental casualty means there's collateral damage. I spent enormous energy trying to keep him alive, and he didn't even care. It wasn't selfishness on my part but a lack of faith in how things turn out. He lived until I was forty-one and single. There's more than one way to be happy, and one must find it. Life is over too soon for serving up platitudes about what people should and should not do. My father was proof of my self-sacrificing nature and didn't know it. I think it's always a mistake to pitch your tent on the grounds of criticism or praise because most people undertake actions of consequence without forethought.

When my father lay in a hospital bed for a month after wrecking his car, healing in body while essentially dying—although of course we were not certain of that at the time—on one of the few days he wasn't intubated with breathing and feeding apparatus he said to me clearly, "Things turn out the way they're supposed to."

Across the grassy mown lawn a robin bounces along. Rockin' robin. Between hops he burrows his beak in the grass, poking, searching. This solitary robin red breast having breakfast in the sun knows a few things. Today is my parents' seventy-first wedding anniversary. Only one of them is left to remember. I call my mother and she doesn't mention it.

"It's okay but it's not home," Mother says of her assisted living apartment. I can quote only one line from Shakespeare's *As You Like It*. Touchstone: "Ay, now I am in Arden; the more fool I; when I was at home I was in a better place: but travelers must be content."

Other things have been stolen from Mother's room, a roll of quarters and some small gold cufflinks neither of us can sufficiently describe. Mother thinks the cufflinks were my father's, who never wore cufflinks; a tiepin was absent from the set before the theft, and he probably did wear that. The address on the empty jewelry box reads Sixth Avenue. Dad could have bought these when he was a traveling salesman of party supplies with Benco, headquartered in New York City, or maybe his boss gave him an incentive. This was right after WWII when Dad couldn't stand still to fill prescriptions and briefly became Willy Loman.

Thump-thump. Today my old TV set, circa 1994, lurches and settles whenever the terrain changes or I must use the brake pedal. I couldn't lift it, so my downtown neighbor Rick rolled it out to my car and heaved it inside. I promised Rick my St. Joe statuette because he's trying to sell his condo across the street. As we covered my old TV with a penguin blanket from World Wildlife Fund, he expressed skepticism about the powers of St. Joe. Distracted, I was thinking I could donate my old set to Habitat for Humanity, the Rescue Mission, or even Goodwill, which I generally try to avoid because their stores are too nice, which makes me suspicious. I drive around town through the industrial corridors but find no takers. I pull to the roadside, thump-thumping, and call Becket, leaving a message, and then Jonna to ask her advice. "Let me call around," she says. My engine runs as I wonder why I only discovered flat screens and HDTV a little over a week ago, while for anyone else it appears to be an inalienable American right. Jonna calls back. "Salvation Army on Williamson—but only if it works. It works, right?"

It did last week, but I'm not sure anymore. On its way out of the condo it fell off the hand truck and crashed onto its tube. After several benign forms of consumer despair I never thought I'd feel, Becket returns my call and offers to get her neighbor Larry to set it on the sidewalk for bulk trash pickup in front of her house. I go there, thump-thumping. She lives at the top of a hill. Becket knocks on her neighbor's door, and Larry's wife wakes him from a nap. Larry does the deed, and I follow my friend inside her house for a cup of tea. I think about my old TV sitting on the sidewalk, cold and alone, remote on top. It's 20-something degrees outside, and I'm dressed for a run I don't want to do. Following the tea, I do it anyway; there's a race at the end of the week. Blustery wind freezes my face. I plod beside the river as sunlight blinks on and off near four o'clock.

Mother leaves a message to say she's gotten her TV messed up again, stuck on AUX, which sounds like "ox" and might as well be one to my mother, who has no idea of what has been abbreviated. She spells it out for me in her message, "a-u-x." By the time I reach her on the phone, the night nurse has figured it out for her. She's happy now and won't have to miss the Greenbrier Open golf match she's looking forward to. Until she was in her eighties, Mother played a couple of rounds a week. On her eightieth birthday I gave her a custom driver, which I fully expected her to use for at least five years. Not quite, as it turned out.

My father died when Mother was eighty-one, and the next year her preferred golf partner broke an ankle. She had sold the cart before then. When she and I played some three-par and occasional rounds at public courses she always won, which is not saying much since my handicap was in the high 20s/low 30s on a good day, but I was forty years younger and in much better practice at that point, and still, she won. She had an uncanny ability to play the slope of the land, banking chip shots and consistently bouncing dribbles from her fairway woods into the best possible positions. Her putting was unbearably flawless, while I had a hard time finding the green, my ball often flying over, again and again, until it skidded into a sand trap.

Mother had moved once before when she sold the house in the town where she'd lived since 1969, but her last downsizing from condo to assisted living was more conclusive and, as Mother said, constituted her "last stop." The two-bedroom condo, perfect for six years, had to be emptied for new tenants, Mother's material goods further reduced to fit into one of two closets. Mother refers to herself as an "inmate" of the new facility. At the time of the move, she was in rehab recovering from a septic knee and unable to help with cleaning out the condo. The same thing happened with my aunt Glade; she fell and wasn't able to return to her apartment. In both cases I was there on the last day, sweeping the kitchen and scrubbing baseboards.

Upon receiving an encouraging letter from a niece about all the activities she could enjoy at her new facility, Mother looked at me and said, "It's not summer camp."

It's amazing to me how much Mother managed to stuff into every drawer and closet of the condo, how many boxes from the last move she had failed to open, much less sort. She says the time got away from her, six years in an eye blink. As my friend quipped when her mother passed away last month, "Seventy-five years of tasteful hoarding." My mother is no hoarder and fairly unsentimental, yet it took me three solid weeks to construct some logic through my sorting, with piles to give away, seal into storage, or distribute to distant family. Not much immediate family as it turns out—it's down to my sister and me, and my sister says there's no extra room in her house; she's taken all she can. At the same time, Mother is not yet dead, even though it felt like it some days when I dragged myself across the bridge to South Roanoke and entered her condo with my lunch bags from Chipotle. Mother's being alive is a wonderful gift after the long haul of hospital and rehab when she could have died numerous times from numerous treatments, but it made the task of closing the condo that much harder. Just when I thought I could part with something, Mother would ask about it, and instead of pitching it toward the Rescue Mission pile I packed it for the storage unit or delivered it to her new room where there was precious little display space.

Waiting inside kitchen cabinets were dozens of crystal and china pieces that Mother had not used since moving to the condo. Once disturbed from their drawers or shelves, these hidden treasures took on weight and expectation like an island of forgotten, guilt-tripping toys. Each item magnified by catching the light seemed to speak and say the same thing: "Take me with you." Even colorful plastic cocktail stirrers collected on my parents' various vacation tours whispered the same plea as I dropped them into the trash. I made the mistake of looking more closely at the matchbook collection and kept several of them from the Mark Hopkins hotel in San Francisco, New York's Americana, Caesar's Palace, and The Royal Hawaiian.

On the final day of packing and cleaning I pulled a heavy box from the back of the guest room closet and opened the top to find it stuffed with WWII mementos, including my father's portrait in dress whites, wearing the very epaulettes, stripes, and stars I also found packed in the box. It held his discharge papers, too, a veritable museum of WWII. God's eye watches my mother's child: I closed the lid again and taped it shut for storage without sifting all the way to the bottom. Some things cannot be excised or plucked from our lives. Some things we have to keep. Some love is without end.

Mother says, "Why am I still here? I can't get any better and I don't get any worse." I have no answer, no "Spirit in the Sky" chorus for her. The body is a betrayer, no longer her home. No home is left. Her face contorts in pain. "For me," I say. "You're here for me." I know she wishes she felt like staying.

Place as Language

Hanging art in my house (or in my room) has always been my way of claiming the space, of turning it into a place that's mine. One of the pictures I've moved with me a number of times is a framed print, "Rainbow Island" by Mike Falco, which was a wedding gift from my late friend William Goyen, author of the lyrical novel *The House of Breath*, and his wife the late actress Doris Roberts. The print shows an Edenic island populated with a number of serene cartoonish animals roaming the mound or swimming along the shore. An idyllic impression is created by sunshine, color harmony, and a pointed omission of the human element. The animals depicted all seem to know how to get along, to coexist without having to decide who's the boss. It is a picture of cooperation, and none of them, not even the monkeys, is talking. Rainbow Island is a fictional place, an imagined place where I'd like to go, but only if I could do so without upsetting its balance. I'll probably never get to Rainbow Island, but when I look at the print it offers me a window into heaven, much as William Goyen's lyrical fiction offered me a new way to consider voice, style, and region.

Near the end of his life, in conversation with poet and English professor Reginald Gibbons, William Goyen explored themes of exile and return, expectancy and loss, echoing Samuel Beckett's declaration, "the artist lives *nowhere*...." Goyen's apparent preoccupation with setting, with his fictional East Texas town Charity and its rural surround, had "become a language...a language of its own; I've created a language...that was never spoken there. That's become my *style*...I was making a *language* out of *speech*." Goyen's artistic vision, his style, set him apart from place-dredged and description-drenched writing, from "those Southerners," as he succinctly put it. Endeavoring to make a language "that was never spoken there" is a distinct and separate project from capturing the reality of a people and a place through cultural representation. There is no intentional mimesis in Goyen's writing, but he did start with the raw material of his birthplace.

Arguably, places would not exist at all "were it not for the stories told about and through them," asserts Patricia Price. "Places, as well as landscapes that allow us to grasp them, are thoroughly narrative constructs."

Price goes further to exclaim, "Places without stories are unthinkable." William Goyen and Eudora Welty might agree on this. Welty in particular has much to say about a writer's point of origin and the continuing influence of that inner landscape:

> There may come to be new places in our lives that are second spiritual homes closer to us in some ways, perhaps, than our original homes. But the home tie is the blood tie. And had it meant nothing to us, any other place would have meant less, and we would carry no compass inside ourselves to find home ever, anywhere at all. We would not even guess what we had missed.

Place and landscape in Welty's appraisal are formative, even indivisible from us.

Through his narratives, Goyen never set out to portray a region or its people realistically but instead to delve, by way of certain particulars of which he had experience and emotional knowledge, into barred regions of the human psyche and spirit, into the soul of speech. Through his stories he honored his home territory of East Texas. Eventually the corporeal aspect of his divining branch yielded to metaphysical concerns, and Goyen, while properly eschewing didactic in his writing, became an agent for the transformative power of art. The setting for that transformation, he believed, is the locus of the body. The writer achieves his effects through an elemental rendering of the world as a weather of mitigated and mixed desires and by creating characters who split the difference between ghost and flesh or the apparent polarity of the sexes. By traveling to peculiar and edgy places in his work, Goyen went beyond the typical debate of regional versus universal in the way Eudora Welty understood and articulated the problem in her essay, "Place in Fiction." Even while she appreciated the spillage that binds place to emotion, she wrote of place that, "by confining character, it defines it." Goyen's characters, though, defy this notion; "the writer himself" experienced "his roots" in a certain place, but his characters are bound more tightly to the mythic and archetypal than the local.

I believe that products of literary imagination can provide access points into our spiritual dimensions. At first glance, my claim is in opposition to Welty's charge that art's responsibility is to make "reality real," but that is only so if we limit the scope of reality to material concerns. William Goyen asserted no special province of spirituality, although one senses several routes in his work. He did attest to Gibbons that losing himself in his writing lifted him from conscious toil into connection with archetypal material and voice: "Now, when I'm really working, really writing, I have the feeling it's coming from outside of me, through me. An absolute submission, absolute surrender. It's being *had*, being possessed. I'm being used." In speaking about being an instrument in the act of creation, Goyen mixed the language of sexuality and channeling, but he did not name the higher power. He also noted that without this type of artistic surrender, he might be dead from madness or alcohol; his service to art had saved him.

In his sixties, William Goyen loped across the Hollins campus, a white-haired, bushy-browed, tall and stately figure who had published *A Book of Jesus*. He projected a potent mix of history and reserve. Like my father, he had served on an aircraft carrier in World War II. It was there on the seas that he started the reading and writing journey that eventually led to his first novel, *The House of Breath* (1950). Erudite and earthy, he held an advanced degree in comparative literature. Fairly calm, approachable, he moved about campus shyly smiling; unlike many others in a stream of writers-in-residence, he exuded humility. He was linked to Hollywood, a place he loathed on principle, by marriage to Doris Roberts, whom he loved without question. He gave a sermon in the chapel that was drawn from his *Jesus* book; his Jesus was a low Christology character. Because he had been a New York editor for many years, he could spot good writing of any kind dead on. He helped more than one graduate student connect with agents and editors. I was an undergraduate at the time.

After World War II, Goyen had traveled out to Taos, New Mexico, and stayed at the art colony of the famous patron Mabel Dodge Luhan. He bunked at the Lawrence ranch for a couple of years. Still haunted by D. H. Lawrence and a host of other artists who passed through the place, the ranch retains its power when I drive out to see it on an impossibly intense morning, cloudlike beings floating singly across the sky. I take my turn lying down on the rough wooden bench, looking up into the branches of the tree painted from that angle by Georgia O'Keeffe, the tree leaned against by Lawrence as he sat scribbling. The interior of the bunkhouse suggests a small utopia indeed. Dorothy Brett, in her tiny hut nearby, probably crossed paths with Goyen here. During his residency at Hollins in the late seventies,

Goyen was writing a book about four women who had shaped his life, Mabel Dodge and Frieda Lawrence among them. Goyen knew Frieda; I knew Goyen. It was sort of like I had known Lawrence, but in truth Goyen's writing burrowed under my skin even deeper. D. H. Lawrence's work had moved me in adolescence, especially its scope, the many genres in which he worked. Lawrence eventually fell under the patronage of Mabel Dodge, who traded Frieda the ranch on Lobo Mountain northwest of Taos in exchange for the handwritten manuscript of *Sons and Lovers*, the first of Lawrence's works that had captivated me. The gritty East Midlands coal-mining town he described was enough like the Southwest Virginia coal town where I was born to strike a deep chord.

After Lawrence's death in France in 1930, Frieda returned to New Mexico and lived on the ranch with her subsequent husband until her death. She later had D. H.'s body cremated and his ashes brought to New Mexico where they are interred in a chapel. Or arguably they are not actually there, and may not be anywhere, but in any case the Lawrence Chapel is dedicated to his memory. On the day I climb the zigzag concrete path to the chapel, the guide says to take it slow; we're at 8,500 feet. I've been out here a week, so I'm not feeling the strain of anything other than our encounter with a strange man we meet at the top. Without greeting us he continues tape-measuring the railings inside the chapel, the distance from the altar to the railings, the dimensions of the door, and so on. He works like a rabbit hopping this way and that, even though he's a large, physically imposing man. And then he opens his mouth, and it sounds a lot like the gibberish of the obsessed. A cryptographer, he calls himself. He leaps from the Temple of Isis to erections and resurrections, to Lawrence's strange novel, *The Escaped Cock*. 1934, the year the chapel was built, he says, was an important year in Hollywood for phoenixes and codes. Lawrence's *The Rainbow* links directly to Victor Fleming's yellow brick road.... I ask the man to step aside so I can take an interior shot that he's not blocking, while he, indignant with the docent's asking him his name, puffs and sputters.

"You know it's *Taos*," my friend Lisa says, "one syllable," when I say I'm going back to *Ta-os* after twenty years.

"There's something there," her husband Mike chimes in. "A spirit." And then he tells me the pueblo doesn't like outsiders. I'm thinking that's entirely reasonable. I'm also thinking that artists and writers are outsiders by nature, but maybe we constitute another sort of tribe.

Taos seems relatively unchanged, the pueblo a welcoming place as I tour it, guided by a college student volunteer who walks us through the pain of near genocide in his strong voice. I stay in the same hotel as before, the one with a replica kiva ladder for a towel rack. I drive around shadowed by a ring of mountains. There's something familiar in this, something like home in the Roanoke Valley but with altitude. The highest peak around Roanoke is Catawba Mountain at 3,200 feet, topped by a popular photo-op outcropping. For more than a decade I gazed toward the peak from the front deck of the red house. Occasionally I climbed that mountain and squinted back down, looking for the wooden rectangle of my deck below. The proportion of valley to mountains in both places is quite similar. Home might be a proportion, a portable proportion. I'm trying this out while wondering what Lawrence found in New Mexico of the Nottinghamshire of his childhood— besides mines, hard-working blokes: outsiders. Romance of the American West. Dry air for his weak lungs, of course, his legacy from breathing coal dust. Subsistence survivors. He finally accepted Mabel Dodge's invitation when he and Frieda were nearly penniless. She paid their train fares east from San Francisco to Taos. And when he arrived, his dream of an artistic commune was revived. Although the British are noted for traveling great distances to get out of their nearly constant fog, it could not have been merely the light, the air, or necessity that produced in him a spiritual affinity to New Mexico.

"All landscapes are haunted by ghosts." Places are always overwritten in time by those "long displaced and dispossessed" combined with "the tales of those who claimed and possessed, and these tales shape, contest, and offer alternatives to the tales of those now living on the land." Patricia Price could have been writing about the haunted landscapes represented in many of William Goyen's stories, particularly the landscapes in the two bookends to his oeuvre: "Ghost and Flesh, Water and Dirt," the titular story of *Ghost and Flesh: Stories and Tales* (1952), and "Precious Door," a story published posthumously, originally the title story of what turned out to be Goyen's last collection, *Had I a Hundred Mouths: New & Selected Stories, 1947–1983*. These are two of the three stories Goyen recorded with the Audio Prose Library (in February 1982). Both stories land high on my list of favorites, owing in no small part to repeated listening. I've introduced Goyen's work to my students through the recordings many times and observed that the author's reading voice never fails to enchant.

When introducing his reading of "Ghost and Flesh, Water and Dirt," Goyen speaks of this story as a prime example of his "concern with *style*":

> I've cared about writing, or telling some tales, some stories, in the language of the people of my region, which is East Texas...because that language is so unique and seemed to be finally a distinct language of its own. And I came to believe that I was even creating a new language, so it was a *stylistic* experience, a *stylistic* work that finally happened...using the very living language of the people around me as I grew up.

There is special pleading in the emphasis Goyen brings to the word *style*; he continued to separate himself from dialectical regional writing while he sought to celebrate the musical patois of his youth. Music more than any other influence shaped Goyen's prose sensibility. He described his work as "song," "ballad," "aria," "rhapsody," "anthem," and "serenade" as well as "meditation" and "prayer." He was a registered songwriter with ASCAP. "Vocal energy," as David Rivard suggests, is consistent with "what we call 'style'—the idiosyncratic, bodily presence of a particular writer that is almost always driven by perception embedded in music." And, as Rivard goes on to say, style is not necessarily embodied in naturalism or psychological profundity.

"Ghost and Flesh, Water and Dirt" opens with a lyrically compressed passage in which the narrator Margy Emmons expresses anguish over the ghost of her husband that haunts her still. His ghost drove her from her Texas home to California on a train, then back again, and finally compels her to tell or confess her story to whomever will listen, "Cause you know honey there's a time to go roun and tell and there's a time to set still (and let a ghost grieve ya); so listen to me while I tell, cause I'm in my time a telling and you better run fast if you don wanna hear what I tell, cause I'm goin ta tell...." Margy, like the narrator of "Precious Door" and of so many other Goyen stories, wears her story like an albatross and lays the burden down before a stranger who will listen and maybe help her to bear it. One of the results of bearing her story seems to be drink, as Margy is "settin with you here in the Pass Time Club, drinkin this beer and telling you all I've told." As her circular tale unfolds, from her first encounter with Raymon Emmons when they bought a gift of shoes together at Richardson's Shoe Shop to Margy's eventual employment selling shoes in the same store, her story turns through cyclical movements, each containing the past as well as the present. The story moves not by realized scenes or extended moments but by detailed summaries of events and recounted conversations that compress time into the urgency of this "time a telling." There's only a glimpse of the present as a setting backdrop outside of the telling itself, when Margy addresses her listener at the bar, a fellow beer drinker who remains unnamed.

The narrator's cyclical treatment of chronology figures in the title's elemental progression through seeming oppositions: ghost, flesh, water, dirt. Dirt, or the burial of Margy's daughter and then her husband, Raymon Emmons, delivers up Raymon's ghost, and thus the cycle repeats back into life until overtaken by water. The vast landscape of water, as encountered by a young Goyen in the Navy, figures in many of his stories. The ghost of Margy's husband eventually forces her to escape their old life and house and town or be driven mad by the insistence of his presence.

In her new California life, Margy falls in love again and finds fulfillment in the flesh, "dancing and swimming and *everthing*" with Nick Natowski, "a brown, clean Pollack from Chicago, real wile, real Satanish." When Nick is sunk on his aircraft carrier, Margy loses "one to water" and is driven back home "to look at dirt a while." And of course "that ole faithful ghost of Raymon Emmons" is there to grieve her once again when she opens up her dusty Texas house. Just as there is "a time to go roun and tell," there's "a time to set still" and listen. Margy plays each role, greets and grieves life, and replays both at once when recounting her story: "I'm telling you, there's a world both places, a world where there's ghosts and a world where there's flesh." The only place where ghost and flesh, teller and listener, exist simultaneously is in her language. Margy evokes the events, breathing spirit into the ghost with the breath of her telling, while she and "strangers (like you)" sit still, suspended in time, drenched in the water of beer. Language is also the place where male writer can narrate as female, representing yet another slippage of form.

There is no barstool listener, anonymous or collective, who witnesses the narrator's spoken monologue in Goyen's story "Precious Door." Instead, this narrator recounts his tale for an implied reader, in conventional story form, but the straightforward narrator situation begins with a subtle twist: the story opens with his little brother who has come "to tell us" that "somebody's laying out in the field." This narrator is first a listener whom two other voices prompt into action, the plot's unfolding triggered when his father tells him to "go see what it is."

Because the boy/narrator is afraid, he asks his father to come with him. They find "a poor beaten creature," a man, they will learn, whose own brother has stabbed him brutally in the side and left him to die. Together father and twelve-year-old son carry the man and lay him on the porch daybed just as a furious storm commences. The hurricane waters prevent the doctor from reaching the man; he dies in the parlor as father and son ride out the storm, having sent the rest of the family to the high school basement shelter. The appearance of this man and the loss of him provokes the boy, on the brink of manhood, to bouts of crying that wring new emotions of longing, hope, and passion from him. The description of the man as "a beautiful young girl if it had been a girl" is a signal moment in the narrative that begs a closer reading of all the description in the story. In the rush of the narrative we might forget that it consists of the narrator's memory, that this telling embodies his own emergent wash of feeling. His love of the stranger mixes with his own awakened longing for love, whether for a male or for a female is as yet uncertain; the description of the man contains both possibilities. The boy's awakening includes animus and anima. The man's older brother, the one who raised him, will die from regret, from enduring love of the brother he murdered.

The boy and his father recite the Lord's Prayer over the dying man, a formula of words meant to restore their connection with order, but what's brought into being in the boy is a passionate longing "to find someone who would take my tenderness. And to have, together with someone, a plan." Over their prayer tolls some tongue of wind against metal, a clanging reminder of what the world can do to love.

The "creature," the "man," the "stranger" is "familiar as kin"; he "looks like somebody." He, by these many names, of course conjures Christ, betrayed by his brother/disciple Judas and stabbed in the side by a Roman soldier. We finally learn that the victim's name is Ben when his brother, wild from grief, blows through the front door of the house, confesses his crime, and gathers his dead brother to him in reconciliation; together they return to the world of water surrounding the house.

The boy tells us that he and his father "looked outside and saw a whole world of things floating by. We ourselves felt afloat, among them." This house echoes the Old Testament ark, the world destroyed by water, as brother killing brother echoes Cain's murder of Abel. The boy/narrator seeing things floating and feeling afloat is but one of many examples in the story of deliberate exchange between descriptive and figurative language, a storm of language and emotion, a flood of feeling. The narrator says he "wept for Ben and his brother so many times he can't remember." He has a brother himself, a brother who found a stranger lying in the field and ran home to try to help him.

The fierce hurricane winds, lightning, and rising waters appear naturalistic, but, like the operation of Goyen's language, the elements foreshadow the legendary, mythic tone of the story's ending. When father and son carry the dying man into the parlor, the narrator builds a fire in the fireplace, an act of compassion. But then we remember the opening paragraph of the story in which we learn that at eight o'clock in the morning when the man was found, it was "already so hot that the weeds were steaming and the locusts calling." It must have been sweltering in the parlor, then, by the time the narrator built the fire, yet there's no mention of the heat, only of the "softness," "brightness and warmth" of the framed faces of kin brought to life by the fire's glow; this is a fire to answer the destructive force of water. The circle of kinship elicits the words "Thank you" from the dying man, and a benediction, "God bless you, pardner," from the father. The man dies no stranger but a member of the family within the fire's circle of kinship.

It's hard to explain the sort of kinship one forges through deep appreciation for the art another person makes. The derogatory idea of a groupie comes readily to mind. I have never been a groupie, a stalker, or delusional about my attachments to other artists, but there are several with whom I've felt particular kinship. It's almost like one breathes the same air at the same rate in the same lungs before the spell is broken. I had a girlfriend once who wanted to breathe through me, like performing CPR. I let her do it, though it was difficult to let go of my own volition and breathing apparatus as I lay like a corpse for a few long moments. I'm making it sound creepier than it was; it was meant to be tender. Of course she wanted to do this in order to feel closer, but it is true that she had lost two family members to early deaths. People can express their emotions in baffling ways. More often than not, if I feel connected to a certain writer or artist I eventually find that they felt kinship among themselves as well, so I've come to believe there may be certain invisible artistic tribes operating below consciousness that connect artists to one another, especially the living with the dead; sometimes these tribal members brush up against each other in space, but often they never meet except through their writing or paintings or music. Time bundles our disparate sticks. I was lucky to have met William Goyen and doubly blessed to have been able to send him my first book of poems that took its epigraph from his work. I heard back from him right before he died from leukemia.

At the end of the tale, the brothers in "Precious Door," living and dead, are "melting into" the "gray rain" and "mist," which is also the narrator's own tears and the veil of his memory. A visual gap on the page follows, and the story ends in a two-paragraph coda. The narrative is still retrospective, but its perspective shifts from personal to archetypal memory. Father and son hear reports of wonders from a passing man in a boat who tells them of the church steeple and "bell, miraculously afloat" that "stood gonging like a buoy near Trinity bridge."

The final paragraph begins with an abrupt transition from specific to collective memory: "And for a while it was reported that a floating door bearing the bodies of two men was seen moving on the wide river through several towns." People in various towns attested, "the raft was whirling in the currents as though a demon had hold of it," or "it rode the crests of dangerous rapids so serenely that it was easy to see the two men, one, alive and fierce, holding the other, dead." The narrator "waited to hear more, but after this, there were no further reports of the precious door." What some saw as demonic, others saw as serene, but the narrator saw the two men not again. The distancing effect and matter-of-fact ending statement evoke a melancholy tone of loss. There, all report of the brothers ends, and the narrator must dwell in language built from his shattering memory, alone with his own voice.

Scarlet Tanager

In this version of the Scottish play, a summer outdoor drama, the witches
are merely two and dubbed Medicine Woman and Native American Girl;
the former carries a broken tree limb staff and sports a gray-blue blind eye
contact, while the latter appears battle scarred, face set in a wounded scowl,
arm in a sling with strategic splashes of blood. As the tragedy opens, sky
darkens and clouds bunch, and I am crossing the amphitheater to find my
portable chair. Medicine Woman states her solemn passage: "When shall we
three meet again, in thunder, lightning, or in rain?" Native American Girl
limps in from stage left, answering with familiar phrases of which I catch
"battle" and "hurly-burly." As I tromp straight down the hill, one of only
three figures standing, I hear the third witch's line spoken by Medicine
Woman: "That will be ere the set of sun."

Cue real rain, as mist rises from humid grass, a subtle soaking that
builds in amplitude: "Fair is foul, and foul is fair...." Pelted with drops on
shoulders, hair, or umbrellas if they have prepared, the audience anticipates a
decision. My hair is soon dripping. A rough circle of tiki torches, pluming
smoke blacker for the fizzle of rain, marks the perimeter of the performance
space. On the ground, colorful surveyor's ribbon outlines a center aisle and
seating sections, tonight with room to spare. Before Act One's end, foul
weather surpasses fair. Hair on the frizz, skirts and shorts stuck to our chairs,
all rise for rain checks, and witches make hasty retreat.

I sit at a picnic table eating lunch, idly listening to my friend Christine talk
about gestural drawing, how the line extends in space, has weight, earnest-
ness, direction—and almost belief, I think. My hand goes up to my head just
as a slender branch falls from the shade tree, landing neatly in my hand.
Timing. I'm as lucky as a baseball fan with a pop-up foul in my glove. I
catch and hold the forked branch of the Chinese elm in tension like a divining rod, a line carving the air. Aimed for my head, it has found my hand
instead. Where will it direct me?

A rare summer oasis opens in the Virginia countryside, cooler temperatures and an accompanying lack of heavy atmosphere. In the distance, blu-
ish-purple peaks of old mountains draw my eye when I'm not fording cattle

guards, trying not to twist an ankle. Navigation between the thick American boxwood hedges of the Virginia Center for the Creative Arts (VCCA) leaves spider webs across my face that many sweeps of the hand fail to erase from my hair. No large matter. In a few minutes I feel something wet land on my shirt and realize I'm paused beneath the gnarled thick branches of some tree bearing fruit of the sort birds eat.

This time it's only piddle, but I have had birds shit on my head and shoulders twice in my life, like a warm raw egg breaking and oozing down. Following this, someone will tell you it's good fortune. The second time I encountered such luck I was sitting in a writing workshop in Mexico with a Grande Dame of poetry pronouncing upon my poem, saying something to the effect that the first line was simply horrible, or perhaps the word "awful" crossed her lips. After having published more than a half-dozen collections I was sitting there for my retooling, in a word. She continued her humorless drone, head down, staring at my poem through the pigeon's morning ablutions with the class quietly busting a gut. I had to excuse myself to wipe the drooling poop off the shoulder of my gray warmup suit. And of course someone whispered that it was good luck.

I stride to the bottom of the hill, turn around and plod back up, beginning to shake the cobwebs from my heavy sleep-gnawed limbs. I haven't had much time for body maintenance the past several months, and the lactic acid buildup of yesterday's afternoon hike aches this morning, though these are the same legs that used to perform ballet moves and daily jogs, the same knees that were adept at squats. Popping at the joints that still propel me, I move along listening to the chirps, cheeps, and more ambitious blurts and intervals of different songbirds. I spy a mockingbird's white stripes on gray, bluebirds and indigo buntings, cardinals, jays, and sparrows, but I don't know who's singing what.

I know I'm supposed to provide the names of things if I am planning to paint this pastoral scene in words, but sometimes it's best to stick to the confines of the moment rather than turn into a field guide. My experience of this walk is not the experience of knowing everything by name; it's of moving through space with many things revealing themselves to me bit by bit, flickering at the edges of consciousness. After picking my way back over the cattle guard, I decide to loop the road. A rabbit hops out and back into the shrubs. On the homestretch I start picking up bark shed from the sycamore tree, Indian paper scattered along the gravel. I used to write on this bark with pokeberry ink at Camp Iva. Sycamores hail from the oldest tree clan on the planet and can live five or six hundred years, growing to a very wide girth. Tubular pieces of bark, peelings from smallish limbs, are good for no more than a sticky note along the trail. Even so, I collect a bunch of this note paper sloughed from the sycamore, thinking about what I could write on the paler, tan-colored inside portion of the bark: an aphorism, something pithy, tightly wound.

Later in the day, meandering past the lake, I see a few folks splashing in green water as I enter a wooded trail. I've been here before in different seasons, fall and winter, with fellow travelers or alone. This morning's rare coolness has been replaced by steamy humidity. After a few minutes under the leaf canopy I stumble down a red muddy path, skidding on sticky wet clay. Before long I scramble back out again, choosing to walk along nearly empty Boathouse Road. No horses here and no cars. My walk is a lazy endeavor attended only by the sound or sight of many birds. A toddler-sized crow fence-sits. Another bird that might be a juvenile something or other ambles over, rosy in color and as large as a jay with a longish twitching tail. It hops over ground cover and through rough assorted grasses. Then a train rumbles by, but I can't see it, and I come upon a restored caboose, now an art studio with no tracks leading to it or away. Over time the tracks have disappeared, replaced by a grassy patch at the edge of a parking lot. The sign reads "Sweet Briar." Two students ride past me like butterflies on mountain bikes, long hair flying.

A moment of decision came over me as I was nudged back on the bed and my pants pulled down. "Never interrupt someone doing something you said couldn't be done," Amelia Earhart wrote. My best friend put her face in my lap and started nuzzling. Aside from this startling act, in the middle 1970s sex was a pretty ho-hum subject; dates were either "hot" or not, discussion of penis shape and size was a typical giggle fest, and no one had heard of AIDS. I had held out longer than most. I didn't smoke pot or pop pills or even snort unless I laughed too hard. I earned good grades by attending to my studies. We could drink beer legally at eighteen, and occasionally I did, but everyone knew that if a paper were due, I wouldn't go out. As a group we took one of our hall mates to see a midnight showing of the film *Looking for Mr. Goodbar*, hoping she would stop bringing men back to the dorm from mechanical-bull themed bars. After seeing the film she pronounced,

"That girl was sick," and life continued as it had before, with her roommates stepping over various cowboys.

Among my college friends were fraternity rape victims who gutted out their recovery without reporting a crime; incest survivors whose abusing fathers arrived with little notice for campus visits; and women who had endured abortions sponsored by their steel magnolia mothers. All of this seemed the price of having been born female. Our sex meant suffering, but we didn't make a habit of lamenting or moralizing the issue. Although my going both ways went unmentioned, at least by me, the group talked freely, and no one seemed to think our various sexual experiences meant we were extraordinary or doomed. We were simply curious and traded information like bees buzzing a hive.

I continue my walk past the Sweet Briar College sports fields, across the highway from the VCCA along the road below a dressage circle, feeling my college-aged innocence return and smiling at the thought of the red-headed waiter I met at the restaurant where I worked one summer. Freckled and lanky, he was a decent lacrosse player. I sneaked over to his remodeled slave kitchen apartment, and we indulged, staring up into the rafters with a fan swirling over our sweaty bodies. Afterward, he would talk about his high school girlfriend. I didn't mind hearing about her and asked him lots of questions about their love making, which he enjoyed recounting. I think he fell back in love with her while we talked.

Driving out of the campus after my walk, I slow for speed bumps and troughs, and just as I look off the road's edge, into the nature sanctuary, a huge branch thunders to the ground. I see it crack and tumble through other branches, taking them down with it before landing. Torn leaves and leaf confetti follow in its path. No clocks in the Forest of Arden, no need to wind them. I wonder if anyone else saw or heard this branch fall and how many times large limbs splinter from trees in the woods on a single clear day, per hour, per week, per month; how many branches are falling, piling up into tinder, rotting for edge habitat? Who hears them fall? Who remembers?

One of my fellow writers at the VCCA residency who wears a pretty dress comments on the actor playing Macbeth: "He's yummy." As we leave, soaking wet, several of the other women make noises in the affirmative. Macbeth is dark haired and deeply tanned. I admit only to myself that I wanted to sit in the rain more out of devotion to the actor than the play, but I don't want to appear as shallow as a woman who calls a man "yummy."

I try to keep my voice and expression neutral. "He was the best actor," I say. "Too bad about the weather."

When the next performance night rolls around, everyone bails on the rain checks but me. I'm not sorry. I resign myself to sitting close to the stage behind a young woman who reads Ezra Pound's *Cantos* during the intermission. I have seen Macbeth with his sidekick Banquo at the local Food Lion buying Cracker Jacks and beer.

We were milling around the artists' barn drinking wine from plastic tumblers, talking, looking at art, as a straight-line windstorm called a *derecho* dashed to Amherst, Virginia, from Chicago via West Virginia, stripping leafy branches, hurling them into heaps, snapping the trunks of many tall pines, poplars, black walnuts, and cedars, while severing the power lines in its path during a record heat wave. All without warning. Three brownouts in succession finished with a short fade to black below the moon, preceding pounding winds that ransacked the trees and ripped shingles and siding. In the aftermath, day by day, piles of green branches wither brown as the moon wanes. My hair, face, and torso drip sweat in stifling rooms where no breeze plays through the screens. We are powerless for ten straight days: no lights, no AC, no phone or computer devices unless we recharge at the church or the library, no refrigeration, no swimming pool because it's filled with downed tree parts and growing danker without an operating pump. Silent bodies of trees, like fallen soldiers on a battlefield, lie only yards from an electric transformer snapped from its pole. The toppled transformer is as useless as the rusted Tin Man with frozen ax.

The cows go on birthing in the fields surrounding the VCCA, at least two calves born this week despite 80-degree nights and 100-degree days. I drive back from seeking air-conditioned respite at the Amherst county library and Ascension Episcopal church and pass a slick black cow lying at the end of the road just before the cattle grate. Her nose presses against the painted white clouds of a sky-blue sign that reads, "The Real World." Behind her a calf less than a day old stands looking toward the sign, bumping her in the behind. I think about the twenty-day-old baby girl I was holding a few days ago, who did nothing but sleep, purse her lips a bit in mock suckling, and poop. As charming as she was to cuddle and watch, she was not yet able to hold up her head, control her vision, or even smile with volition, her brain only thirty percent of adult size, her legs unable to bear her up. By the time a chimp is weaned, it's ready for puberty. We humans demand more parenting.

Later, I hear that the new calf, still sticky with afterbirth, fell through the grate and got its legs wedged while the mother cow watched from the sidelines, mooing. Baby fell into another world where she was powerless. It took a two-legged to lift the calf out. At least we're good for something.

Soon there's a dull nausea and headache taking the place of greater consciousness on my part, and I reach for salty snacks and electrolyte infusions, still trying to power through the writing I'm here to do. I'm sedentary in order to conserve strength. Slouching in the armchair, I then lower myself to the concrete floor where it's no longer cool. Eventually, I swallow pride and drive home to air conditioning's bright purr and a house for refugees. A. doesn't seem that glad to see me; her mother's camped in the guest room, so we have to sleep together. Usually, our sleep patterns mean that we do not: she stays up late, I'm down by ten. I call this storm-induced proximity, toss and turn on my corner of the mattress from anxiety but at least not heat; at some point, I reach over and pat A. when she is sleeping, as I have done many times before. I catch myself, because this doesn't feel any different to me, the warmth of her sleeping form beneath my hand as unaware of my tenderness as ever. I drive back to tough it out with the other fellows for several nights, confused as to where I belong, but run home a second time, my head literally swimming on the hottest day in thirty years, day nine of outage. I want to sleep, to live, and all I feel are hot flashes blending into heatstroke. On day ten the power company crawls to the end of the line and finds a bunch of sweating artists, writers, and composers marooned on Mt. San Angelo, and I rejoin them.

Day one, starting over, reincarnated post-storm and post-post power, I'm back in my studio wondering if the realism of consciousness, the narrative of the endless moment practiced by James Joyce, which landed *Ulysses* in hot seas, was what depleted the exiled Irish author before age sixty. I'm wondering if the same sort of hunger for consciousness is also responsible for Virginia Woolf's watery exit in the river Ouse. These facts are unknowable, lost civilizations of the interior. Is it possible to think so hard you disqualify yourself from happiness?

Aaron knocks on my studio door to say goodbye; his residency is up, most of it spent sweating. Even so, he has kept up his running and biking in the heat. The same heat has sat around my temples like a leather strop, tightened hourly to make me forget other aches. I give him a package of peanut butter crackers for the road, which have slightly staled in my desk; I realize this later when I crack open another package of the same vintage. "Send me some poems," I say. "I've enjoyed your humor." Aaron drives away and I close the door again. I find myself wondering what fiction is without fact, and what is fact's identity once it has been suspended in a solution of timeless lyric intensity. All the same, if I could write one book as rich as Woolf's *To the Lighthouse* or half as profound as the derided experiment of *The Waves...*

Osage oranges drop out of season after the *derecho* blows through. Instead of the child-brain-sized fruits I remember from October, these June orbs pummel as small and hard as baseballs. They wobble, rolling along the paved road when kicked, fluorescent yellow-green, seemingly unnatural and ghoulish as though they would glow in the dark. I once saw something that color pool on the ground under my broken car radiator. Some of the green knots of fruit pile up next to the split red cedar trunk that's draped over a fence. The blood-red streaks of the tree's splintered interior highlight the wood's orange and amber striations. Into the downed branches an indigo bunting flitters, iridescent feathers shimmering like dragonfly wings. High on the power line the bright male's brown mate perches to sing.

Many consecutive summers of teaching in Bath County near the Cowpasture River form the hub of my creative ecosystem, *eco* as in *home*. Yearly trips to that river mark the place where my energy restores. This summer's writing workshop collects a smaller participant group, and for the first time in eighteen years Charlotte is not here. She's scheduled for her second knee replacement surgery; nothing but this could ever keep her away from the river. Our tight group more than survives: we carry on writing, talking books, holding class and conferences, and drinking wine as usual during extended happy hours—tally-ho! And this afternoon a group of five drives over to Warm Springs, to the Jefferson Pools, to "take the waters."

The Gentleman's Pool House opened in 1761, and there, Thomas Jefferson took the waters in the European tradition, sipping from the drinking pool after soaking in the waters. Like so many things Jefferson built, the first pool house is of course octagonal. The second, larger, circular pool house of batten and board opened later for the Ladies. Ninety-degree water with a heavy dose of magnesium must be responsible for the crystalline aqua color that magnifies and distorts my limbs and sends streaming bubbles up from the rock bed. Tiny yellow bubbles gather strategically, like a spit of bikini over my black swimsuit, and I wonder if iron or sulfur accounts for their color. We have no idea why we always have to pee like crazy after floating around for twenty or thirty minutes, but we all agree we do when Jenny broaches the subject.

One year a large group of us soaked naked in the Ladies' bathhouse before they banned the buff, or "God's suit," and Charlotte and I laughed so hard we were cautioned with removal. Posted signs remind us kindly not to disturb the tranquility of other bathers, and by all means NO Swimming! Not swimming presents a challenge, as the water at 4'10" covers my mouth; I bobble and water splashes up my nose as I try to tiptoe. My enhanced buoyancy, lifted by mineral salts, means I navigate with a neon-yellow noodle pillow woven beneath my head and arms, avoiding the squeaking of upper-arm skin on Styrofoam and all swimming-type motions as much as possible. This is not an effortless sort of drift; I must avoid flipping over like a turtle or bumping into someone else's noodle.

Segments of sky appear overhead, amalgams of gray and white clouds chasing by. The oculus at the top of the roundhouse makes a strange reverse God's eye: I look up at the sky but only see a swatch, a sample of something so vast I could never see it all. Intermittent blasts of sunlight turn our clear blue-green oasis into a kaleidoscope of watery light that wavers and illuminates the white board walls in irregular ovals. I'm not wearing my glasses, so as far as I know everyone here smiles contentedly with eyes closed. I control nothing and want to know less; physical sensations take over from my mind, and with quiet heart I pose no questions, seek no answers.

Then a chill wind blows and clouds darken. The pool's serious attendant warns of a storm's approach. We are not ready to be born again into time, for conversation to reset, to towel off and redress to play the part of ourselves as our friends and family, husbands and lovers expect. No one moves toward the ladders. It's our choice to keep floating through the storm at our own risk.

☙

After plunking down a deposit on an apartment tucked in what was then a funky part of town, and unbeknownst to me a block from the house A. owned at the time, I walked through the three rooms at the top of the early twentieth century mansion that offered refinished oak floors, windows over-looking a tree-lined street, and a spare sort of elegance that sufficiently can-celed out the marital ranch house. I liked not knowing my way around and seeing different kinds of people walking the urban sidewalks. Some of them appeared to be homeless. At least I would not be that.

Before I could move into the apartment, I felt a certain dread come over me. Living separately would externalize the end of the marriage in a definitive way. Surely, a better-built marriage could withstand a much fiercer wind. I did not want to be a *divorced person*; I did not want to fail at mar-riage; I would not be a quitter. I was so young I felt old. Delusion is the state of being alive: I could suffer being cast as a witch, but I didn't want to be *divorced,* in a word, the only divorced person in my family for all generations up to that point. I broke my just-signed lease and stayed home another stormy year and a half. Struggling in my relationship with A. now brings it all back. What have I learned beyond storm survival? Duck and cover, but someone always leaves.

A butterfly lights on a bush beside me and I stop to study it. Definitely not a moth but a butterfly I don't remember seeing before, although I'm fairly cer-tain it's common here. The yellow double wings with marked black stripes and swallowtails should be easy enough to look up. In July when I meet this butterfly, I'm wondering whether it's summering here in Virginia or if this is a stopover on a journey already begun. By the end of August it will need to flutter far to the south. Every day I look into the butterfly bush that's bloom-ing with purple plumes but never see another creature quite the same. I try looking it up from memory and am never confident I've found the right one. I settle on the Eastern Tiger Swallowtail. The name pleases me, and the website tells me this Tiger has been previously spotted in the same county.

Yummy Macbeth, dubbed the new Thane of Cawdor, accepts a traitor's ti-tle. King Duncan twice places his trust in a traitor by the same name. This time I sit through the whole play without compatriots. When Macbeth was merely Macbeth and no Thane, he seemed a battle-weary loyal with noble aspirations. With new ambition aroused he quickly crosses over to murderer, hands drenched in the king's blood. Was his true character always false of face and false of heart—"and nothing is but what is not"? Or, with dagger dancing through the air before him, did one dose of power and misinformation corrupt? It was the king's fate to trust the wrong people. Fool me twice...and I'm dead, said the king.

All of Poe's unreliable narrators amount to self-justifying Thanes of Cawdor. Wait long enough and you will play all the parts, known and unknown, true and false.

I read that the two major symptoms of alcoholism are *guilt* about the past and *fear* about the future, but aren't these universal issues? Like any anxious person, I admit I have both guilt and fear in some measure. On my last night at the residency, I stage a sort of intervention. "I'm having a happening," I say to the only other person within earshot in the VCCA barn kitchen. "It's called 'Burning your losses.' If there are things you can't let go of, losses of opportunity, or a relationship that haunts you, write them down and tear them up. I'm going to burn them in my cauldron." I point outside the window to an empty clay planter on the concrete stoop.

"What's done is done," the writer says. "I'm afraid I'm going early to bed."

She is the same one who called our local Macbeth "yummy." No weird sister, she. I offer to do her burning.

At ten, just home from the play, I peer into the designated cauldron with my flashlight and find her torn scraps left for my torch. I add my own portion to this stew and go about assembling a pitcher of water for the sizzling and fizzling finale. I don't want the fire department in on this. I strike through half the matchbook to get every little piece burned properly, but I'm patient with my boiling cauldron. I stir with an alfalfa straw that occasionally catches fire, smokes out, catches again, and chant to myself about letting go. When it's all ash I douse it for safety. Only one half of my problem appears to be worked through at this point, but with any luck I've burned out the hut of guilt crowding the song in my soul. I trust I still have time to work on fear of the future. I almost laugh thinking maybe I could get out of something like that by dying. "Out, out, brief candle!" No dice.

I switch off the flashlight and sit in the dark. Fireflies zip like falling stars across the lower portion of the sky. The Big Dipper appears, and in the low distance the red planet, Mars. The multiplied candles open out of their dark boxes. Seeing the Milky Way means looking down the thickest slice of the sky where stars upon stars add up in layers of time. This is our neighborhood, our galaxy and super cluster, Laniakea, "immeasurable heaven." In all of this sparkling, I wonder how people lose their own fire. Why do people stop knowing what they want? What douses their desire? I keep looking up as fireflies and stars strike matches to each other, sharing life above and below, meeting in scars.

My fat paperback dictionary cracks open to *irony*. "1: the use of words to express the opposite of what one really means. 2: incongruity between the actual result of a sequence of events and the expected result."

A swerving storyline: this two-page spread in my cracked dictionary, duct-taped together, ends with *it*, at the bottom of the page opposite *irony*.

Who really needs a definition of *it*, I wonder. With so many words missing from this compact pocket edition, I could choose hundreds of words with which to replace *it*. I've carried my pocket Merriam-Webster around for at least fifteen years; I would claim thirty, but I remember having to replace it once with the newer edition: "it 1: that one—used of a lifeless thing, a plant, a person or animal, or an abstract entity (it's a big building) (~'s a shade tree) (who is ~) (beauty is everywhere and ~ is a source of joy)."

I reread this entry several times in sequence, ending on *joy*; I change my mind about our needing *its* definition. I know I cannot look for *joy* and expect to find it, but somehow I do find it.

When the giant old oak at Nimrod Hall in Bath County, signature of the place for more than a century, had to be chopped down, Frankie cried bitter tears. When the men finished paring the limbs and then severing the trunk, heavy as sin on their saws, thick tree parts lay in the long beds of several trucks, and the black snakes hidden in the rotten cave of roots slithered to find new homes. We're left to wonder whether the *derecho* that ripped through Bath, same as Amherst, might have felled the tree if it had still been standing this year. As consolation, missing its generous shade, Frankie and Jimmy added a pergola to extend the lower porch. Now more of us can enjoy this new outdoor room.

Several hummingbird feeders relocated from the second-story porches afford us closer looks at these Fifth World gravity-defying marvels. Their dances with the plastic feeder flowers or the red petunias in the hanging baskets make me hold my breath. I plop down beside Jenny with a tree-imprinted mug of hot coffee. She tentatively extends her camera toward the nearest hummingbird, so close we can hear its throaty hum.

"I've been trying to get a good picture," she says. "I can't stop looking at them."

Flowers cannot propagate without hummingbirds to taste their nectar; we cannot keep our balance without hummingbirds. Jenny and I sit still as they flutter and flit, and hover, leaving ghostly afterimages above our heads. We listen to the low notes of all this flying energy.

I tell her about the day a hummingbird flew right into my shirt at home on my sixth floor balcony. "So far up, I don't know why it was there."

One little hummingbird nips at the feeder's fake flower and then reels backward in the air, up, down, motionless, before darting to another place, wings so whirred with dervish speed they verge on the invisible.

"They seem like insects," I say. "Their wings—"

"Blur, I know," Jenny says.

Jenny dances in a special fitness program. Every day she wears the sweatshirt of the organization to breakfast, like a fetish blanket for a child. She wraps herself in the program's movement theory to banish fear of her mother's and her sister's daily struggles with muscular dystrophy.

Together we watch the hummingbirds feed on sweet nectar like bees, lapping it with the tube of their tongue. They prey on insects and spiders for protein, with a high rate of in-flight metabolism second only to insects, but up to eighty percent of a hummingbird's time is spent quietly perching.

Medicine Cards reveal hummingbirds as harbingers who are bringing back vanished animals to the planet, righting the ecosystem's imbalance, and signaling the end of white two-legged impositions. Impossibly, humming-bird means *joy*.

I finally tell the group of accomplished women who are cresting forty and afraid they will always be alone that all they have to do to get a hundred prospective husbands is to announce they are lesbians. They look wildly back at me.

"No!" they sing in reflexive unison, as in anything but *that*.

I stab at my breakfast. "It's totally true," I say. "We want what we cannot have."

The other sage crone at the table nods her head in the affirmative, says, "No challenge, no date." We know the younger women are too available to be attractive, too eager to be caught to arouse a chase.

In the field below the main house of the VCCA, one of the recently born calves develops an attachment issue. Number 123 eyes me intensely—with longing or suspicion—for several mornings in a row, nay for a couple of weeks, as I waddle the cattle guard and stride down the road threading the fields toward the *Washington Post* I pray will be left in the rural box. Sometimes it is. This early morning walk is my ploy to get to the paper before the other fellows wake up and smell the coffee. Daily eye contact with the calf becomes part of the scenery as I trek to the bottom of the hill and back. I don't stop to think about what it means.

On my final morning's walk, the calf with #123 tagging its ear starts a ruckus, howling in the distance. Standing like a balky toddler with heavy diaper, the tan calf pitches a small fit while the rest of the herd ignores it.

"Run to Mama," I say under my breath, and the cranky little calf hurtles toward me, growing bigger and bigger. It's too late to say I didn't really mean it, to take back what I wished for. "Shit," I think, as I cast my legs fast uphill, forgetting the newspaper altogether. "Shit and double shit."

I cannot help but love that iconic picture of Vladimir Nabokov bearing down on us with his butterfly net. Who would ever need more metaphor for the blessed pursuit of elusive art? Though he was curator of Lepidoptera at Harvard, Nabokov's scientific research was not well regarded. But in 2011, DNA sequencing studies vindicated his theory of the evolution of Polyommatus Blue butterflies. Indeed, these blues did fly from Asia to North America and eventually to Chile in five waves. If not for the trap of words, Nabokov would have spent his life chasing butterflies.

Scarlet tanager: Picture the black wings, and the body with dew-slicked head as bright as a ripe cherry. Sun infuses the skin of the fruit with reflective sheen. The feathers glisten. I want the scarlet tanager to speak for itself. I want the scarlet tanager to tell me what it means. Brief candle flickering in the branches, alighting in the world, the bird means what it is. And when it is gone you will miss it.

Natural Disasters

In the office of dead and dying bees, I sweep the fallen stinging creatures from my windowsills between two shuffled pieces of paper, thinking *balance in all things.* Although beset by my institution's endeavor to eradicate all actual paper from these premises, and thus all signs of the productive but messy inner life of this hive, paper in all stages of construction and deconstruction remains plentiful in my office: blank, bound into monogrammed pads, crumpled balls smaller than fists, the backsides of rejected manuscripts useful for scribbling phone messages, stapled research projects stacked in uneven towers, paper-clipped sections from a colleague's promotion dossier, assorted memos, student transcripts, meeting notes, printed emails, program designs, budgets, spreadsheets, course descriptions, more college memos and so on filed in cabinets or metal desk tiers, student drafts inked or penciled with my encouragements, and humble cast-offs awaiting the blessed recycling bins. From time to time a student surveyor from the Environmental Sciences department appears and asks permission to gaze into my trashcan. If she spies any discarded paper she's empowered to jot the infraction into her report using the antiquated pen and notebook carried in her hands. I hope she makes a good grade.

Various versions of paper amount to ongoing proof of my utility, and in this context my necessity, but seldom do I have the pleasure of putting any of these sheets to practical use so that my papers might be pressed into service, standing in for, say, a broom and a dust tray. In this bellwether moment, I hover, pausing in my task, afraid lest, merely sleeping, the mostly desiccated stingers will resurrect as I carry my practical sheets speckled with broken-winged things. I tilt them gently into the trashcan. Will they yet fly away?

I can almost see it, the splinter inside me for months. It's surfacing after applications of baking soda paste, which shrinks, prunes, and bunches my skin like wrinkled magic tape. I'm still waiting for the splinter to entirely unmask itself, salted from my largest organ, arisen to ride the waves. I feel it pushing deeper instead of daring to be named. There's a lump, laced with scaly transparencies of ragged cells, above the joint of my second finger. The baking soda paste has begun to shed me in a patch shaped like a tiny imaginary continent. Harder each day, obdurate, the lump sustains a dark pupil, an odd feature, pock of an ancient sea, perhaps proof there was once water and therefore life on my planet.

In the same office with an occasional buzzing near my head from a straggler that looks nothing, really, like a bee, I watch a video of a dolphin giving birth. The birth starts tail first, a nuisance to the mother who tries to pry the appendage loose by rubbing against the watery floor as though her baby were a waggling skin tag. The little tail flexes, almost folds in two but doesn't break; its mother keeps applying pressure to dislodge her offspring without the solemn help of gravity. Tail, body, and head at last plop free and a swimming contest commences with the new mother speeding up, much lighter now, as a blood cloud spreads behind her. The newborn tries to keep pace, a smaller twin to the mother's muscular undulations. My thoughts dart to predators and then I remember that these creatures only seem free but are swimming the confines of a large tank, which is why I can witness such miraculous moments. I am happy again, at least as much as possible given their captivity, but I worry as the loose formation of bodily fluids swirls farther from the mother and out pops a little afterbirth goo followed by a bit of flesh flotsam that's as stubborn about letting loose as the little dolphin performing its tail-first debut.

Complicated, all of this, and yet the dual swimming looks easy, even joyful. The just born shadows the motions of its mother. They breach together to blow some air, to inhale. I gasp. Not a marine mammal myself, much less a fish, I have been holding my breath throughout this unfolding drama. I used to dream consistently of finding myself underwater and realizing after a short struggle that I could breathe there. I wonder how the baby flipper knows at merely half a minute old to wait until it surfaces to take its first breath. Humans really aren't that smart, all considered.

"If a writer stops observing he is finished," quoth Hemingway in a Madrid café. In the same interview with George Plimpton, he declared, "Certainly it is valuable to a trained writer to crash in an aircraft which burns. He learns several important things very quickly. Whether they will be of use to him is conditioned by survival. Survival, with honor, that outmoded and all-important word, is as difficult as ever and as all-important to a writer."

With survival the bottom line, the absolute necessity, even without honor, I wonder why so many of our species keep trying to die through cigarettes, booze, drugs, gluttony, diets, extreme sports, risky sex, bungee jumps, zip lines, mountain climbs, fast cars, skydives, and motorcycles. Some of these methods, of course, are meant to make one feel more alive, others meant to numb emotions as though they would never pass. Is life a suspicious gift with too many strings attached?

If the shopworn biblical metaphor for the body is a temple, house of the spirit, then the world is the body of God. Take this world as house, each town and feature on the map: explore these rooms one by one. I grew up in Richlands near Raven and Red Ash, not that far from Dante (pronounced *dant*), Cedar Bluff, and Jewell Ridge, among the Appalachian Mountains and along the Clinch River. The Appalachian region stretches across parts of thirteen states, uniting north and south, and the Clinch River meanders down to Tennessee. The first thing I fished from those waters was a monster bearing rows of shark-like teeth. We called it a dogfish after the shark, but it was probably a catfish. Easily entertained, I learned early that anywhere makes a good place for a miracle, if you want to call it that. Now I tramp around my loft living room each morning in full view of mountains to the north, east, and west, watching Norfolk Southern trains pull coal from seams and move any number of hidden things piled two shipping containers high in the opposite direction. Pick a room. Take a walk through the body of God.

Sunday afternoon I stride up a street adjacent to downtown through Roanoke's oldest suburb, the Old Southwest neighborhood. The houses on Miller's Hill date to the turn of the last century; the 400 block of Day Avenue has been targeted for redevelopment by the city. One by one these once stately homes are coming back to life, exteriors restored and interiors updated. I will be moving here, but I don't yet know it. This walk is a walk into my future, and a return, but I am blind at this point, blind to so many things. The original contractor for this block, coincidentally the same company that built our loft, got into a dispute with the city and the project stalled out, but the rehabilitations, house by house, have continued with smaller contractors, a worthy effort to convert a sore block of old housing stock from slumlord exploitation back to single-family dwellings.

I crest the hill past the looming Baptist church that guards the corner, my knotted Achilles tendon smarting a bit, but I keep my pace. It's been little more than a month for me in the running program I started to keep my mind off my troubles and weight off my thighs. Today I'm charged with a forty-five-minute walk following yesterday's group run on the greenway by the Roanoke River. The trees along this street, like the ones along the trail, are decidedly changing color, orange and yellow tinged. Walking around this neighborhood where I used to live, I usually see some porch-sitting friends or meet someone on the sidewalk, like James pushing his two children in a stroller coming home from church. I head up and down blocks, sensing the little dash of summer that remains in mid-October.

Meandering back toward the center of town, I pass a bagpipe band on the steps of Green Memorial Methodist and am confirmed in my idea of downtown living, the almost daily surprises it holds. Our town is thoroughly saturated with festivals and outdoor activities, copious races for good causes, and civic parades. One must embrace navigation of blocked streets on week-ends. Foot traffic often proves more efficient than driving.

Walking is a good way to come to know a place. When I spent months in foreign places—Prague, southern Spain, London, Malta, France—I walked as much as possible, although there were other ways to get around. The walking gave me grounding, and I had lots of unscheduled time in which to wander. I walked so much that I dreamed the paths and streets upon returning home. These routes I imagine trace riverbeds in my mind. I can follow water's path, remembering.

I come upon a scrap of notepaper on the ground. I pick up what I think to be litter only to read the scribbled start of something like a poem: "On the last morning / I imagine her / between the trees // I rise to walk / in dark...." The last two lines are either circled or marked through and the final two words illegible. The rest might be considered sentimental sap except for these oddities: the handwriting makes the word *last* read as *lust*, while the word *her* looks as much like *hell*, affording this translation: *on the lust morning I imagine hell between the trees....*

I round a few more blocks, passing a clutch of competing banks. A little bird has done a perfect swan dive to the sidewalk. Nothing seems amiss aside from one buckled wing that tells me how it died; a wisp of downy feather on the plate glass above is a clue. With a discarded plastic bag in hand I scoop the bird and find a very dirty sparrow, soiled because it lived in the sooty city with frequent diesel trains and constant exhaust. Only I see this fallen sparrow. There's no burial except a toss into a trashcan, nonetheless I bless the bird and keep walking.

Every night for a number of years a woman slept next to me for at least some part of those hours. She said Sunday nights felt "achy" before we moved in together. One night in the historic house of many colors a waterfall rippled down a twenty-foot wall above the grand staircase below the complicated roof. There had been a drought for a while, but after we moved into the house it began to rain. A few days earlier some workmen had removed a long-dead bird from a roof crevasse. It was nothing but tiny bones and a few lousy feathers stuck together, no identity left. *What a blessing*, I thought when the rotted bird was removed, but apparently it had been sealing the roof from leaks. It took gallons and gallons of viscous black goo and a team of roofers to do what the wedged dead bird had done by itself, weighing nearly nothing and accidentally applied to the weak spot by the pressure and ingenuity of the rain's hands.

From Hem (-ingway) again: "From things that have happened and from things as they exist and from things that you know and all those you cannot know, you make something through your invention that is not a representation but a whole new thing truer than anything true and alive, and you make it alive, and if you make it well enough, you give it immortality. That is why you write and for no other reason that you know of."

One night in the new condo-loft with the amazing view of the city and successions of mountains beyond, I was seated in front of the central three-panel window eating dinner. I picked up my plate and headed to the kitchen sink. Moving back and forth between the kitchen and the dining area, I snuffed candles and cleared the table. After washing the dishes I went to bed but had trouble sleeping because of the hissing wind, gusting between fifty and seventy miles per hour. In a nod to historic tax credits that forbade the updating of the building's facade, the original double-sash windows were coupled with panels of new interior storm glass. I got up, returned to the dining area, and slid the storm window completely shut behind my dining chair despite strong, surging wind caught between the two layers of glass. A. was in her studio.

I rolled back into bed, pulled the covers over my head and shut my eyes. Soon, there came a reverberation of smashing glass, and in an adrenaline-drenched moment I ran to the source of the sound. Shattered glass thrown like lightning spears covered and surrounded the dining table. Large pie pieces and small slivers had embedded deep in the drywall at angles; some had scudded over my placemat and lay scattered around my chair. Not safety glass but regular single pane that could pierce your heart.

The next day A. got stuck in the elevator trying to receive a repairman up to our floor to replace the window. At the same time, about forty-five minutes away, a shooting rampage was unfolding at Virginia Tech. Thirty-three died that day, including the killer who once sat in a creative writing class until he proved too creepy and antisocial and was removed to individual tutoring. Of all the weirdness I've encountered in more than thirty years spent teaching, I never imagined a student capable of mass murder. What do we do when the unimaginable happens and happens?

Now it's Hurricane Sandy. I walk outside my office and gaze through the large Palladian window at the building's end to see dark strings of scumbled clouds. With a change to close focus, I see stinkbugs in the foreground, scuttling little dinosaurs dancing glass. It's hard to believe that large amounts of this campus, including the library, were once underwater in the 100-year flood of 1985, professors and students in hip waders, passing soggy library books down a conga line. It is either impossible to prepare for such disasters, or some of us are always preparing for disasters to avert, worrying so the worst won't happen, digging fallout shelters and oiling the hinges of storm cellars, making sure beach houses are built on stilts for storm surges that do not come rather than the much more powerful hurricanes that do. You can't spend your marriage preparing for divorce; we buy insurance for everything and hope never to use it. In elementary school I learned to "duck and cover," but I more vividly recall the image of Smokey Bear admonishing me not to play with matches: "Only YOU can prevent forest fires." Bambi lost his mother when the forest was set ablaze. Cue images of charred stumps, deer and birds and rabbits racing from the flames.

I hear on the radio that "Natural disasters call for leadership." I email people I know in New York and New Jersey to see how they are holding up, what damage they might have suffered. After a few days, Christine writes back that she dodged the storm but is spending time in Far Rockaway Beach helping a friend clear out her wrecked house. After a couple of weeks when her power's restored, Sharon finally answers from New Jersey.

Sent home from work with my evening class canceled because of this fierce weather, I trudge the distance to my car in weird yellow light. As I drive the loop road that marks the campus curtilage a predominately white owl flies mere feet away, dipping in front of the car. I see no more than its broad back jotted with dark gray spots and a body large as a tomcat's; its great expanse of wings only flaps a few beats to the top of a tree. Appearing out of the storm, this creature seems more mythical than real. A shiver loosens inside me. I blink, and the owl disappears without my seeing its face.

Con Edison cuts power to lower Manhattan in the wake of flooded subways, like they did the weekend before 9/11. In *The Towering Inferno*, did the skyscraper collapse into a heap of explosive-contaminated concrete powder? No, it did not. Call it natural, an accident of God, unnatural, an accident of man, or just a disaster of the destructive imagination. I declare, however, that it is no longer possible to decide what is a natural disaster and what is human havoc; one turns too quickly into the other. Carbon energy leads to global warming, which leads to weather events. *There was an old woman who swallowed a fly.* Weather used to be considered a no-brainer act of God; like running into a deer with one's car, weather falls under the non-collision clause. Most everyone but diehard crackpots and energy lobbyists agree that we are making bad weather worse with our carbon emissions.

In *Knowing*, Nicolas Cage plays MIT professor, John Koestler, who sends his son off with the aliens to reseed humanity and then dies with his parents and sister, drowned in the rush of a gigantic tidal wave. In another of my favorite disaster flicks, *Dante's Peak*, a volcano erupts, chasing a family down a mountain slope, but I give *Twister* the nod over *Dante*, *Towering Inferno*, and possibly even *Titanic* for drama, special effects, acting, and backstory. People will build their houses on sand in view of what might destroy them and rebuild in the same spot again and again. People will destroy marriages, setting themselves and their partners adrift, for no big reason aside from internal combustion. Reparation after disaster is nearly always impossible to manage: too little too late, like going to counseling after the marriage blows up, as most people do in a burst of forensic feeling. Politics trumps the purpose of federal agencies: "Natural disasters call for leadership." Okay, I heard that already. Before all power has been restored to Manhattan, the head of Con Ed resigns. Who will be accountable for the disasters brewing in my life, I wonder. I used to stand in front of the mirror and sing, "I'm starting with the man in the mirror...." Well, it's at least a place to begin. But "It takes two to tango," as my father used to say somewhat ominously.

"Many aspects of her existence, as if in the wake of a natural disaster, had been disorganized, upended, torn apart...to some degree, wrecked beyond repair...." I read Maggie Scarf's *Unfinished Business: Pressure Points in the Lives of Women*, and sigh a lot. With two women, I imagine you get more pressure points: "...an attack of depression can be...compared to another kind of disaster—to floods, earthquake, typhoon, and so forth...in that there's a lot of mopping up and a lot of restoring that has to be done in its wake." Knowledge, knowing—not very satisfying when it doesn't avert disaster. John Koestler figured out that the string of numbers scratched by a prescient girl meant dates, locations, longitudes, latitudes, and the totals of the dead from various disasters, yet he was swallowed by a wave. Is this what wisdom boils down to? Scarf continues, "In some cases, things never are the same again afterward. The damages can't be made good and all of the losses replaced."

"The one who remembers" is the shaman or storyteller of the tribe, the keeper and healer of psychic lost places. A mental patient is often described as having *lost it*, mental illness a form of being lost, of wandering. Home is frequently the source of the problem, and finding a way to be at home in the world is the answer. To suss out the situation of being ourselves, sometimes we have to take the long route, circle back and spiral around the mountain asking, *Who am I?* I took a class by that title and at the end of it had a political screaming match in a restaurant with a fellow graduate over the outcome of the Gore/Bush election. Who the fuck *am* I? Sometimes we need a shaman to talk us through it. I think of modern talk-therapy as a form of shamanic ritual in which we can lay our burdens open to someone who has proven useful as a guide. At several junctures in my life I have made such psychic journeys. It can be fruitful to take these trips accompanied by a therapist trained in the art of listening deeply, who asks for no more than a fee and the light of truth from where I sit. We all need a witness who doesn't render judgment.

From where I sit this morning at home in a downtown loft sipping coffee, I can see a coal train rattling by. Though the enterprise looks tame enough at this stage, dark, irregular chunks heaped and sparkling like the diamonds they could be in a million more years if let be, I know the movement of coal represents an unnatural natural disaster that's been going on for years back in the hills where I grew up, in the Appalachian chain, the conterminous parts of western Virginia, West Virginia, east Kentucky, and Tennessee. Coal extraction goes on elsewhere as well, but I'm speaking here of what's close at hand: coal has made a fortune for absentee owners, an energy empire for corporations concealing slag tarns, early death, and mounds of grief—mountains leveled; valleys and rivers filled with shale and shame, limestone, and poison runoff; sludge pouring into children's bedrooms, pounding like flashfloods down hollers in the dead of night. Water aplenty, but it's not fit to drink. And for locals, these coal jobs are the best, perhaps the only, employment available. Good folks are in a bind not of their making. They have little choice but to defend their livelihood while protesting chronically hazardous working conditions. Black lung and cave-ins don't kill mine owners unless they're underground with the workers at the time. Fat chance. And then this happened in my state: a coal baron took the money he made in the mountains and threw a huge addition onto the art museum at the other end of the state. This kind of largess ought to be illegal.

The larger disasters of coal will color the future beyond these hills and have the potential to spread, from stoic hill people to the planet at large, the ironic recipe of economic inequality that equals physical extinction. This morning in Beijing the smog blots out the sun, the pollution level meaning no safe breath for anyone. From space the winds blow the smog everywhere in a borderless free-for-all. This morning the local paper says our smog is from Alaska! Our carbon energy footprint can potentially make Earth uninhabitable; 2012 was the hottest year on record in the States (until 2014, 2015, and 2016), 3.2 degrees above average for the last century. John R. Christy, director of Earth System Science Center at the University of Alabama in Huntsville, tells us that the need for cheap energy as people around the world struggle from poverty will undermine any efforts to curb coal production: "carbon emissions will continue to rise because of the undeniable benefit carbon energy brings to human life." Undeniable benefit: severe weather patterns, extreme storms, historic drought, and blazing wildfires, but no world's end, no final reckoning?

In another of my favorites, *The Day After Tomorrow*, a small collection of refugees only survives a sudden deep freeze by sheltering in the New York

Public Library and burning books, lighting one off another, never letting the fire in the giant stone fireplace go out. Despite a pack of wolves escaped from the zoo and a stone-cracking flash chill that freezes flesh on contact, this group prevails by book fire. A couple of leftover pay phones offer the only outside communication until the ensuing floodwaters cover them too. Without that bank of pay phones, the son of a government climatologist would not have known to stay inside and would have wandered off to perish with the group that walked into the snowstorm's eye, thinking it was over. No satellite signals, no electric grid to charge devices. I am thinking hard on how much excess technology we can shed and still function when the blizzard hits. I sit in Jim's chair with gray and brown hanks of hair falling around me while the customer in the next chair talks about how he and his wife didn't want to start texting, but now they do. "You can have ongoing conversations," he says. "It's their language," says his hairdresser, meaning his children's generation. "Dust in the Wind" plays in the background. I'm losing parts of myself that are supposed to grow back.

When Gurney Norman writes of the part of Appalachia he knows best as "the last unconquered place," he's not speaking of energy removal, of the rife colonialism of the coalfields, but of the soul that remains, of what makes a local cultural identity persist in its folkways, music, and stories. He's collected these stories and told as many himself. Italian academics embrace his storied place, while Americans tend to cling to some stereotypical version of a monolithic South, conflating old plantations in river deltas with the mountainous regions. Tin ears can't distinguish one accent from another, but no matter its origin—mountain, valley, or shore—the Southern accent remains suspect.

The literary South most of us know was constructed in the last century by William Faulkner, Eudora Welty, Flannery O'Connor, and their descendants. James Still rests on a shelf seldom disturbed and the status of Appalachian literature waxes and mostly wanes from notice. Read James Still's *River of Earth*. At least read that. Read Denise Giardina's *Storming Heaven*. Read Lee Smith's *Oral History*. Read *The Coal Tattoo* by Silas House. Read Wendell Berry. See the films *Coalminer's Daughter* and *Matewan*. Before you picture, once again, *Gone with the Wind*, while humming ironically about Mr. Bluebird on your shoulder, please read *River of Earth*. There are many selves and many Souths. The truth is that nobody can agree on what Appalachia means or is. And most people don't know where it is. It lends itself to mythopoeia. It rises up and bites your ass, only this and nothing else: a contradiction, a wild walking lexicon of extremity and the *barely composed*.

I sip my coffee, look into my computer screen sometimes uncomfortably glimpsing my reflection, and remember something that many have proposed or noted: the dissolution of place in digital unity, a new *placelessness*. It sounds to me like we'd all be poorer. Simultaneously a bumper sticker has become a movement: "Think Global: Act Local," especially if it's farm to table, something we can eat. Are chic eats a boon for people from unapproved places? Maybe. The question of where we belong must extend beyond the limit of the original dirt between our toes and also beyond the virtual sphere, where we construct ourselves with keystrokes, words, and images and reconnaissance is as easy as cruising websites. As Adams writes, "To walk through a place is to become involved in that place with sight, hearing, touch, smell, the kinetic sense called proprioception, and even taste." I fall back on the senses in order to know what I know. Perhaps our tending toward *placelessness* offers certain proof of our having reached the point Gurney Norman refers to as "global regionalism." No one can say place has disappeared or been dismantled. Boots on the ground; in other words, let's take a walk.

Most of us, as long as we are able, persist in traveling to gain definition, listing places we've lived or been on vacation the way we used to exhibit merit badges on a sash, except those had to be earned over time and most with an effort of hands. Save for exile, military service, and forced migration, travel these days usually means privilege. Among the privileged, being rooted in a place and staying put unless you hug the coasts of California or New York is generally suspect. Beyond this sort of snobbery, we must still have some real human need for moving around in space, for breathing different air and letting journeys work on us. Traditional mountain people don't leave home that much, being well equipped for the innovative requirements of rough survival but not rich. I have a feeling these folks will find a way to outlast the technology-enriched rest of us whose smart asses will not be saved.

One night in the new sixth-floor loft an earthquake sent something large and weighty crashing to the floor in the condo above our heads. Simultaneously, many secrets were pent up there as well, agreements that were destined to become disputes; first the developer bellied up, and two years later the contractor, leaving us to puzzle through the debris of soured deals. We'd signed a stack of papers we had not thoroughly understood.

Beside me during this time, peripatetically, slept a woman with many fractures from family secrets. She slept late at night if at all. Sometimes she fell into frenzies in front of the computer screen, finding shreds of information, building cases and amassing details in some periodic table of past wrongs. I raised my voice against injustice and offered commiseration, strategies for reparations. Eventually, I imagined myself bleeding on the floor, but it never really happened that I needed as much of her attention as the past absorbed. Inevitably, I was deemed a liability. The waves swamped me with sad longing and then receded for spells. I fell into resentment, became irritable and caustic. It seemed that our grief would never really end. But worse, most of our grief wasn't even between us. So aggrieved, she was, it felt like she'd taken a lover. And if she had, I'd be the last to know.

I found myself in the basement of our building during an April flood with water pouring in among my stored artwork and boxes of duplicate domestic items, while A. was MIA, attending a day-long meditation session during which I was unable to reach her. Shaleen, a condo neighbor, came down into the basement, appearing at just the right moment, and we hoisted my belongings above the waters, for hers had been safely stored on higher ground. It is important to understand that everything hinges on moments of much-appreciated assistance such as this, more than on long aftershocks from disaster on which we tend to dwell.

In a few months, a second trembler rolled through the sixth floor from south to north. A., who survived the 1989 L.A. earthquake with a protective angel hovering over her, was in her south-facing studio, and I in my north-facing library/writing chamber. The quake rolled her out of her studio and down the hall to the front, where I opened my door to ask, "What was that?" It sounded like the plumbing meant to rattle apart.

She said, "I thought you had fallen down in the shower."

"No, I'm right here."

5.9 on the Richter scale, the epicenter was located in central Virginia, near the town of Mineral. The top of the Washington Monument cracked a bit and had to be closed for repairs. Think: alien invasion, *Independence Day*. The monumental phallus breaks off, sealing the president's fate. And you call it just a movie.

A few months later I find a crack in the shower where the tile walls meet at the corner and fill it with sanded caulk. East Coast earthquakes are few in number, so few we forget about the Mid-Atlantic Ridge most of the time, but crustal collisions gave rise to the Appalachians, once tall as the Himalayas, 300 million years ago. I never find any other sign of visible damage.

So many parts of the landscape have been claimed for agricultural production, settled and developed, that at this point there is nothing left to grab. Mineral rights: sold. Water rights: earmarked. Paradise: long ago paved. And for nature's bounty we get national parks. BLM wilderness areas. Within boundaries, like a zoo, we visit the natural world, what has become of the "natural world." Hikers in a conga line of light, wondrous metal walking sticks, technical clothing, and properly treaded boots rampage up and down Half Dome at a rate that erodes granite. While driving my usual truck route to work, as I ribbon through freight movers, body shops, storage facilities, shooting ranges, and cabinet-makers, I muse. Just past the day-old-bread store, on the grounds of the largest car repair shop, I see a dead raccoon that probably got hit on the road and crawled just far enough to die of its injuries in cool grass. I can't help thinking that it's only a matter of time before what we like to call *nature* reclaims this strip of asphalt, these bath refitters and light manufacturers, a matter of time until kudzu snakes the lamp posts and loops the power poles together in a mockery of Christmas tinsel, leaving raccoons to safely abide. There seems to be no question at this point that humans have been the poorer neighbors.

In our downtown arts district, one can hear on a summer evening the dulcet periodic blasts from police shotguns removing starlings from their perches in the stinking pear trees that line our street. Starling droppings damage vehicle paint and crust sidewalks. It's true, they do make a mess, but please, where are they supposed to roost instead? Like me, they have migrated into the city. From the balcony tucked in a notch of the building, I watch the starlings' frantic flapping as they bundle together, stumbling like startled drunks through the air as the shotguns continue to pop, pop, pop. Walking to the parking garage I pass a squirrel caught in a quandary, running away from me, trying to find a tree. I can see that its tail has already been stripped of fur and badly broken. The snapped mast scrapes along the sidewalk as the squirrel skitters, frets. Across the street from our building a deer leapt through a plate-glass window, ran raggedly bouncing wall to wall, and crashed back out leaving a bloody trail. It came down from the surrounding mountains, perhaps nosing along old Lick Run to the city, and then did not belong, got stranded between two buildings, caught between rows of windows, and followed its lost reflection through glass. Having removed their natural predators except for ourselves, we notice a heck of a lot of deer around here, deer that eat every green shoot, every tulip bulb, most herbs save thyme, sage, and mint, all vegetables and roots. Deer plowed into the side of my car, breaking the mirror, when I lived in the country, and rut-crazed bucks flung themselves into the cars of friends. Still, I know there are way too many of us two-leggeds now, even if locally outnumbered by deer. For all the Virginia hunters in coonskin caps, for all the educated men lacking sufficient testosterone-drenched ritual, there are plentiful deer to hunt with bullet or arrow, fresh bloodied venison to skin and vital parts to sever one by one, enough primitive pretenses to indulge with vaunting tenderloin. Were there food enough for deer on the mountainsides, I know that a stray, very lost deer never would have wandered downtown and bounded through glass.

Five years into our life in the sixth-floor loft, a pair of cicadas cracks open in the condo. At first I find just one abandoned skin, slit as with an X-ACTO knife down the back but still clinging fiercely to a short limb like a crunchy thumb on my potted spindly palm. A. collects the specimen and covers it with a makeshift bell jar.

Cicada nymphs can take seventeen years to crawl out of the ground where they once dropped as eggs. But in the South the cycle shortens, and pretty soon I start reading and hearing about the thirteen-year cicadas being back, specifically brood XIX. When I lived in the country, I had a habit of setting my houseplants outside every late spring and through the summer. I can remember a particularly noisy year when the cast-off exuviae of cicadas seemed to be everywhere, even crunching underfoot at the gas pumps. Their mating in the tall trees at the fringes of my property raised a ruckus of shrill shrieking that not even the folk cure of bagpipes could have silenced.

Accidentally, I carried stowaway cicada eggs in potted plants with me through two moves. Months later I find a second dried skin. When nymphs crawl out of the soil they find a place to attach. It can be a leaf or a twig or, in this case, expensive slipcovers stitched of Belgian linen. In the world of nature, life is said to find a way, but it seems more like a neurotic script unfolding when the past signals its way into the present hour and something hatches from the depths of us, determined to have its bit of light and air regardless of the cost. I never saw the wet, red-eyed teneral phase when the creatures extracted themselves from a tunnel of soil and then cracked out of their own skins. I never saw them pump up with fluid, expanding nascent wings until they could fly. And if I heard these two cicadas that awoke on the sixth floor from potted dirt, I thought their screeching was the sound of trains braking on the tracks. I can't yet know if they managed to find each other, mate, and drop eggs back into my captive soil. Time will tell. What's buried will swim up.

Jonna calls to say that she feels enormously upset and frightened by the fact that a rodent appears to be living in her kitchen, possibly beneath the dishwasher. The large black cat named Baby camps there and stares. Lacking full appreciation for her terror, I offer that it's fairly normal this time of year beyond the first frost for mice to seek shelter. She has already cleaned out a drawer full of droppings and doesn't want to acknowledge that what she's calling a rodent is probably a rat. Having lived in the country, I have encountered numerous moles, voles, mice of the brown wood and gray house varieties, and, yes, rats. I am almost immune and not the right person to appraise her tragedy as such. I offer to set a trap.

"I can't kill it," she says. "It's got to be a Havahart."

Unprepared for tackling an existential rodent problem, I know this will be an impossible conversation. Nevertheless I say, "Yes it's sad, but it comes down to this rat or you. And it's your house." This is the same conversation we've been juggling for years concerning extracting oneself from sociopathic boyfriends.

On *Sixty Minutes* I watch an interview with a North Korean escapee from District 14, where he was born in a gulag. He tells how he was so conditioned to camp rules that he turned in his own brother and mother when they planned to escape. He never got the promised extra rations for his ratting. Instead, merely a boy, he was beaten by the guards who took credit with the higher-ups for the intelligence he had passed to them, and subsequently he witnessed the execution of both his mother and brother. He explains that he never felt connected to his family as such, his parents having been selected for breeding by the officials, and the camp's children held as common property. Dreaming of full plates of food and little else, he lost grounding in his brainwashing and at last found a way out; he crawled over his comrade who was electrocuted by the fence and walked alone through barren, cold wilderness, finally arriving in the west where he was given political asylum. He suffers from PTSD and depression, says the plentiful food on his plate is never enough to fill him; the sinking in his gut remains. He says he still doesn't know about love. *What is it?*

I can't know while watching this interview and feeling the sadness collect in my chest that in a few weeks, every channel will have news from Connecticut's Sandy Hook Elementary School, bad news that will bring us right up against Christmas: a shooting by a lost twenty-year-old son who will first take the life of his mother and then the lives of twenty-six others, mostly first and second graders. *What is it?*

Ms. Rikki Lee Jones with the congenitally crooked tail came to us from the alley behind the house of complicated roofs, located in the historic district where we lived for three years before building the loft; she just appeared. She lapped water from a large blue ceramic bowl in the garden that was fitted with a fountain. Every day she drank a bit deeper and stayed longer. She is a beautiful shade of taupe pointed with dark chocolate, and no one claimed her when we asked around. We took in the foundling and named her after a singer. That's the way it had to be.

Every night for years a woman slept next to me, and then she stopped. She stopped at the height of the sunspot cycle, the super cycle peak. She said, "I don't owe you the rest of my life." At night I could hear her breathing in the next room. I closed my door until it clicked, but the cat opened it. The cat opened the doors we shut between us. We petted the cat and both tried to get the cat into bed with us, but she demurred. Even though Ms. Jones had variously shown some appreciation for her rescue from the elements, Siamese cats prove difficult as projection screens.

After two months of fooling around with it, I finally go to the doctor about the knot in my finger only to discover that my primary care physician, a Doctor of Osteopathy, no longer keeps a scalpel in his office. He refers me to a surgeon. I'm thinking it's only a tiny splinter, but I keep the appointment after having the required X-ray. A few mornings later I'm in a well-lit office with my middle finger strapped down for an effective numbing shot.

My splinter turns out to be a blood clot. The surgeon, quick in telling me she's a mother, irrigates it thoroughly and applies a single strip of sticky tape to close the slit. "Most of the time these clots absorb on their own." Mine obviously had not.

For a week or so the little bit of swelling above the second joint makes me think the lump lingers, but eventually the tape falls off in the shower, the redness fades, and the regular contour of my finger returns. No more bruising when I play around on my drums. Now it's only my right elbow that aches. When I am thoroughly healed, a Martian meteor exhumed long ago in the Saharan desert passes tests confirming the presence of water: new measurements, new instruments, and a new conclusion = life. The rough pyramid of rock, scorched black, encases an annealed rock within, which looks like translucent amber. Sparkling chunks float suspended inside the meteor, in a core that equates to ancient water.

Aurorean light to the east offers pink and purple streaks out my windows. I flip open the computer and read scattered news: a beeswax and zinc compound thought to have been used medicinally for the eyes has been found in a small metal disc exhumed from a Roman Mediterranean shipwreck from 140 BCE. I imagine opening this blackened tin that has been passed through the ages and applying the healing balm to my tired, bleary eyes. What these eyes done seen.

I arrive at the college to find a woman and two men in white jumpsuits wielding spray cans; they ask me to stand back. I'm wondering how they got into my office. Waiting in the hallway, hoisting my heavy briefcase from shoulder to shoulder, I peer in as they move about in a unison dance, motioning toward the largest window that's draped with fading prayer flags. The men silently don ventilation masks; the woman does not, but turns toward me to convey that the white powder from the cans will kill the yellow jackets within twenty-four hours. "You might see a few stragglers." She reports that their nest is tucked into the space between the window sash and the plaster walls; the ingenious insects are crawling through the crumbly old mortar between two bricks.

"I thought yellow jackets lived in the ground."

"Holes," she corrects.

"Most of them were already gone," I say. "I put them in the trashcan." This is not strictly true, but I hate to see their annoying buzz wiped out entirely. If they had wanted to sting me they probably would have already done so. Periodically over the summer when I visited the office I swept up numbers of their dead, officiating at what I thought were mass bee funerals before I knew they were yellow jackets.

And just as quickly the human swarm departs, taking with it everything except the residue of white powder sprinkled over the windowsill that seeps into my row of loosely filed class notes on the shelf below, killing every old idea. I try to shake the substance from the paper folders. I run to the restroom to scrub white powder from my hands.

Lost Places

El que pierde su tierra pierde su memoria. [He that loses his land loses his memory.] —Juan Esteban Arellano

I.

The Richardsons of Illinois have been planting a corn maze or a maize maze (or simply *amaze*) for more than a decade. Families come to wander miles of paths through the corn, a sterile variety selected for its softness in case anyone takes a notion to bang someone else over the head with an ear. Every year the theme changes. The Beatles on the occasion of the fiftieth anniversary of their stateside invasion was quite popular. The Richardsons provide maps to follow, of course, and markers along the way if you are keen enough to catch them. A banner over the starting place proclaims, "Get Lost Here."

As kids scrambling the woods, my best friend Greta and I made whole days of digging holes. I'm not sure now where we were going with it, what solemn aims we held within, neither of us naïve enough even at nine to think we'd reach China. We may have discovered some natural depressions that in warmer seasons filled with murky water and tadpoles and sought to make them deeper. The digging was not easy going; roots and stubborn layers of shale hindered our short shovels and sticks, preventing us from carving the perfectly honed holes to which we aspired. Maybe we psychically connected to nearby deep-pit mining operations, which furnished the underlying purpose for civilization in the heart of Appalachia. Groceries and schools, the liquor store, clinics and hospital, storefronts, and Dad's drugstore at the strip mall: the whole economy hinged on coal. At my house, mining was not much spoken about beyond short explanations for men's smudged faces and dusty overalls I occasionally glimpsed in public places. It went without saying. We kids were simply connected to the land. Great kivas and underground ritual or burial sites, Paleolithic pit homes and cave dwellings, would not have surprised us if we had come upon them in the woods. We would have thought some other kids got there first. Drawing designs on rock walls with shale chips came with the territory, and in our pockets we brought home fossils and harder shards of stone we called arrowheads; occasionally one of them actually was. With slingshots of forked sticks and rubber bands, we took aim at squirrels and other small prey, letting scattered rocks fly. We didn't hit them. When left to wander we went to ground through endless games of hide and seek, hours of bike riding, combing the landscape in every direction in our silent deerskin moccasins, which were actually nothing more exotic than cheap sneakers.

Every conscious animal will make a shelter. If "place is the house of being," as Martin Heidegger wrote, and being a person means "to be there," inseparable from being placed, then we were scratching the root cause in digging around on the forest floor to make ourselves at home. Everything begins and ends in a room, even when there is no word for room, as with the Hopi, whose language denotes instead a range of different things happening in a dwelling, the doings and goings on there. In winter, we carved igloos with our mothers' kitchen utensils, took teacups into ice rooms and sat on dirty white chairs of packed snow. In summer, once we'd hollowed our dugouts sufficiently, we wove roofs for our pit homes with gathered sticks and branches, lay down in them, and hid. From what I do not know—only that it was essential to achieve maximum invisibility, and, once we'd achieved it, we quietly waited.

I woke later than I'd planned on July 25, 1993, starting out south from Green River at 6:40 A.M., headed toward a gravel parking lot above Utah's expansive Maze District of Canyonlands National Park, with nothing but Sunday morning hellfire on the radio. Arrived at the Horseshoe Canyon rim via 30 miles of dirt road in fair condition at around 8:30. Hit the trail at 8:45 after saddling up with water. Prepared for a steep descent into the canyon, an 800-foot drop, then another 1.8 miles to the Great Gallery. It sounded rather easy, if solitary, as I signed in at the trailhead. I bounded down, down, down, quads working, core strong, making up some time skating loose rock before missing the main trail. Footprints led in two directions, and I found neither markers nor cairns after the steel barrier to wheeled traffic at the base of the bowl.

I wandered for more than an hour until a little box canyon dead-ended in rock walls. I looked up and spotted a tawny mountain lion skirting the ledge. Brief eye contact like two flames sizzling. I quickly mustered all of my sangfroid in reversing my steps lest I join the uncertain fate of the stray deer

I'd heard rustling tall grass, sounding a lot like lunch. Nearly running, I scrambled over animal tracks and scat piles. I was going down in defeat as to direction when I popped out of the brush and saw a couple coming toward me, heading briskly. They passed at a clip as we exchanged the basics. I tried to keep up, but I was winded from my retreat maneuver and they were practically running, having left two dogs in a hot car. Tracking them, I found the trail again and eventually passed Mike Lee, a hydrologist from Alaska, whose name was printed above mine in the trail register. He had stopped to photograph the composition of the canyon walls, not the pictographs I sought but sedimentary rock, a rock sequence from the youngest at the top to the oldest at the bottom. What he could see that I could not: 20 million years ago there was a startling uplift of as much as 10,000 feet that formed the Colorado Plateau, and the landscape around us was a record of ongoing erosion. Our trail wound through Cedar Mesa Sandstone, near-shore (white) interwoven with river/lake deposits (red), below the Carmel Formation and Navajo Sandstone of the Horseshoe Canyon Trailhead. We had entered from the Jurassic era and now followed a trail through the Permian. With my detour into the box canyon I had turned an hour-and-twenty-minute stroll into a march of nearly three hours before I even reached the Great Gallery, but all of this had taken so much longer. Some of the soil beneath my weary feet had traveled from as far away as the Appalachian Mountains, deposited by wind and water.

The high gallery was worth my getting lost to see: a red, darkly burnished, hovering figure was waiting for me. A grouping of other figures, as if wrapped in blankets, levitated from the earth. Or were they floating down? Giant slabs surrounded me. Even in my fatigued state I felt something imbue me just from looking at these ancient pigmented shapes on the rock, a transfer of energy from the hands that made these images, witnesses from another world; maybe it was because I wanted to feel more than tired, but it was inspiring to look deeply at paintings made so long ago by people called primitive. I snapped pictures of a white-painted figure with iron-red horizontal stripes, worried that noon sunlight might blot it out of my shot.

With the mountain lion added in, I probably walked eight miles down, around, and back up to the canyon's rim with blisters to take away. I met Mike, the hydrologist, again when I was almost to my car at the end of the day. A jeep pulled in as I was peeling the boots from my feet. A woman jumped out of the passenger's seat and asked if I had hiked alone. I had. She returned something like a frown of admiration.

At thirty-five, sitting in the laundromat writing at the end of a strenuous day, I still felt that I lived inside an invincible body. I didn't need to consider that the mechanics of the situation might change. Jotted for proof in my journal, it was at least 110 degrees in the Maze District that July day with nary a tree for shade, much less a passing cloud, and my notes don't mention my feeling the heat! I had found the prize, the panel of floating painted figures in a shallow alcove beneath a canopy of rock. In Moab, I bought a beautifully fired vase painted with the main figures from Horseshoe Canyon. A week later I was back in Virginia reading a wire report about an entire Boy Scout troop and their leader who drowned in a flash flood in a remote area of the Maze, near Horseshoe Canyon, Utah. The wash where they camped turned into a torrent in the middle of the night. The area is noted for rapid, dangerous shifts of weather. I had hiked through there, covered the same ground. We passed in different time zones, "like two lovers who have missed their rendezvous," as Simone Weil writes of God and Humanity. "Each is there before the other," she adds, "but each at a different place, and they wait and wait and wait." If either place or time is separated at a crucial juncture, we will miss each other and we will miss our God, and sometimes we will miss death. I feel most alive when sweating through it, when in motion, and most vulnerable when I am waiting for something to happen, like my life turned inside out. I have to find ways to keep moving, even as I grieve, even as I love most that which I am leaving, that which has left.

In the narrow Catawba Valley where I lived for twelve years, by chance I saw my second mountain lion, this time an eastern one perched on a bluff near midnight like a fierce, shy blessing over the winding road. Just before I ducked my car down a hollow to cross a bridge, the headlights struck and lit up the big cat like a match head; its eyes burned bright, acknowledging its territory—which I had thought was also mine.

Some writers seem to have something to say; else, why brave the isolation of study walls, hour upon hour of the desk and chair like wandering a maze forever without a key? The maze is a zone of contradiction. Seated in a café among boisterous couples, web surfers, and texting coffee drinkers, a writer knows no company but her own thoughts, lost in an antiquated thing: the inwardness of headspace. Devoted *nefelibata* ("cloud-walker"), more and more I write to express faith in life, in its unfolding. I've noticed that writing makes reality *realer* without copying it; maybe writing lends me more copper in my metal blend, so that I become more than a flash of lucky color, a penny lost in the street. The real conspires to prod you along when you are attentive, sending all manner of synchronous bits of information your way once you open to a subject. What Kafka said about breaking up the frozen sea within us is true enough. What Goethe said is truer, even if the quotation can't exactly be traced back to him: *Begin it.*

Writing is an action with a long life before the reaction is over. Carlos Castaneda's path with the heart is the only path, the only way to walk. It's a shot in the dark or, as George Garrett wrote, *whistling in the dark.* Sometimes it takes a lifetime for the reaction to even begin, and then it begins silently, as someone reads to himself. Just do the first action, I say, in the wilderness of faith, without fanfare or enormous preparation. Step away from the vehicle, pack only a power bar and water, lots of water, and start down the trail out of devotion to the deeper realm into which the movement sends you, drops you. Whether the landscape is writing us or we the land is impossible to know. In New Mexico, 6,000 varieties of wildflowers bloom. Away from the ego and any notion previously held about what a self might be, I start typing and become lost in its rhythm. I am no longer *I, as my little dog knows me,* as Gertrude Stein put it so well. I don't care who I am as I am breathing and typing. I am walking this interior.

Plodding along twenty miles of ragged dirt road in northern New Mexico in a rented Ford Tempo, on my way to see Pueblo Bonito in Chaco Canyon without any idea of how much there was to see, before me stretched a scarred and layered landscape baking in July heat below a scraped sky. I had no idea that Chaco Culture National Historical Park stretches more than 60,000–70,000 square miles, the largest archaeological site in the US, and that Bonito, the largest pueblo, was but one of dozens of ancient standing structures. The place had not been on my radar; in the year 1993 I was bent on following the petroglyph/pictograph trail, but a ranger in Petrified Forest National Park recommended I see Chaco. According to my flapping map there were only two roads in, by southern route or northern, and while I had found Route 57 up from Gallup at Thoreau, I felt lost in a shrub-littered landscape as the sole motoring human. It was not an unpleasant feeling.

Greasewood, sage, and bunch grass littered with invasive tumbleweeds surrounded me, along with a fierce sense of what I can only call presence. The landscape, however severe and withholding, was alive, living.

I stopped the car, rolled out of the driver's seat, and snapped a photo: rocky, dusty road gradually bearing left, gently rising toward and over a mesa; wispy clouds scrubbed in with a dry brush floating in the far blue distance and coalescing in a milky smear at the horizon. Miles away to the upper right of the picture a gap opens between mesas and the canyon widens. In the foreground of the photograph the car door casts a deliberate morning shadow on nothing but pinkish tinted dust. The little bit of green in the surrounding land comes from knots of perennial grasses, sub-shrubs, and woody shrubs native to the Colorado Plateau (Stipa oryzopsis and Hilaria jamesii, Gutierrezia sarothrae and Ceratoides lanata); collectively, they look dry enough to burn if you think the word *fire*. Although May to September sees most of the annual rainfall, the total is seldom greater than 15 inches, averaging 8.5 throughout the Colorado Plateau with elevations ranging from 5 to 8 thousand feet. I know this now.

Back inside my car I turned on the air conditioning and adjusted the static on the radio. Headed up from the south, the worst route with the longest stretch of rutted dirt, my modest set of wheels continued to be the only vehicle along a road devoid of structures, with cattle guards lending bursts of intense rhythm to my general unabated rattling, until I finally passed a white pickup loaded with a Zuni family moving in the opposite direction. In the near distance a wedding cake butte jutted from the canyon like the Emerald City, only it was not in any way green. I would learn its name.

Twenty years later, I'm driving the shorter northern approach into Chaco in late May, and this time my rented Chevy SUV tackles thirteen unimproved miles, playing tag with the compact car just ahead. I finally pass the sedan after many larger vehicles have blown the dust off us both. From the other direction, RVs and giant SUVs zoom by doing at least twenty-five. I keep the faith, gripping the wheel soundly, and bounce along at a safe but decent pace of fifteen to twenty-five miles per hour. At one point a posted speed limit of thirty appears like a mirage, and I think *you have got to be kidding*. These curves could easily scuttle any fast-braking vehicle and send it surfing dirt waves into a ditch.

Once arrived and inside the visitor's center, I make my way to the welcome film and settle in to watch "The Ancient Ones." In a few minutes the family I passed on the road wanders in and sits behind me. We learn that ancestors of pueblo people—who until recently have popularly been referred to as Anasazi, a Navajo coinage for *ancient enemies*—believed in two levels of existence, above ground and below, with the living above and the place below populated with those whose spirits invest the land and us. I turn to greet the threesome behind me after the flute music signs off. A gray-headed man with a nearly grown daughter between himself and his wife tells me that fifteen years ago he had to turn around, didn't make it all the way down that road. Today he's dressed in shorts, the women in dresses, for walking around under the midday desert sun. Later I see the three of them gamely covering the ruins of several Great Houses without hats.

Twenty years ago as I was leaving Chaco I stopped to help a Navajo woman in a truck with a flat. The jack that came with my Ford Tempo wouldn't reach high enough. She had a baby on board and two other children. Another car stopped; a man rolled out and introduced himself as Greg. He worked a bigger jack and said that he and two friends had tried to get to Chaco the August before but had been wiped out by a sudden squall. Stuck in mud ruts trying to cross Escavada Wash on motorcycles, they had to be carried out by a horse truck and trailer. Soon after I revisit Chaco I'm talking to my friend Christine, and she tells me that when she tent-camped in the canyon a fierce rainstorm nearly drowned her. It isn't the kind of place you fool around with—it will do with you what it wants—yet I've felt no bad energy there, no fear roiling my gut or tragedy vibes. Some claim the place is haunted, tainted, and defiled. It's certainly mysterious and holy, unstable, open to interpretation. If you're meant to get to Chaco, you will.

An affinity for lost places seems to have been born in me, like an ache for solitude. With a population of only 1,000 in my hometown of Richlands, Virginia, you'd think I'd be pulled in the opposite direction, and many are, but Bali Hai calls me. Places others might find unappealingly remote sound promising, like "God's Thumbprint" in Burkes Garden, Tazewell County, Virginia, where on Lost World Ranch they are raising Appaloosa llamas and possibly the largest herd of double-humped camels in North America. I would add Hidden Valley along the Jackson River in Bath County; Utah's Virgin River Gorge; Horseshoe Canyon in Utah; or any western ghost town.

I realize this list has the ring of piña coladas on the beach only to me: Camp Iva near Bluefield with its frigid spring-fed swimming pool to test your mettle; the frozen library in *Doctor Zhivago*; a hidden strip of beach on the southern coast of Spain; Druid rock formations in Scotland primed toward constellations; really, any prehistoric ruin or simple stone circle. In Iceland, roads have to be routed around faery circles by law (my kind of place). And then there's a picnic in a ruin on Gozo; second-run B movies on sunny summer afternoons that transport me; graveyards and kudzu-immured battlefields, especially Antietam in Sharpsburg, where General Lee's first northern invasion ended in troughs of blood along the creek (1862). True to the mountain spirit of resistance, I am no Civil War buff, yet in walking the battlefields of Antietam, I felt that there, indeed, dead soldiers, blue and gray, must still rise and wander beneath the moon.

Mesmerized, I study an aerial photograph of Pueblo Bonito snapped in 1929 from Charles Lindbergh's plane on a low flyover. This photo was taken during the period in which the canyon was quickly, too quickly, being dug by old methods of massive earth removal, its treasures, found in only 150 of 600–800 rooms, tagged and shipped east to the Museum of Natural History in New York and the Smithsonian in Washington, DC. This happened once in 1896 for four years and again in the 1920s for six, with the latter dig decisive. Some of those treasures—black and white pottery, including intact chocolate jars and olla water jugs, copper bells, and thousands of hand-polished turquoise beads—are slated to return and occupy a small display inside the Visitor's Center, but the rooms we tour will remain empty. Destabilized by car-sized boulders having sloughed off, Threatening Rock forever sits upright but precarious in the background of Lindbergh's photograph, a dark jagged seam barely sewing it to the rest of the bluff behind Pueblo Bonito. I'm staring at this scene shot for *National Geographic* by Ann Morrow Lindbergh on her honeymoon, and the picture's only a little blurry.

Soon, I'm walking around rooms ancient masons built in five different phases of construction, the last style called core and veneer, and for a long moment I float without having any notion of who or what I am or why I keep returning here, not just to Chaco but to earth itself: the woman who fell to earth. In a mere coincidence, of course, I was born less than twenty miles across a ridge from Saltville, Virginia, site SV-2, pre-Clovis culture, where fossils were noted as early as 1782 in a letter from Arthur Campbell to

Thomas Jefferson: mastodon remains, giant short-faced bear, and mammoth; a tibia tool from a musk oxen and evidence of cooking. I feel myself wearing thin, my stretched molecules nothing more than fine mist smeared beneath a turquoise sky blurred by clouds. I'm drawn again to Chaco, to these handmade, sunbaked bricks stripped from the cliffs, to ancient standing structures through which I imagine daily life built from the inside out in human-scaled rooms, none larger than the length of roof beams allowed, beams mostly long removed for firewood or rotted. Chambers connect, strung one by one to reach grand, highly planned proportions without keystones, arches, columns, or corner bonds, and seldom a foundation. I stand within an enigma that has provided a steady hum of theories.

There's so much I don't know about Chaco, that no one knows about Chaco. Every bit of scholarship tries to answer the question. G. B. Cornucopia, ranger hat as level as his gaze, stands near the sparking fire circle as the sky darkens, recounting the many voices heard in Chaco over a million years. I study his bearing, erect with weathered face, and I think he has to know something after spending so many years here, but all he claims in the end is mystery. Back in the campground I tilt my head, loading the brilliant sky into my memory; its multitude of flickering candles keeps striking new fires, and soon I am blinking back tears: this sky is only possible because Chaco has been designated an International Dark Sky Park. Unlike any other, this light, these lights, have traveled and persevered to fall into my eyes. I want to be a dark sky park of the imagination, a designated place without light pollution, a body of star glory.

Leading the tour, Ranger Cornucopia, dubbed "Mr. Chaco," says the architectural phenomenon of Chaco was "not just utilitarian" but "symbolic, artistic, grandiose," done for "other reasons," perhaps to make "something grand. We know what they did, but we do not know why." Archeoastronomy drew him here years ago.

If there are solid facts, they might reside in the numbers that map aspects of this place. Without leaving ontology altogether, I talk myself back from the brink of nonexistence with factoids: 2,400 archaeological sites in 32 square miles, suggesting a highly sophisticated and organized multicultural society sustaining art and public works, built over a period of 400 years, roughly between 800–1200, with the peak of population and activity between 1075–1115, coinciding with a period of heavier rainfall, though the general weather patterns have not changed. There's scant evidence of human squabble, with only one cleaved skull turned up, practically none of the gristly horrors that have been found elsewhere in the region, in multiple settlements to the north, northwest, and south. It appears that only turkeys were sacrificed in Chaco, despite a Mayan dagger having been unearthed and pounds of black on white and black on gray pottery ritually broken. Only about 40 percent of the pottery was fired here, but far more was broken. Consequently, Chacoan society was probably organized around allegiance and ideology, not forced labor, although most societies have winners and losers. Perhaps with Chaco, at least for a while, there were only obsessives, laborers after a cause to which everyone subscribed.

Of the archeological sites lying closer to home in the greensward of my native terrain, Daugherty's Cave alone holds 10,500 years of settlement; there's also the site in Saltville near my birthplace, not to mention Cactus Hill to the east, a prickly pear dune holding one of the oldest sites in North America, but there is nothing as well preserved or as vast as Chaco anywhere. There's something about the windswept forms and reduced color in northwest New Mexico that drives a needle into my complacency, even into my contentment, piercing past sadness, regret, and every false notion of self-importance and ego until I have to come up through my strata again and decide to be. Reveal to me a stripped-down version of myself, and I want to be reborn. I crawl into the womb of my quarter-dome tent and try to sleep as winds rattle the fabric.

Twenty years ago, fresh from a scarring bit of romance that took more from me than I could acknowledge at the time, I glued myself back together under a hot sun right here in Chaco. Nothing's really changed, just cycled back, and here I am, still standing my ground at noon to blend with my shadow. I didn't know I was dead, but when I come here I want to live again. Thankfully this time it's May not July, but oddly it's the old wounds instead of the fresher ones that bang up from my insides with sharp spells of anguish in the middle of the night, festering boils of *what if* that demand to be lanced. This landscape, this waterscape, called "place where the rock is propped up," "the place that the people think about," and mostly "the center place," takes me down to the root of all the pain I can ever feel, to the reasons I am here, to all of my lessons forever spiraling the path. I've left and been left, with neither part played in innocence. Self-pity is a bottomless well of regret. I saw my father wallow there time and again, without a visible weapon, threatening to kill himself. It was shameful to me then, that a child had to comfort a man, and here I sit with that history. Some tribes tell the legend of the Great Gambler who wagered and lost their souls. I crawl from the navel of the earth with the ancient ones to reach the fourth world. They are the ones who came here and found hard life, sickness, little food, and darkness cold. From the third world they heard footsteps on the roof of their world, planted a tree, climbed a ladder, poked a hole, and sent water bird to scout. There's no going back to the third world from the fourth, or to the fourth from the fifth. Emergence is continuous.

Threatening Rock fell the year my parents were married, in 1941, crushing a whole bunch of Pueblo Bonito's rooms. Although scientifically monitored with metal stakes, it fell a few years after the prayer feathers meant to hold it were removed. At three in the afternoon on January 22, the photographer ran out of film and made a trip from the canyon to fetch it. The propped-up rock fell when he had gone, the way some people wait to die until the loved one watching over them has left. Some say Pueblo Bonito was built in the shadow of Threatening Rock so that one day the rock would crush it to signify a new era. Women rarely made it past the age of thirty, men past forty-five, in this canyon. All of the six seep springs still providing water in Chaco are saline. Ranger Cindy Winkler says the Chaco story is written in the wind. "Listen to the wind," to what the wind says. We stand on the site of Pueblo del Arroyo and listen hard. The Hopi say the reason we are here is because it is hard.

I call my mom to check in and she tells me she's had "that crazy dream again." The one where she's trudging and trudging and doesn't know where she is because the setting keeps changing and she can never arrive.

"This time I was driving a car," she says. "I'm just lost. It's the same theme every time."

I remind her that one time recently she did arrive at a house where the porch light was on, and all of her family came outside to greet her.

"Oh, yes," she says. "I got there once. They were all waiting."

Her arrival kind of shook me up, since all the family she dreams of are long dead and buried, but I don't tell her this. As long as she's still trudging through that field, lost and frustrated like the rest of us, I figure she will be with me, on this side of the equation.

"Yearning for a place is a decision to enter history," Walter Brueggemann writes. The place my mom yearns for is in a dream, a house populated by the dead not the living. "And if I go and prepare a place for you, I will come back and take you to be with me that you also may be where I am" (John 14:3, NIV). Most days I'm not sure where she wants to be. To reach old age is to live ambivalent; most days Mother can take it or leave it. "I've lived too long" is her major physical complaint. And then there's unexpected fierce clinging, healing and recovery from illnesses that you think would kill any healthy fifty-year-old, yet the ninety-plus slogs on. Some days I wonder if my caring for my mother keeps her bound in her body, if her frustration is against this bind: my love balancing her fear.

The camera, a Bellini from 1901 bought by Anton Orlov, contained eight already developed but never before seen photographs from the World War I period. Orlov believes film and paper prints will ultimately preserve images better than digital media. These artifacts emerged intact from the camera's time capsule: soldiers on horseback; soldiers posed either side of an undetonated iron bomb; images of ruins and WWI planes.

If I could do it safely without damaging her, I'd like to open my mother's head by a clever hinge and view the images inside, her private newsreel from 1918—the year of a worldwide flu epidemic—to the present hour. Behold my time capsule, fragile and tough, my mother, better than a *camera obscura* in her ninety-fifth year, still lucid, still perpetually trudging through recurring dreams, begging the question of whether we ever arrive. The porch light's still burning over the door, the messages we are holding will one day spool free, releasing us from flesh and skull.

A labyrinth set into the floor of Chartres Cathedral in France was probably once complete with an image of the Minotaur. I stood with it beneath my feet and thought about pilgrimage and true places, hesitant to take a step. A well in the cathedral basement marks a Druid ritual site that the present structure subsumed. I gazed down and down, into dark waters, the shape of the well a funnel, a wormhole. "The sacred center is thus essentially a nongeographical entity, a created thing, ultimately an illusion, yet, paradoxically, also a place more real than real," writes Belden Lane. I want to get there, to the sacred center place, but I have never found anything significant without walking toward it more than theoretically. Reality has real terrain, layers built upon layers, the twists and turns of time that lie beneath what can be seen. Erasure and renovation—nevertheless, my feet have to trace the ground. Let's go for a walk or a jog. This is my personal primitive peripatetic journey without an end, what Paul Adams has called "a dialogue with the earth, a direct imprinting of place on self." I will keep plodding. The significant difference between labyrinths and mazes is more practical than academic, the former not a puzzle but a contemplative unicursal path, one way in and one way out, while mazes mean to confound us with choices, producing multicursal anxiety if not the experience of being lost: we test wrong turns and hit dead ends. Surely then it was the latter, a maze of significant design and some supernatural proportions, that held Asterion the Minotaur, though every reference to and utterance of *labyrinth* still evokes his prison.

Asterion, "the starry one," with head of Taurus on the body of a man, was no love child. His mother Pasiphaë hid within a wooden cow on wheels covered with cowhide and cast a spell of disguise to lure a wild bull to copulate with her. As gross as this sounds, it was Poseidon who had cast a spell on Pasiphaë, arousing her lust for the very bull arisen from the sea that Minos had failed to sacrifice. It really wasn't her fault; she was a pawn, and yet...why *do it*, especially with a wild bull? She was compelled by the spell. Young men and virgins were served up as the starry one's food. Several times, I have been in the position of serving myself up to spiritual cannibals in attempts to turn them into saints of passion, joy, and loyalty. How presumptuous of me to have gone in armed with nothing but persuasion, and how wise it was of Theseus to have tied a ball of red thread to the entrance gates of the labyrinth and unspooled it behind him as he searched deeper and deeper. Theseus slayed the monster with his fists in the farthest corner of the cunning cage Daedalus had built but also found his way out by the gift of Ariadne's skein of thread (Callimachus, Greek Poet, third century BCE) or *clue*. The clue furnished by Ariadne was never furnished to me, and thus I have approached monsters without protection. Hard lessons bear repeating it would appear. I was trained as a child that the Minotaur was also my dad. As such, he evoked my sympathies and fierce longing to fill the place where a healthy father might have parented me instead; after all, he was still half human if broken by war. *This was not his fault*, our oft-repeated mantra.

In the movie *Labyrinth* Sarah believes her half-brother Toby will be sacrificed to Jareth, the Goblin King, if she does not finish building a labyrinth. The burden is all hers to bear. Guilt and grief can take many forms, the madness of silence choked down with what one already knows by gut and crux. Parents can be goblin kings and queens, entrapping their children's psyches, and yet what child can forget them without sacrificing some essential part of the self? Parents can leave their children on their own in the woods, subject to witches in gingerbread houses, but the more pervasive question is can children leave their parents?

In other words, I should have known not to take on anyone else's monsters, my own being weighty enough. Prior to self-sacrifice I should have gotten a *clue*. It's always been the deep end of the ocean. Sometimes marvelous things can be fished out of there at the edges of the known world where beyond there be dragons. Karma will still instruct one, even backwards. I am a late bloomer in matters of emotional self-preservation, but these things I know: you must enter the labyrinth of others' hearts unarmed, for this is the only oracular truth, and yet I advise making friends with Ariadne. You never know when there's a monster yowling in there. I have lately learned to cover my ass with thread.

Twice now I have just missed the final breath. My father slipped away in a hospital bed with no one present but my mother holding his hand. This must have been the way he wanted it, as everyone else had just left for lunch. When his children returned the curtain was drawn, his eyes closed for good. It had only been minutes since I had tried to meet him in his long stare, bloodshot but still pale blue. While someone remarked that they thought he was getting better I knew his tide was going out soon.

When my aunt Glade died a few days after her ninetieth birthday I had only just been at her side, having come to the nursing home for a care conference. After reviewing her condition with the roundtable of nurses, nutritionist, social worker, and resident staff, I went to visit with my aunt who informed me, "They told me it was my heart that's the problem." Around the words she struggled to breathe.

"I think you have a great heart," I said and she laughed, but followed up with "I guess I'm just going to have a heart attack." It shocked me to hear this, but I tried not to show it.

"Well," I replied. "You made it to ninety!"

"That was the best shrimp salad I ever ate," Glade said. A. had made it for her birthday party a few days before, and boy had the birthday girl relished the dish.

"Did you enjoy the coffee?" I asked. I had dropped off a cup of her favorite in her room before hurrying to the care conference.

"Best coffee I ever had," she said and showed me the empty cup. Of course it was the same black coffee I always brought. I stood at her bedside in my coat explaining that I would love to stay longer, but I'd lost my pocketbook the day before and only discovered it missing late that morning.

"Oh, Cathy," she said, "I'd do *anything* to help you." She said it with such sincerity. This is love. I told her that of course I knew she would always want to help me, and I appreciated it. I had to fetch a replacement driver's license before the DMV closed. I'd already cancelled my credit card—and also hers, which I carried in order to buy her supplies. I squeezed her hand goodbye.

As I drove into the DMV parking lot across town, a sudden rainstorm released hard drops onto my windshield and my phone rang. The nurse told me to come back, that my aunt wasn't doing well, and I knew with those words she had already left us. I retraced my path through an increasing volume of rain and found her eyes shut, her body situated in bed with the privacy curtain drawn around her half of the room. The bedside tray was rolled back, the empty coffee cup discarded.

"Sometimes God will break you down," May-Lily says, reflecting on an afternoon spent on the roadside between Asheville and Charlottesville. This side-of-the-road business finished with two tow trucks and no engine diagnosis until the following day. Her evening included hitching a ride to the Super 8 motel and watching *The 40-Year-Old Virgin*. The next time I hear from May-Lily, after we've managed to meet up and spend an evening seeing live performances of bluegrass and gospel music, she's got a new situation, a flat tire she says she wasn't butch enough to change. More finesse or more force, what's needed? The secret is loosening the nuts first, that way you can jump up and down on the tire iron without knocking the car off the jack. Yet it's still hard to decide what to tackle. The locked lug nuts turn out to be rigged, requiring a secret Prius key; this is no not-butch-enough matter. Three miles per hour courting the rim, and she's talking to me again when the police pull her over in Asheville. Just before we ring off I ask if the thing with cars breaking down is *chronic*. "Yes," she answers. "It's karmic."

More than six months after cuddling my neighbor's newborn in my arms, I'm spooning puréed green peas from the organic baby food jar toward Saba's mouth. Her mother, Shaleen, tells me she may not like them. "These are her first peas, ever." The tiny taste elicits a mixed reaction, puckered cheeks and a brief frown. "Do you like them?" her mother cheers her on. Saba replies by warily forcing them down, but they do go down. I scoop another portion of sage-green peas that match her dinosaur shirt and move the spoon toward her mouth. Success in small measures, she takes the second bite without puckering. And then a brave smile beams through with the second swallow complete. Pretty soon Saba leans into the peas, chasing down the spoon. "She likes them," Shaleen says, so proud.

Side-by-side illustrations of cells in a dictionary entry: one plant and one animal. Most of the numbered, labeled parts match; just five out of fourteen labels pertain to only one or the other of these cells. Resemblances are therefore more striking than differences. Plants and animals, including humans, share a plasma barrier as well as mitochondria DNA and a number of nuclear membranes and nuclei, though the plant version of vacuoles is larger and more plentiful. Girl babies carry their mother's multi-generational mitochondria that will pass down intact should they have a daughter. Knowing this now touches off a bit of a yap and a yammer inside me for the child I never had, as it means my mother and grandmother and sweet ole etc. before them stop their cellular journeys. Great-great-something grandmother Josephine Kasey, whose black Irish eyebrows I appear to have inherited, will be finally plucked.

Mothers also keep cells exchanged from each fetus they carry. Thus, mothers have foreign cells circulating in their bloodstreams forever, or you might say these cells become a discernable part of them. Is this why mothers can hear the baby cry? A cry of self to soul, a cry evoking biological empathy.

Love your mother.

While parents continue to see the miracle of creation in their children's eyes, on the border of Switzerland and France at the European Organization for Nuclear Research or CERN, spinning protons approach the speed of light. In the confines of the Large Hadron Collider, 16.7 miles in circumference, the residue of these fierce collisions turns up evidence of the Higgs boson or God particle. With confirmation that this long missing link that ties together all the universal forces—strong, weak, and electromagnetic—is found, we will crack the code of the behavior of subatomic particles and piece together the grand framework, although, as a subjective part of it, we can never see the whole design. Jesus replied, "You do not realize now what I am doing, but later you will understand" (John 13:7, NIV). Nothing is out there that's not in here, but I am concealed even to myself. "God is a circle whose center is everywhere, whose circumference is nowhere": in one of my early college papers, I tried to trace this phrase to its source and failed. Failing made me want to major in philosophy, but when I went for a conference with the professor he informed me I was more interested in religion. In beginning philosophy I found its end.

When my aunt Glade was a teenager she had a steady boyfriend with whom she corresponded throughout WWII. He came home and asked to marry her, but my grandfather said no. Like my grandfather, the young man didn't have a college degree. It seems silly, but my grandfather's word stood, even though I learned, when data from the 1941 census was released, that only five percent of the US population had graduated college at that time. Not surprising, since our colleges were founded to train preachers and teachers. Only after the war did the GI Bill open the floodgates to higher education. My aunt Glade was the youngest child; she and my mother and three older sisters had graduated college, a point of pride for my grandparents.

The years passed; Glade never married and never mentioned Jimmy, the young man she had loved. In her late eighties she read in the newspaper that he had died, and managed to attend his funeral. They had long ago lost contact. Struggling in on her walker to sign the guest register, she was met by Jimmy's widow; he had gone on to marry and raise a family. When Glade respectfully introduced herself, noting their mutual friends and the sadness of the family's loss, the widow replied, "He talked about you every day of his life."

I study the shining repair, the tracery of liquid gold light in this once broken ceramic bowl, inherited by my father from his mother. The bowl contains a swimming swan and was shattered by my father one Fourth of July when he was suffering from his demons. I remember the Japanese concept of wabi-sabi, which honors signs of wear and tear in objects mended over time, and the art of kintsukuroi, of repairing pottery with gold or silver infused lacquer. Like my father, this bowl is more beautiful for having been broken and mended. His cracks showed continually, and only my mother's love would

hold him together. There is no other life than to have been and be constantly ready to be broken by the world and repaired with silver and gold. Whoever loves me finds a heart mottled with shining stitches. Kintsukuroi: I lay
down my burdens and pick them up mended by the method, knowing I will
again hold the water of joy and overflow.

My twelve-year molar sends electric jolts through the whole left side of my
mouth, through the branching nerve path upper and lower, until the pain is
everywhere and nowhere. Hot and cold sensitivity woven with dull throb-
bing keeps me slurping tepid liquids for more than a week. I rue the day I
agreed to have that perfectly good mercury amalgam replaced. The dentist
diagnoses TMJ and bruxism. Terrible tori, those Indian mounds of stray
bone under my tongue, make it hard to get a good X-ray. "Most of your
teeth have hairlines," my dentist says. Lovely. I endure another week of
weirdness and adult purée, including copious amounts of adult beverages,
blaming myself for this strange "clenching" I do in sleep and wondering why
the minute the plane wheels touched ground from Italy I began to moan in
pain: great diet plan, though, after all the pasta, pizza, and vino. My sleeping
body has its own agenda, its own involuntary journey. The pain dulls on an-
algesics: I can eat toast and chew scrambled eggs. Along about the third
week, shooting throbs resolve into the lower left back molar, number eighteen; it feels pressured, like it has the bends. I trudge back to my dentist, who
points me toward the endodontist, who confirms the dead tooth with a bit
of frozen cotton. My failure to flinch means number eighteen has expired,
the pain up to this point spent rocket fuel.

   "Do they ever rise up like Lazarus?" I ask the endo-doc when she later
telephones at my request. I'm wavering about the root canal.

   "If they did, I'd be out of business," she says.

   "What about prayer?" I ask.

   "Go for it," she says.

   "You wouldn't necessarily be out of business," I say. "You could raise
teeth from the dead."

   "I'll do absolutely the best job I can for you, but there are no guarantees
in medicine or dentistry—"

   I'm thinking, thank goodness for all those other guarantees in life…

   She adds, "If it's cracked, I can't save it. Just promise me you won't look
at YouTube videos."

"I already have," I say. "Root canals leave dead things in your head near your brain," I quote. Through the phone, I hear the doctor's heavy sighing.

Should we ever meet again face to face, I will be sedated and she will be masked, digging around in my mouth with sharp instruments while I drift along unable to quite care. She will suddenly speak to me. "Your tooth has a distal crack, iffy, 50/50, what do you want me to do?" I won't be able to answer properly or remember that she's already given a dire prognosis for fissures. "Do you want to try to save it?" she'll ask, an echo from a galaxy far, far away. *Save it*, I think, or do I say it out loud? I have no idea. I remember that she's already told me she no longer pulls teeth. She plays cello in the symphony. I hold my mouth open for another twenty minutes while she prays over Lazarus in her elaborate way.

About nine months before my partner formally ended our relationship, she came to bed very late and so churning of mind that I could hear the volume of her thoughts. They rankled me from a sound sleep, and somehow I knew that she had decided against us, or rather against me. It's never an easy pill to swallow when you have been ousted by a theory. I knew she had been poring over Internet sources for several months, discovering Mayan-styled astrological prophecies. Things didn't look good for our same-colored glyphs and twin portals. The verdict was going to be human sacrifice. I could feel the jagged dagger striking down into my chest. She raised up my still-beating heart in her hands, silencing a mighty mean god. Not my god, but hers.

Although later portents would point to our profound connection, this particular trial of a night proved a turning point, a no turning back point. Can it really be like this? You wake from sound slumber, so startled that the full force of your intuition is baldly present, raw with the truth: in the place of love, this bomb going off. Your partner of nearly ten years wears a certain squeezed expression of mental anguish. Your number's up: you lost. You're out. A concept has overtaken love's flawed reality. You wake from your dream of sticking it out through the thick and the thin, the trudging drudgery of dredged emotional soup, strained and clarified into the glory of togetherness, this beautiful thing called *we*, which indeed you saw as the only prize worth having. There is nothing you could read starting with *www* that would ever make you leave her. There is nothing and no one who could make you leave, though you have threatened to end it and cajoled. No one but your partner could cold-cock you awake with pain like this.

❧

She said she wanted to help me find my pocketbook, but at age ninety, my aunt Glade was trapped in her nursing home room, in her bed, in her body, unable to turn over, arrange pillows, or even pull up in bed without assistance. I saw the intensity in her eyes when she told me she would "do anything" for me. It touched me so deeply I tried to keep the conversation light, balance intensity with laughter. She was always as generous with humor as with love and money. Unlike my earnest mother, my aunt saw the funny side of life. But that night after I had made the passage to my mother's apartment in order to tell her that her last living sister had died, and sat with her for solemn hours while she wept, and gone by the funeral home to start the arrangements, I fell onto the couch before the TV at home for a few minutes of bittersweet numbing.

Close to ten o'clock I got a strong feeling that my pocketbook was no more lost but somehow found. Earlier in the day I had called campus security and then the snack bar adjacent to where I remembered having left the little black purse on a chair. One of the cooks distinctly remembered seeing my purse in the exact chair I described, but by the time she went back to check it was no longer there. I thought someone might have turned it into lost and found, but no one had. And yet before going to bed I checked my email one last time, and there was a message from a student I didn't know writing to tell me she had just discovered my pocketbook in a chair; she was studying late in the student center and would leave it with security before she left campus. Shivers went through me.

The next day, I picked it up and found nothing missing except the cash, fifteen dollars. Whoever had stolen my pocketbook had returned it complete with all the credit and insurance cards, on one of which was printed my Social Security number. Of course I believe that my aunt chased them down and boxed them about the ears immediately following her myocardial infarction. I just know she prodded a guilty human conscience in her first angelic act.

II.

On the map, Chaco Canyon looks like the Milky Way lost in a vast cosmos of desert, a hopeless kiss. Its arid parcel in northwest New Mexico stretches a hundred miles, with the central architectural area covering three square miles and nine thousand years of settlement, in terms of space and time. This morning the rumbles of construction in the center of Roanoke wake me at 3:33 A.M. A train ambling by combines with jackhammers and generators to vibrate the whole building up to the sixth floor where the ruin of my life is well in progress. But you cannot tell much by looking. The same furniture's in place, and the house, if anything, is cleaner and less cluttered with only one two-legged living here. The plump Siamese hears the signal of my changing breath as I wake and does a brand of snuggling in which she whisks her tail across my naked middle-aged belly several times and then bounds away to scratch at the perimeters of the rug pads, making obnoxious percussive pops as she roots out kernels of recycled material before vanishing into the high sierra of the condo. Annoyed but sleepy, I don't track her. My horse has thrown a shoe, all hope grounded. The fingers in my ears tremble when the generator on the street below roars up again to fuel excavation of gas and sewer lines. I can't escape the sound that rattles my chest. By city ordinance, this drilling work takes place in the middle of the night to protect office workers from interruption. And now that over a thousand folks like myself have heeded the beckoning siren of downtown living, street repairs and upgrades are constant with no adjustment for sleeping residents. I actually brought it up with the City Manager, and he made reference to the ordinance with no nod toward updating it.

I fall back on my hoard of pillows meant for two and dream or remember the young husband pulling a wagon cooler on wheels for his family's day trip in Chaco, wondering what he could have experienced of the stillness of the place with two children and a wife anxious for cold cuts. They spread their bread and fruit and cheese and peanut butter and packages of meats across the next picnic table, while I reached for an energy bar and drank some water from the hot jug retrieved from my car, map spread before me anchored by daypack and notebook. A little gray and vaguely yellow bird jittered around, discovering the apple core I'd tossed to the center of a spiky bush. Hat never left my head those desert days.

I wake up again and it's morning in my city, with the purrs and grrrs of various engines traveling streets, rails, and sky, comings and goings tracing toward and away in dancing spells. Today's sky—laced with puffing streams of low-hovering clouds over the peaks of smoke-blue mountains—is painted a painless blue of a sort not out of the tube. The eastern morning sun bores through the line of living room windows, penetrating UV film to the side of my face with its thatch of spider red and a diffuse scar from bouncing off tree bark in a brutal game of Blind Man's Bluff that left my child self knocked down and bloody. I don't know why I ever thought I could write about the mysteries of Chaco, its rough buff colors, pinkish earth and rivulets of dust, ghost water, dashes of surprising chalk-blue lichen on sandstone cliffs. With these unlikely combinations of color, it's part of a region with the greatest range of biological habitats in North America, owing to its altitude and humidity extremes.

This clear air vivifies my native landscape, soft green fringing below the indigo gray-blue zigzagging hills I've studied for years without seeing them clearly enough. Below the dimensional cloudscape and the gradually lightening sky that says nothing of yesterday's violent storm, here I am. Yesterday, sprays of hard rain from the west electrified the balcony as if a fire hose set on high aimed straight for it. Rain blotted the building from the visible world, and I from the mountains. All of my new plantings reeled and learned to bend, the cherry tomato bowing the lowest, dipping from its pot in the plant stand. That fierce blasting water was over in less than an hour, every appointment and plan erased in a small space of time in which we lost power. This morning, I drive Mother to her eye appointment, dodging downed limbs and lines to find that the office is still dark.

I run a short stretch of the city's greenway, following others around a barrier. Mud mounds and rivulets mark the low bridge along the Roanoke River where a crew is finally attending to a giant pile of debris from several spring storms that have left tree parts wedged, forming a dam between the bridge piers. With a truck and winch, they hoist the huge logjam, piles of limbs tightly entwined like beaver houses between snapped trunks. I run a little farther beyond the aging skate park. Will I ever get any faster? I run back and forth following the same path. It is never the same. Susan finds a giant turtle wandering from the grass onto the asphalt path and posts it on Facebook. Someone else spots a heron. An eagle. There's fruit to pull down from the trees and eat, black ice to avoid in winter. There are days this path is closed altogether and we have to go around. *It is only necessary to know that love is a direction and not a state of the soul....* I keep running.

"A horse, a horse, my kingdom for a horse." Confirmation arrives that skeletal remains discovered under a car park in central Leicester, formerly the site of Greyfriars Church, are those of King Richard III. DNA samples as well as radiocarbon and genealogical studies concur. The quite intact skeletal remains exhibit King Richard's mortal wounds from the 1485 battle of Bosworth as well as the hunchbacked monarch's crippling scoliosis. Evidence left us from his decayed flesh: piles of worms infesting the soil where his bowels lay. He may have suffered from intestinal parasites. What's beneath the visible world? Have we built our church on nothing more than a passel of wormy old bones?

At Chaco, only two burials seem to have been given higher ceremony, which is possibly indicative of their higher status. Speaking of which, the taller, more decorated human remains might have been the healthier Pueblo Bonito dignitaries or another ethnic group altogether; three or four distinct linguistic groups lived and worked in community there. These remains are protected from DNA tests in accordance with Native American customs, and on some level this is unfortunate since speculations about ethnic diversity in the canyon could be informed by the testing. On the other hand, what might such findings disrupt in terms of claimed historic connection to the place by many and various tribes? The trade-off of knowledge against connection so far has not been worth it. There are perhaps things we are better off not knowing.

My mind swims through questions the way the air wells and swirls as humidity dispels, roiling in visible heat waves. 850–1150: Chaco is under construction. Why choose such a desolate location for at least thirteen towns (pueblos) and numerous great kivas? In this place there was variably too little rainfall to sustain agriculture for a large permanent population, and yet the structures were grand, covering acres, piling up small interior rooms to as many as six stories. The number of structures suggests a population larger than the land could provide for in dry years, although there is evidence of dams, divergence of water for irrigation.

An estimated 214,000 trees were felled for construction, ninety percent hand-carried, probably by teams of at least six men, twenty to sixty miles from the Chuska Mountains, with no wheels to ease their path or water to float the logs. We're talking about literally tons of wooden roof beams balanced on notched branches and dragged. Much of this wood was cleared from rooms long buried and burned for firewood by Richard Wetherill's excavation team, which began its digs in May 1896, removing hundreds of intact artifacts before the passage of the federal Antiquities Act of 1906. These treasures were shipped east to the American Museum of Natural History in New York.

So many rooms with unaccounted purposes: some rooms were no doubt for storage, others for shelter for permanent residents or pilgrims, but of the six hundred or so rooms in Pueblo Bonito, only thirteen suites with connecting chambers may have been suitable for family groups. In Rm. 28 of Pueblo Bonito, 116 vessels were exhumed, including cylinders containing chocolate, a product of Mexico. In these many rooms, corn and turquoise beads were stored in vast vats, along with Pacific shells, pottery, ceremonial staffs, and colorful feathers. But why so many rooms with relatively few, perhaps only 800–900 permanent residents, in the canyon? Some theories point, on the high side, to as many as 6,000 residents, but this appears to be too many mouths to feed. Debate continues, as do my questions.

Do the more than 400 miles of north-south roadways tracing natural breaks and mesas, mounting over great stairs carved in the rock, point like compass needles to other Great Houses, outliers, and longtime migration routes? Are these pilgrim routes in and out of the canyon actually processional routes for sacred journeys? The roads widen to as much as thirty feet as they approach the Great Houses. Without land-moving equipment, how did they build roads so incredibly straight that they can be picked out in photographs taken from space?

This much is certain: a score of research years has rearranged the body of knowledge along with my molecules. My physical and mental body at thirty-five was a different body from the one I now inhabit; for one thing, my hip tends to ache. Right after I visited the Southwest in 1993 I was thrown from a Sea-Doo at Smith Mountain Lake and cracked my hip on the side of the craft. The bruise surfaced over a series of weeks. When the bruise was so deep it had yet to bloom into color, I could barely walk. Now it provides me with an arthritic yelp when I sit on hard benches, turn a certain way in sleep, or run down hills. I stare out from the same eyes, but they've gotten sharper in the distance and blurrier near to hand. I no longer actually see the thread go through the needle's loop; now it's a blurry thread, a needle head I stab on faith. My consolation horizon line is less of a smear than a ribbon of light, as my distance sight improves. I'll take the long view.

Around me this time in Chaco, the group gathered for the tour are mostly residents of adjacent western states. I greet the closest woman. When I tell her I'm from Virginia, she exclaims with wonder. She has just used the example of my state in saying that no one had come from that far away, and in her next breath Hello, Virginia arrives on cue. She and her husband moved from the east, or came from "back east," as she says. Naming a place any of us claims as home starts to sound fictitious, largely meaningless. We are nomads. We learn that even the first peoples were immigrants from Asia.

Right off the blocks, Ranger G. B. Cornucopia, who has lived and worked here the longest, a constant amid morphing conjecture, tells our group that climate change was not a factor in the migration that occurred by the mid-thirteenth century. He affirms that the weather was not substantially different from what it is now in Chaco; in fact it's been the same for the past two millennia, although the ancients endured cycles of draught and extremes, with -38 Fahrenheit the historic low and 100-degree days typical in high summer. Mr. Chaco pooh-poohs any theory with the word *abandonment* in it; the Chacoans' was not a mysterious vanishing. At least twenty contemporary pueblos trace their ancestry to Chaco, including the Zuni, the Hopi, the Acoma, the Laguna, and sixteen other pueblos, sprinkled in two language groups to the Rio Grande. The Navajo came late, but they have stayed in this area the longest and also lay claim. Navajo crews do much of the restoration work in the canyon with methodology passed down generation to generation. I'm weighing whether or not one can still be thinking of oneself as an immigrant after cultivating a place for four hundred years; human lifespan and memory being what it is, we can fail to see what's vast, and maybe underestimate our impact. In order to answer my questions and know what things mean, I have to know what time and space meant to the people who built this place. Fitted with the blinders of who we are now, of who I am, how can I ever know? Knowing I cannot, I still want to imagine.

"No one vanished," Ranger Cornucopia concludes with some well-earned disdain in his voice. They didn't abandon this place en masse but dribbled out for various reasons. Maybe it was more like the dwindling of an Italian hill town in Umbria, I think. So many hill towns are empty now, and not because they aren't structurally sound; it's the economics. Some people move away to find work, and then more and more folks follow, until the quorum it takes to make a community has drained out. When the schools are as empty as the churches, you have a ghost town with only a few old straggler-souls left behind.

"No," says Ranger Cornucopia, "there was no evidence of human sacrifice," disappointing the father who asked the question, he claimed on behalf of his squirming boy. "You have to go down to Mexico for that," Cornucopia shoots back. A few of us laugh in small measures. "These were not the bloody Maya or the Aztec," he says. In fact, the Chacoan buildings predate theirs. These ancients erected some of their elaborate Great Houses on landscaped mounds, creating more grandeur through the appearance of relative scale and perhaps better drainage for the irrigation and plumbing ditches that laced the valley, emptying into Chaco Wash. Learning of this landscaping design, my mind immediately turns to Thomas Jefferson's terraced lawn at University of Virginia, its illusion of one grand expanse.

The Great Houses, plastered with light mud containing gypsum, must have glowed at sunrise and sunset like a heavenly city, reflecting the sun's pinks, oranges, and reds. With so much ingenuity, this highly developed urban plan can hardly be labeled primitive, yet it's just past Basketmaker III, 450–700, that we find Pueblo I, 700–875. Paleolithic peoples from ten thousand years ago sought shelter in Atlatl Cave, foraged for food, and hunted bison in the canyon. Their projectile points have been dated. Researchers have also identified two hundred fifty early pit houses in and around Chaco and thousands of shelter sites from north of Mesa Verde to the Mogollon Rim. This whole part of creation rocks the American cradle, which is why the region is known as "the land of many houses."

Many of the structures in Chaco align perfectly with solar and lunar events, with cardinal directions, and with solstices, as did the time-telling rock on top of Fajada Butte, until tourists wore down the ground with the weigh of their curiosity and forever altered its position. "Same with Washington, DC," says our ranger. "Cosmological implications. Ask the Masons." After the ancients built these walls, they chiseled out corner windows to track certain astronomical alignments. Corner windows along with T-shaped doors were picked up again at Aztec Ruins, which was built quickly over a brief period of thirty years, situated within the drainage of the San Juan River north of Farmington in Colorado. Aztec Ruins, misnamed by the Spanish who thought North American Indians were Aztec, and the closer Salmon Ruins, also to the north, came of age in the period overlapping Chaco's decline, built in Pueblo Bonito's image.

_◈_

Mom says, "I feel terrible, like my head is burning up. I bet my face is red as a beet."

"You don't look flushed," I say. "It must be the BP medication. Side effect."

And she says, "Really?" Then, "Good." Her voice wavers, unconvinced. "I had that dream again," she continues. "Different location but the same theme. Always weird."

This dream was of a golf course: wet fairways and greens, and she had to slog through mud, picking up golf balls. Then she was lost and had to find her way. "The scenery kept changing around me," she says.

"Where were you going?"

"Home, I guess," she answers.

"Where is that?"

"Just home," she says. "You know. Back."

A kiva = any round room; their uses changed and evolved over the years. Older pit houses were repurposed as earthen kivas and later as above-ground kivas with ceremonial functions when masonry houses replaced earthen shelters around AD 700–800. Kivas, as well as other rooms, were continually remodeled, round rooms reshaped into rectangles, their walls reinforced and thickened. Square the circle. At Aztec Ruins, I saw three interior kivas with three reinforced walls similar to the one at Pueblo del Arroyo in Chaco. The reconstructed Great Kiva at Aztec Ruins National Monument is forty-eight feet across, the same diameter as the Chartres labyrinth, and ringed with fifteen rooms. I stepped inside and felt the quiet take me, turn me inward. The song of one flute fluttered around my head. I climbed down to floor level from the anteroom using a replica wooden ladder, like the one preserved in the museum, and paused to consider white and red painted walls, low curving benches along the walls, and T-shaped windows. The reconstructed roof—ninety-five tons supported by pine beams—probably rises a bit too high to be historically accurate, but other than this, the space looks ready to entertain the whole village for a seasonal offering, perhaps to cele-brate a birth or mourn a death. I tried to feel traces of ancient others in that reconstructed space but could not. I stood alone for a while until some other tourists appeared, heads dark against sunlight, popping into the doorway at the top of the ladder. I climbed back out before their voices reached my ears.

Striking dark green bands of tabular stone run along two exterior walls of the Great House at Aztec Ruins. These bands would not have been visi-ble when the structures were in use. Mud plaster that protected the walls from the elements here as in Chaco would have hidden these curious waver-ing tracks of stone. Some say the bands represent snakes, and some say the river, so necessary to survival. Settlers trickled up from Chaco and Salmon Ruins in drought years, closer to the Animas and a convergence of three riv-ers. I can count three visible green bands, and maybe, the guide tells the group, there's another row of rock beneath the ground, below excavation level. If so, this detail points us toward another interpretation concerning protection and the four cardinal directions. The Navajo say this world is the fourth, or the fourth band. Rows of rock echo Chaco, the place before, which is guarded by Fajada Butte's dark bands of coal.

My $99.00 DNA results return a month after I've spit into a sterile vial and dropped it in the mail. The first report is rather vague and unsatisfying: 85% British Isles, which maps the whole of them in one fell swoop. Thus my greater part could be Irish, Scottish (probably not), English, or hail from Wales in some combination. 10% of me is identified as Southern European, pointing to Portugal, Spain, and Italy; 5% "uncertain," as in we don't yet know how to parse this, or our samples haven't turned it up enough times for comparison. Immediately, of course, I focus on the 5% of unidentified, uncertain material, wishing I could choose something profound to uphold the other 95% dilution. Despite the fact that a family DAR member traced one side of the family back to Old Bohemia, this information has not yet shown its face in my DNA analysis. Those branches may have been lopped for efficiency, drowned by other strands, or in my case colonized by the Brit-ish. As more and more folks spit into the vial, some finer tunings may emerge. European explorers knew of Chaco by the mid-seventeenth century; by 1774, a map identifies the canyon's location. Since my lines have been in the New World a long time—by 1740 at least one Hankla infant had died in

America—I imagine it's going to come down to English and Spanish flags upon further refinement. As for the uncertain 5%: a star system in the carbon neighborhood. I'm hoping to hail from Antares, a red supergiant.

I have only weeks to wait before a more refined version of my results arrives: 98% Heinz 57 of Europe. The largest portion of this matches Western Europe, bringing in the Czech, the Dutch, and parts between, and, after a heavy draught of Guinness: Scandinavia, Spain, Great Britain, Italy, Greece, and Finland in descending order, plus an exotic 2% dash of West Asia to round out the Southern trade route all the way to the Holy Lands. I begin and end in a contested place.

Ranger Cornucopia's Pueblo Bonito tour winds us through a stretch of small chambers or pens in a row where bird skeletons were discovered. In Chaco's wide weather variance of 100 degrees, none of these macaws transported from Mexico, and probably kept for their feathers, could survive more than three winters. Twenty years ago I was told that the permanent population in Chaco reached ten thousand, and nothing about these colorful imported birds. Now the population estimate has shrunk to less than one thousand, and birds and chocolate have entered in, evidence of an ancient trade route that stretched far south, intersecting ethnicities and cultures.

Only the past changes; only the present moment's eternal.

Everything has its consequences. Hitler told his architects of monumental projects that they were to build, "the word in stone." The science of archaeology depends on finding the word left in the rubble. Is it so hard to care about these scattered and worn stone piles for their own sake aside from admiration for the substantial feat of labor they represent? Visibility instead of protection could have drawn the ancients to this canyon; the pueblos backed up to the cliffs, and threats from above would have been hard to defend. Chaco offered a central location in the San Juan basin, a plentitude of basic building materials from the cliffs coupled with rich silt for crops, a relatively high water table, and perhaps a seasonal lake effect at the mouth of Chaco Wash. Ten thousand years of agriculture means the crops Chacoan farmers tilled, their corn, beans, and squash, looked nothing like what we picture with those words. Our corn derives from ancient corn, but theirs was an ugly husk with at most ten kernels and about ten times more protein, nutrient rich. Though there was less corn to go around, they didn't need as much. By comparison our corn is sugar water. The thought of organizing the labor of thousands of scratch agriculturalists for building structural testaments over hundreds of years seems as impossible at Chaco as it was on Malta, where we are supposed to believe that ancient Sicilian farmers floated over to the isles and proceeded to organize themselves into stone masons for the next thousand-plus years, building above-ground temples and associated underground sites in roughly the same period.

At Chaco, Navajo restoration workers pass down their knowledge to apprentices and can identify the work of individual masons and several phases of stonework in Una Vida, Pueblo del Arroyo, and Pueblo Bonito, the oldest structures. Each phase reveals a high level of planning and execution. At first, stones were simply stacked, wider at the bottom and then narrower as the walls ascended a couple of stories. Later, core and veneer masonry, roughly piled and mortared interior walls encased by intricately fitted thin dark tabular stone from the high cliffs, allowed stories to climb as high as six. In the last phase of construction, workers used loaves of softer tan-colored sandstone from the canyon's lower walls, the higher denser stone having been stripped. Generations of builders tore down the cliffs as they raised these walls, and in the last phase they had to use inferior material. The exterior appearance, even with all these phases of masonry brought together in one structure as in Pueblo Bonita, would have been seamless because the walls inside and out received a coat of white plaster. The engineering didn't stop with the walls; the Great Houses are situated for passive solar heating. These people were highly skilled technically and probably even more spiritually evolved to work cooperatively, passing down knowledge, to execute a city plan drawn long before they were born. The project of Chaco is the equivalent of a cathedral.

The Navajo say, "The Bible is the land." The land is their holy book. Landscape holds memory, each feature bearing meaning. I believe ancient Pueblo people chose the location of Chaco Canyon because of its sacred mountain, Fajada Butte, a block of sandstone banded with black lignite coal. I have learned its name.

III.

Sitting at a picnic table with Fajada Butte rising from Chacra Mesa in the background, I'm reflecting on my past several days in Chaco. Up on the cliff, during my longest hike, I could see anyone approaching from miles around

in all directions and would have been able to pass information along by signal fire if I'd had reason. I gazed toward South Gap, which divides South
Mesa from West, toward the distinct gash named South Road, imagining
pilgrims lining the route and wondering how long it would take them to
arrive after they had been spotted. Chaco was not a place for surprise attacks.
After hiking up to Pueblo Alto and New Alto, and viewing Pueblo Bonito
and Chetro Ketl from Chaco Plateau above, the highly visible location of
Chaco for trade, ceremonial gatherings, the dissemination of culture, and
food distribution is much clearer to me. When I stood over the canyon to
study and photograph the generous half-moon patterns of Chetro Ketl and
Pueblo Bonito, I was not alone up there but passed by several groups, boisterous boyfriends and girlfriends, older couples, and even young kids. For a
while I walked along with a young man in dreadlocks on kind of a vision
quest. He promised to email the photograph he showed me of a rattlesnake
in the campground, big around as my arm, long as my height. I agreed to
send him a picture of himself atop the cliff like a rock spirit.

Far more than my learning about Chaco, my time here is about being
in Chaco, being with Chaco, being Chaco. My friends Mike and Lisa agree,
while most people I know who've been to the center place only wish to go
once. My well-shorn feet hit dusty red earth as I weave paths followed by
thousands of ancient people in grass-woven sandals. The Menefee Formation is what we share, a Mesozoic geologic formation littered with clam-
shell fossils, shark's teeth, marine sand, and an occasional dinosaur bone.
Dust from Chaco sticks in my tread, sifts into the fabric of my hiking boots
and into the wool fibers of my socks. Later, Mike will tell me we need to
rinse off the tents with the hose. When the wind pitches, gusts of sand drive
into my teeth and my hair, which separates like pieces of straw in an hour.
Hiking reminds me that traveling on foot without horses means that just
about any place is as remote or accessible as any other. When human steps
measure the time between places, the journey itself matters. Walking and
taking in the vistas, I pay no more than a small price in bad roads, dry skin,
and scarecrow hair in order to see the tough beauty of this world. I can live
without a shower for a couple of days, especially while eating Mike's dinners,
grilled over ashen chunks of wood from his expertly latticed fire. What's
spare here and now was concentrated with habitation, human, plant, and
animal, and rich at its height. What echoes with absence was relatively re-
plete: populated, civilized, organized, and grand. "Chaco was not an isolated

place in AD 1000," Ruth Van Dyke reminds us, but perhaps instead "an ancient farming oasis," or a "relative oasis," as W. James Judge writes, with a number of fortunate conditions coinciding, including expanses of bare sliprock for brick; *rincones* or level side canyons suitable for irrigation farming; and at the canyon's western edge Escavada Wash, where the water table surfaces. Chacra Mesa, just east, offered accessible hunting and an array of plants.

Isolation came later, starting in 1140. Many of these dates were derived through dendrochronology, the study of tree ring growth. The map of Chaco Canyon is a time machine, yet, if I were to go back, I couldn't land at any particular moment and see all of this construction in working order at the same time. These sites were not coexistent but overlapping, sometimes supplanting each other, waxing and waning. Some houses emptied out and were then reoccupied as others were continually expanded and renovated. They erected the later sites in far less time and less elaborately, while Pueblo Bonito was under construction for hundreds of years by thousands of hands, constituting a multifaceted biography of a people in a place that covered acres. For all its grandeur, Pueblo Bonito has only one door and perhaps one symbolic tree, a ponderosa pine planted in the plaza near a large public kiva. One door to many mysteries: I marvel again that so much earth and rock could be moved and mounded and shaped into palaces by the work of hands wielding only obsidian blades, another import. Mexican Toltec pyramids held stores of obsidian. *Tolteca*: artist or wise man; *toltecayotl*: art and culture, civilization. Toltec culture (800–1000), which also includes monumental architecture, overlaps Chaco Culture and must have been its counterpart and trading partner.

Sunday morning in Chaco Canyon: no better church than this. I contemplate the butte before me; it's a fleshy pink and buff-colored asymmetrical layer cake racked by winds. There was once a house up there near the time-telling stone. Gusts ruffle my papers and lob grit onto any exposed patches of skin. Not many sounds here but the wind. Perfect temperature, eighty degrees in the sun and lower in dry shade, with the cooler wind threading through waves of rising heat from the sandy soil. If you study the bricks of these Great Houses you can see waves from the ancient sea. Above me quite a lot of clouds are gathering and darkening over this arid place. I'm reminded of sudden mean squalls that send water rushing through the washes, entrapping cars and motorbikes in quickening mud.

How could I have felt so tortured in the middle of last night, so mired in my own dark places? The past is written in stone, a monumental language. These structures equal a written history of a people without a written language. Last night, I met myself from twenty years ago and felt all the numbed-out pain I could not feel then. But sitting here this morning, I am evened out, peaceful. The old business of fragmented living crops up and then recedes into this landscape held tight by Fajada Butte. The sacred mountain can contain anyone's desire; it can neutralize my pain. The ancients couldn't take this butte with them, so they took its banded pattern and their well-developed pueblo design. They transplanted corner windows, the grand scale of the kivas and plazas and pueblo plans in half-moon or D shapes. But outside of Chaco in whatever direction they moved, their subsequent civilization never seemed to thrive as it had within this canyon; it was never again as centralized and organized. When the people dispersed, strife and skirmishes sprang up, even slaughter.

I remember biting down on something so hard it stunned my upper and lower back molars to the root, to the anchoring bone, almost to my shoulders, reverberating to my spine. I thought I'd broken my jaw not just a tooth. Maybe it was an almond shell mixed into the bag of raw almonds on which I was freely chomping, or just a hard nut to crack. I don't remember, but the shock comes back to me in waves of shooting pain at the back of my mouth. The compressed feeling of a collision in my mouth went away in a day or two, but I know that moment was decisive. What's done is done and cannot be undone, but every dying isn't the end; a boy with an unhealed wound in his knee found a small, coiled seashell embedded there like a question encasing a live creature. I sit here with something amazing in front of me, a sacred mountain, and something transmuting within.

Lurching up the road into Chaco, I met cows grazing the edges, dust so thick sometimes I thought I would get stuck in the rivulets and dirt drifts. The point was to arrive. The point was to start down the trail leading to the heart, to choose the path with a heart. The point later became to remember an instant, the unchanging moment in a windstorm, the moment we locked eyes at a crowded party and whispered, "I do" without ever admitting it. And the fact of that ancient knowledge forgotten over time: what they knew they had held, beheld, believed, promised, achieved without ever writing it down. I often return to that moment of locked eyes when two strangers sought to see into one another with a promise arising unbidden from inside the earth's heart. It reminds me of something true about falling into someone, about losing oneself to be found. This morning my blue-faced watch stops. Like the time-telling rock atop Fajada Butte, it no longer tells time. Our lives are measured in minutes, hours, days, and breaths.

Today would be my father's ninety-fourth birthday, fourteen years after his death. In 1993 I brought him a T-shirt from Arizona's Petrified Forest covered with rock art. I found it in his dresser drawer unworn. Dad was not a T-shirt kind of guy. After he died, Mother was efficient about getting rid of his clothes, perhaps too efficient; in her dreams he came back looking for them, asking her where she had put his suits, his leather shoes, his golf shirts and hats.

Were Ancient Puebloans planning to return to all the rooms in Chaco and reclaim the treasures they'd left behind, including 60,000 pieces of shaped turquoise? The height of Chaco's construction boom corresponds with a period of frequent rain, but the rains had come and gone before. Burn marks in the Great Kivas indicate the people weren't planning to return: fire marks departure, an ending purification rite. But were long generations after them meant to re-inhabit the Great Houses or meant to stay away, leaving only spirits to dwell? With some limited exceptions, no one did come back and they took little with them. Everything they left behind—beads, shells, macaw and turkey feathers, sandals, and clay pipes, pots, and ceremonial staffs—was removed by archaeologists in whirlwind digs, shipped east if not deliberately disposed, thrown like trash into Chaco Wash. Scoured by weather, the Great Houses will return to ground as the desert deposits gradually refill the rooms. Archaeology these days can carbon-date from samples and see into the ground with lasers. Sites not previously dug would probably rest in peace if not for fracking operations now encroaching.

Whether Chaco was mainly a ceremonial, religious center housing seasonal pilgrims, a trading and agricultural crossroads, or served as the regional tax collector, not many goods for trade were manufactured there, but many things were transformed: sandstone into bricks; sand, silt, clay, and water into mortar and plaster for exterior and interior walls; turquoise into vats of hollow and bird-shaped beads; gypsum and iron pounded from rock for the main paint colors of white and red. It took tons of precious water to construct any of these structures. Forty percent of what's visible can be measured in the weight of water. Mortar filled the spaces between the bricks and plaster covered the walls, requiring water, and more water. Great White Houses were kept up, cracks repaired, repainted: more water, buckets and buckets of water. Which begs the question of storage. Maybe there really was a lake formed by an Aeolian dune dam and reinforced with sandstone bricks that blocked the canyon at Escavada Wash as Van Dyke speculates. Today, for modern-day inhabitants, there's a water storage tank perched on the cliff.

I run through all of this again in my mind as I wander the flat, sandy path to the ruin of Wijiji, a Hopi-named site opposite Fajada Butte on the far end of the canyon from Pueblo Bonita. Wijiji was of late modular design, with a kiva in the center of a rectangular room block. There will be no signs of water during my hike beneath darkening clouds except for the vivid colors of wildflowers blowing red and yellow and even blue just outside the trail's confines, and the bright yellow-green of a companion lizard. I asked the attending ranger to recommend a three-mile hike, and this trail fits the bill. At the trailhead, I write my name on the record just below a couple from Utah.

Soon, I meet the retired couple on the trail and learn that like me they are visiting some sites in the Four Corners area. I ask them about Utah, where they are from, and learn that Horseshoe Canyon is no longer remote; it has full-time ranger protection and dozens of daily visitors. The washboard road I traveled twenty years ago has been paved. It's hard for me to believe I was in Canyonlands' Maze District so basically alone for an entire day, seeing exactly five people plus a mountain lion. This count includes the two-legged latecomers to the parking lot. Can twenty years mean the difference between remote and endangered? I want some places to remain hidden, at least difficult to find, out of general reach, only earned by sweat, research, or happy accident. I want some places to escape the marks of our wear and tear, four-wheelers, the entitlement of earbuds and Internet, and only bear human traces once every thousand or so years. I want to keep alive the possibility of being lost. May the road to Chaco never be paved, I pray.

I wake in the middle of the night, teeth clamped tight against teeth, jaw locked. Damn it, I think, the dentist is right about the clenching. All this time and I never knew. I didn't believe her. Had no evidence other than the distorted moonscape of tori beneath my tongue. Lying here on my back with a jutting jaw and a tight ache in my bite, I accept something new about myself. As per usual during this time of life, it's not welcome news. Maybe tomorrow the sun will come out.

In the high desert of northern Nevada near Pyramid Lake archaeologists have dated a group of petroglyphs back at least 10,000 years and possibly back 14,800 years. Paleolithic man was a geometric artist, striking deep diamonds into chunks of limestone. Meteorological symbols? Climate notes? Pure design: art for art's sake? Made with what tools? These are deeply inscribed patterns. The oldest site in North America, the oldest reference for human marks, yet it photographs as if it were etched merely a few hundred years ago, and we have no idea what the patterns mean.

Between New Mexico and Southwest Colorado stretch 25,000 square miles of evidence of ancient communities and migration routes, multiple rock art and hearth sites and potsherds poking from the earth, from the magnificence of Horseshoe Canyon's Great Gallery of floating figures to various newspaper rocks chocked with spirals and birthing figures, and, hidden in natural alcoves, the occasional red hands and stars. Forging creeks, I traced sites in Shay Canyon. At Mesa Verde, I followed the petroglyph trail at Spruce Tree House. A small Plexiglas display window in Cliff Palace revealed a very fresh-looking mural with red and white pigment in a zigzagging pattern. The Plexiglass had weathered and was scarred more than the mural. I was able to find all five sites listed in the rock art guidebook for Potash Road, and then slide into Moab for the night, dreaming of broken turtles, zigzags, three-foot-long bears tracked by hunters with bows and arrows, lizards, stick men with spears, leaping antelope figures, spherical people with antler heads, and endless spirals upon spirals. Those rare, scattered handprints—like the clusters of haunting red hands I have seen in *National Geographic* from Australia's outback—are thought to be prayers, offerings to other realms of being, and the more common spirals = endless paths through this world and the next.

Outside of Arches heading south, I climbed up to the cliffs above the Colorado River, to find a few more pictographs of antennae people in the Barrier Canyon style I'd traced in Horseshoe Canyon. These figures were holding vague spheres. Vandals had scrubbed the rock surfaces, almost erasing the ghostly images. A picture taken before the vandalism shows the white, nearly translucent spheres and red figures behind them. There's some chiseling and some etching of rock along with the paintings at this site. Along Kane Creek south of Moab I explored several good panels, although one was so tagged with contemporary graffiti that it was all but destroyed. However, the third site down a bad gravel road around Kane Springs Canyon yielded a freestanding newspaper rock. I scrambled down the slope seventy-five feet to a large boulder decorated on four sides. This rock held a birthing scene with a baby being born feet first.

Looking at the weather map, I see the latitude line stretching from the bottom of Virginia to the top of New Mexico, splitting New Mexico and Colorado, and leading on to southern Utah and Arizona. I look east to west, following the latitude from Roanoke to Durango, Colorado. What is it about this line that defines a certain continuum of place? My friend David tells me he had a thing about the Four Corners when he was a child and doesn't know where it came from. Raised in Southwest Virginia, he now lives in Albuquerque after a couple of decades' detour to New York City, but he still hasn't made it to the Four Corners Monument. It's a bit hokey, perhaps, and maybe it's not even really there, not exactly where the imaginary corners really meet, yet it holds the promise of a place with many houses. Not just Chaco Canyon, Aztec or Salmon Ruins, Mesa Verde or Chimney Rock, Hovenweep, Painted Hand, or Sand Canyon, but everywhere you look on the map marks a place of settlement. There is an invisible pattern of civilization in what looks like open space between contemporary towns: layers upon layers, across and below. Below my motel in Cortez, Colorado, a ruin was unearthed when they dug a swimming pool.

Bath County, Virginia. If the spiritual and physical worlds collide, it happens in landscape figures or buildings that come to represent more than their function. Quietly tucked on the Dickinson farm near Nimrod Hall (circa 1783) lies an enormous Indian mound in the front yard of a farmhouse. I've passed it many times in trespassing beyond the low bridge, slipping through rows of tasseling feed corn. This year when my class is walking down to the Cowpasture River for our float via inner tubes to the swimming hole, Katie asks me if I know about the Indian mound. I say I do not, as I have not connected the weird mound with anything as formal as an "Indian mound." The mound rises up about fifteen feet from the lower level of the field like an elevated stage and covers about a football field's length and width. We walk between rows of towering corn and face the mound; its soft green sides and rounded corners are obviously those of a landscaped feature, well considered and executed. I'm wondering what's in it, if it's a gravesite. Katie tells me she's ascertained through remote viewing that the mound is not very old. I have little reaction to this announcement, as I have heard about the Monroe

Institute on Afton Mountain but maintain little interest in government-sponsored snooping though time and space.

This summer marks several points of return and potential ending for me. I return to Bath County for the twenty-first time with a group of writer women, many of whom I've known that long. But something is brewing here; the owners, now in their eighties with children and grandkids entrenched in other ventures, have been working on the property's sale. As a result the writer group wonders whether it can return next year and where it will go if not here. For me, this has been a central place, at the fulcrum of high summer. I go to the river and wade, baptizing myself in its flow. If place is created by the conjunction of time, self, and space, then this place is truly for me a *place*. Not exactly Chaco but somehow akin, a ritual center, a pilgrimage destination, a starting out and a going back in cyclical fashion that lends meaning to the rest of the year. Successive layers of experience here have made it more than just a pretty setting. Even with these many layers of place that I carry, stability seems to be wearing as thin here as in the rest of my life, with the dream house (condo, loft) now up for sale and the relationship that built it over in spite of our enormous efforts. So defiantly faithful I have been, and yet my touchstones are vanishing from other forces bearing down on them.

As soon as I get home from the Southwest it erupts into flame, forest fires stretching over thousands of acres. I get an email petition to stop fracking for natural gas on public lands, including the lands surrounding Chaco, which are heavily resourced, extracted, refinery stacks rising among the badlands, with Halliburton trucks frequent on the main perimeter roads. All of my fierce clinging vines will be torn, my branches pruned.

Former Minister of Defense of Canada Paul Hellyer testifies on June 5, 2013, that extraterrestrials are real, that at least four distinct species have been on earth for a long time, and that two of them are working with the US government, The Tall Whites who live on a Nevada base near famous Area 51, and The Greys. In an earlier speech (2011), he connected ET technology with the energy crisis. He's rather quickly, too quickly, dismissed as a nut.

Captive to time, humans tend to measure it through geography. We are nomadic space travelers aging as we move. Why is it so difficult to believe that life might have been seeded here from elsewhere? Space meets time in us. Gradually, we must stay in place as time chisels our features, wrinkles our surfaces, pocks us with the marks of wind and rain and snow, the landscape of the body's woes. I cried a river over you, storms shaking my shoulders, my unmovable mountains erupting like volcanoes of dread, and now I'm all cried out, gone dormant. Hazel eyes crying in the rain: *No more,* I said. If you want to leave then go, go quickly. If I cannot let go entirely, it will be my own problem to solve, my Rubik's cube, my encoded situation. *To remember to remember* means the land itself contains the memory. The architectural structures may be visual extensions of cosmological ideas baked into the landscape but not necessarily the natural shape of things. My body approximates the body of an ancient one whose stature was also small, 5'3"–5'6"; a resonance of their human scale can accompany me, but I can never mindmeld with the ancient worldview. And on a basic level, what I see is not what they saw. Perhaps they saw Great White Houses aglow in Chaco, plastered exteriors visible for miles in contrast to the reddish or light amber landscape and sage scrub in the same place where I see exposed sandstone brick walls blending into the landscape colors. I squint through my sunglasses, try to see what I cannot see. As I leave the Visitor's Center, the swinging door thumps me hard in the heart as I adjust my hat. I don't know if it's telling me to go away or to come back. I will go away but also come back, and back, and back.

Plopped in front of my TV, I lounge at home in pajama pants, letting my eyes pan over news and fragments of movies, readying myself in a light doze before sleep. It's been a long week and now it's nearly ten o'clock; I'm supposed to rise early to meet my running group. From the back studio, down the hallway without precedent, comes a flying creature with the Siamese cat trotting below. It seems to resonate with the TV's flicker and glow, flapping above or maybe attracted to the screen. As I ask it, *What are you? What are you?* I'm thinking birds inside are bad omens. What was I watching? A *48 Hours* report about the deadly year 2012 on Mt. Everest, and the last thing I remember seeing on screen: a photo of a woman whose frozen body was left tied to a guide rope and draped with the Canadian flag, though she was born in Tibet. She had insisted on summiting, failing to heed her Sherpa's advice to turn back; icy winds caught up and her oxygen ran too low. And with my next thought it hits me that flying above me is no bird but a *bat*. In Chaco bats and moths were the pollinators as there were no bees. Bats are fraught omens and difficult to catch and release. I never know what's coming next, down the hall, around the bend. Today I felt the first note of fall in the air and it's barely September. With a wingspan of a foot, my bat looks unsettled and jittery in its stunted interior flight. I doubt echolocation will serve it well here on the sixth floor. As I reach for the phone to call for reinforcements, I forget to breathe and lose track of the bat. Searching, while awaiting my posse, I have to turn on every light in the dark house, open and close every last door.

Feeling afraid for the first and only time on my journey west, I wanted to flee back to the shelter of my rented SUV. My route expanded northwest from Aztec Ruins to the great Sage Plain above the Colorado River Plateau, turning a tad west again to Hovenweep. On the southern Utah/Colorado border I hiked Painted Hand settlement, outliers Horseshoe and Holly, Sand Canyons, Castle Rock, and Saddlehorn—all in two days. On the trail to Painted Hand, wildflowers, blooming prickly pear patches, and desert rose bushes in delicate bloom added color and warmth to the bare rock. I followed the obvious blazes down a steep drop, through passages as narrow at the bottom as the width of my boot, to the little cave bearing the faintest of painted red hands and a constructed tower above it. Even with those red prayerful hands, the place spooked me in the middle of a beautiful spring morning, and although it was difficult to leave quickly without endangering myself, I retraced the carved stairs and scrambled up the rocks, nearly running as soon as the terrain flattened out. I rationalized I was turning back in haste because I stupidly forgot to bring any water, thinking a one-mile loop no challenge. Later, I read that these fortress hovels and towers were the sites of ruthless raids, bloody massacres, and worse: children and infants were incinerated in a tower at Castle Rock. Black on white ceramic mugs and cooking pots were found containing human DNA. Here were the cannibals, the victors eating their prey. After Chaco, 1100–1200, things deteriorated into dog eat dog in the Four Corners region. I walked trails of slaughter with a heavy heart, without knowing about traces of gnawed human bones, disarticulated skeletons buried in shallow earth. Another text rose in the riven air around me, written as a lone raven perched the Castle at Hovenweep, in the shadow of Sleeping Ute Mountain, briefly spotlighted by a shred of intense sunlight that shattered the cloud cover. Clouds lumped together and formed dark burls that never quite let loose with rain.

Mom and I ritually watch the nightly news to see if the country we have to call ours is going to drop some bombs on Syria's latest mess. She sits in her chair squinting toward the TV and releases her commentary with some spit: "I think John Kerry's got a new wife. A younger one." On screen with the sound down low, Kerry's face in bad makeup approaches the surface and color of stale bread, a puffy white protraction of old patterns: an eye for an eye, but I hope he can do better.

"I think he's had a facelift," Mom says. "I'm sick of looking at him."

In my guide booklet for Casa Rinconada, the largest excavated kiva in Chaco, I read "This is a sacred area...do not enter the kiva." Reminded that I've surveyed many sacred tribal grounds as an intruder, an *other*, I cast myself back to the Great Kiva of Pueblo Bonito, down into the mystical center of *the center place*. Why does it yet speak to me? In the back studio of this loft in Roanoke, Virginia, the daytime bat hangs quietly upside down against the window, covered by a coffee-colored, translucent solar shade. I think of Rilke's poem and yesterday's class discussion: "You must change your life." In that famous last line, there's nothing to equivocate. Releasing a bat to daylight wouldn't be kind to this creature of transitional energies. Occasionally it makes a buzzing sound and crawls a little, but basically it clings to the top of the shade. The last time I saw a bat any closer than this was in the alley, dead, and I remember one I dredged from the metal trashcan in the alley behind my house when I was a kid. I was showing proof of bat to my best friend; my father had killed it with a broom the night before as it flailed around our upstairs bedrooms having wriggled through a hole in the window screen. I can close my eyes and see its eyeteeth grinning from its bloody mouth below a little snub nose, its surprising brown fur, like that of a flying mouse, and ears nearly the size of a cat's. I want this encounter to end better between my bat and me.

We await the dusk hour to try again for release. A. has returned to help me; she and I will set this bat free. The bat must navigate by its powers of resonance, undeceived by surface appearances. It guards the gateway to new life, and all I have to do is open a clear path. Throughout this day I abide with my revved-up heart, sit with my fear. I don't ultimately know what the bat will do. Fly straight for my face? Smack the billed cap from my head that reads "Mile 0" from Key West?

Here in the kiva of my imagination, I have to dig below dunes of dirt the wind has re-deposited. Earth preserves but conceals the lower part of these previously excavated walls. What was once revealed by the hurry to reap artifacts has been sifting back to ground more slowly, but it's going; the sand will fill it in. This sacred kiva would have had a cribbed roof supported by logs, topped with juniper bark, rock, and sod. Nothing is left but the round shape of rock walls, the interior bench, the contours of ritual hearths, and the unmistakable shape of a fire pit. This half-buried place connects original dwellers of Paleolithic pit houses to the masons of such large ancient urban imagination and also to me. I too have built what I thought to be a sacred place, and I too must leave it. I have to excavate below the tops of the door openings of the kiva to find the sipapu that I know is there but cannot see. Sipapu: a small hole or indentation that signifies a portal to the under-world, a birth canal to the world before this one. This small indented open-ing threads me back to the ancestors. Whether mine or in someone else's direct line, they are this land's ancestors, and thus I hope they will adopt me. I cannot be *other* if beloved. Most of what matters in this life, most of what we cling to, is invisible.

I hope my reverence for this place makes me a part of it more than merely an appropriator: this land is my land even if it is not, but I don't sing the conqueror's song. In time, my DNA turns up even more oddities: my Spanish ancestors settled in northwestern New Mexico in the mid-eighteenth century, near the pueblos. Pueblo people and Spanish settlers farmed and fought the Apache and Comanche together. By being here, I choose it, or it chooses me, much like the bat. I wish I knew how the bat got in here, but it's with me nonetheless. Unbidden, it just appeared, conjured from a ritual death of the old into the new; a shaman's initiation can be rough stuff. Like this bat, I am learning to sense my way through dark un-familiar places and in time earn my right to heal and be healed. All of what I call myself must die away as I linger here with my possessions squirreled around me in this lofted palace, this ghost ship remembrance of the dream house love built. This is still a place from which I gaze upon the shape of my adopted Virginia valley ringed with soft mountains, eroded into rich valleys long ago. I go back to ground and throw myself into the great kiva. It's wait-ing for me.

Ridiculous, not quite sane, I'm poised atop the circular wall with all the other sunburned tourists, staring down into a deliberate round hole in the ground, below the ground-floor level, where there might have been a seed pot painted with spirals or delicate black curving lines, a spiraling plant design. I feel hard-packed ground beneath my weary muscles and bones. In A.'s abandoned studio where my new painting slowly progresses, the bat rests upside down, my prisoner, waiting for a key, a push. I lay myself down in the womb of this earth, my mother-home. I wonder again what I was digging for all those years ago in the hills of Virginia if not for simple contact of flesh to earth. And I wonder whether it's possible for me to find my way back, to follow the captive bat when it finally senses open space with the fire escape door flung wide, breaks through imaginary boundaries and soars into the night.

The Gorilla

"Can't Find My Way Home"
—song by Steve Winwood

The Onion reports that a man in Roanoke, Virginia, has lost his nightly battle with a giant gorilla. He tried to keep up his normal daytime routine for his family's sake; he fought valiantly night after sleepless night, but in the end the gorilla out-wrestled him.

May-Lily writes in an email that she cannot find connection for long because those with whom she manages to connect at an intense yoga retreat or a songwriter's festival go back to their daily lives afterwards, and what's kindled flickers, browns out too quickly. She has lost her quotidian routines through the deaths of those close to her and other dislocations. No living parents, no strong sibling or other familial bonds, no partner, no pressing job commitment.

You say, *I would love such freedom.*

She says, *I think I will have to take up drinking.* She tries to learn to drink. It goes poorly. Headaches ensue before drunkenness can take hold and distract her from feeling.

Who are we without our vast to-dos and obligations? Is every day's checklist the only thing keeping us from despair? Or does our busyness keep us from noticing ourselves? What are our selves? *I am, I am, I am.* Who am I? I am that which asks the question: *I* am asking who I am. Alienation is the state of not being at home. Descartes said, *I think therefore I am.* Sartre noticed that there were two *I's* in that sentence: bifurcation, or at least a dissonance of the I's. The 800-pound gorilla? Popeye said, *I yam what I yam.*

In the film *Gerry*, written and directed by Matt Damon and Gus Van Sant, two young men, played by Damon and Casey Affleck, set off hiking to find a landscape feature in the Argentinean desert. Seeking their own "fresh air" away from other hikers, they detour and lose their way for several days and nights without water, marooned in the remote landscape, walking an endless labyrinth. "The power of space is great, and it is always active both for creation and destruction. It is the basis of the desire of any group of human beings to have a place of their own," Paul Tillich writes. If every group needs a territory, every desert takes a sacrifice. Each young man calls the other "Gerry."

The film tries my patience with interminable shots of these actors trudging through desert terrain. No change-ups, no long shots interrupt their close-up slogging, and no close-ups interrupt the long shot operation of one Gerry when he must rescue the other Gerry from a steep-sided rock he's managed to scale but cannot climb down. In other words, low budget.

The men talk sparsely, tell each other not to cry, test their power and leadership, fail to help each other cope, help each other cope, die when they are right, live when they have been wrong about which direction to take. The dust and dirt and baking landscape dissolve the men's life forces, reducing their auras, their visible glowing blue outlines. Cloud formations roll across the land, which is jutted with rocks and jags of heartless hills. The clouds endlessly roil. In this landscape the Gerrys are lost because its features—mountain chain, ridges, gorges, ancient dried-up salt lake, red rock formations, dunes, scrub-scattered low hills—hold no meaning for them beyond a void to be conquered by their will and stamina. In *Dry Place: landscapes of belonging and exclusion* Patricia Price writes,

> The vastness could also be perceived as fearsome, much as a woman who is not bonded or constrained by male authority. And it is particularly in the uneasy eroticism of landscape construction that the instability of the coding "female" emerges. To be constructed as void is to be constructed as potentially terrifying…. Perhaps in part because of the mysterious, dangerous forces perceived to be at work on individual men in the desert, men seemed to prefer to stick together in the extreme homo-sociality that is typical of Western myth.

These lost boys navigate by the sun and recent imprecise memories of their various fruitless turnings this way and that as they force-march and backtrack in multiple wrong directions and ever more precarious circles. They do stick together, at least for a while. If the boys had any attachment to this place, they would have names for the rocks they are passing, names for the cliffs, names for the vast dune expanse; the names would tell them where they were and they would not be lost.

If they were Mojaves, tattooed and adorned with white and cobalt blue beads, each topographic feature would have a name attached to it that told a story, and the stories would provide an anchor for the men's trudging. Their steps would offer a story map and perhaps they would even retrace a geoglyph, like one of more than two hundred known to still exist in the lower Colorado region. There is no one lost when to walk a landscape is to narrate and read the map of oneself in the context of one's people.

Finally, these white boys must stop. Clouds race on, dispersing the light of morning, noon, afternoon, evening, night. The sand ripples, reforms, hardly disturbed by four heavy, now limping footsteps. Their thirst grows multidimensional; it is so encompassing, so pervasive that their thoughts desiccate like shrunken heads. Conquered by vastness, conquered by space, one Gerry appears to kill the other out of anguish or mercy. In a few more steps, just beyond this ambiguous death, a road we've forgotten that cuts through the vastness offers dust trails of traffic, rescue to the lone survivor. This road is literally just over the hill.

For a spell the phrase "space of time" obsessed me. My interpretation of this phrase was a visceral measure of time/space issuing from time. In the phrase I sought relief from entrapment in space and time through crossing their axes. "Existing means being finite or being in time and space," writes Tillich. Ah, but "space of time" offered me something quite different, perhaps release from the wheel. I saw the phrase everywhere. In literature, particularly, I believed it was pointing toward the space-time continuum.

Even in the works of Gertrude Stein, I managed to find the phrase "space of time." I wrote a long prose poem pondering the idea of remembering the landscape of the future. The future is not a place, exactly, but what is time if not a place? If the future were merely a time, we would have little use for projecting ourselves there: *there*, into the future. But where is it? As Tillich said so succinctly, "Time and space belong together: We can measure time only by space and space only in time. Motion, the universal character of life, needs time and space. Mind, which seems to be bound to time, needs only embodiment in order to come to existence, and consequently it needs space." He goes on to remark upon the tension between the two: "Human soul and human history, to a large extent, are determined by the struggle between space and time." Eventually, his God conquers space through time. I'm still trying to grasp whether his God is mine.

My remembering is an action of mind demanding space. We humans can remember little without spatial orientation for our thoughts. The house of memory is populated with gloves, umbrellas, and all manner of odd things to correspond to the names of other things: to remind us of appointments, a giant calendar marked with odd symbols appears; chairs set around a dinner table keep our guests' names organized for easy recall. Each object placed in our house of memory prompts a connection that might otherwise be lost.

What happens if I say, instead of "space of time," *time of space*? I'm not sure.

I just remembered I left my red checkbook in a drawer, in the lobby of the building where I live. Because I tucked my checkbook out of sight I forgot it yesterday in the five minutes it took me to take the recycling around the corner to the trash alley. Why did I remember my checkbook this morning while doing something unrelated six stories up? I need it *now*. Now that I've remembered it, I need it with some urgency, though it was forgotten hours ago. I shuffle into the elevator wearing my sock monkey slippers. As I descend six floors to the lobby, I think that I should always have my phone with me, even inside the building, in case the elevator gets stuck. I would be here in my pajamas and sock monkeys with uncombed hair and a thirst for coffee. I circle back to the point in time where (when?) I stuffed the red checkbook in the drawer. I open the drawer: the red checkbook is where I left it. But I cannot reclaim the hours passed. In point of fact, I am about twelve or fifteen hours older. Over the gargantuan knock-off furniture hangs a horrendous mirror—hung so high that it only reflects the lobby's brass chandelier. If I jump up and down I catch the reflection of the top of my head, severing it from my face; I can only see a wisp of hair flapping. This morning, I do not jump. No dislocations of self from self, please, none this early in the day. I, and my attending monkeys, ride the elevator back up to the coffee pot without incident.

When Jesus said (in Matthew, Mark, and Luke), "Take up your cross and follow me," either he meant everyone must bear up under a personal crucifixion, a symbolic death of the self, or he meant that everyone must die to the world as they know it to know him. The lady, or the tiger.

In Roman times, carrying one's cross was a humiliation, marking one for ridicule and harassment on the way to a certain and particularly cruel manner of public death. "Then he said to them all: 'If anyone would come after me, he must deny himself and take up his cross daily and follow me. For whoever wants to save his life will lose it, but whoever loses his life for me will save it'" (Luke 9:23-24). This passage seems clearer than simply "Take up your cross and follow me." Commentators agree that Jesus meant his path was challenging, demanding personal sacrifice in exchange for spiritual life. A ransom for my hostage soul: this makes me very nervous. I have to wonder how my soul left me so that I must buy it back. I never said, "Go if you want to, just go!" I promise I never had the opportunity to comment. If my soul left, it left in the middle of the night while I was sleeping. It fell in love with another, packed up and left behind my back.

So secretive, my soul! I have to wonder why it did not mate with me for life, like my body, even if it is "just a rooming house," as Valerie Harper said after her diagnosis of incurable cancer.

Listening to novelist Claire Messud discuss Albert Camus in Algiers, I hear that Camus's father was lost like so many others in The Great War, WWI, some months before little Albert was born. I remember pulling *A Happy Death* (*La mort heureuse*) off the Community College library shelves. The novel had just appeared in an English translation in 1972, ten years after Camus's death. It would have been his first novel had he published it in sequence. Knowing nothing of Camus or existentialism, I read the book as a young teen because the paradox of the title intrigued me and I was beginning to study French. In a scant hundred pages the main character Mersault explores the meaninglessness of his life, commits murder to gain monetary advantage, marries without love, and deliberately chooses to live in solitude. In confrontation with his own indifference, he abandons even himself and finds the self-erased happiness of a "a stone among stones" as he dies. I didn't know what to make of this plotline. It impressed me in a puzzling way. When I returned the book to the library, I felt vaguely furtive, as though some adult would pull me aside. The book's morals were decidedly non Main Street.

I lived in a very small (dry) town during my middle and high school years, and from time to time I glimpsed my reputation being constructed as suspect from evidence of my studiousness and "exotic" looks. I wouldn't flatter myself, but recently I was stopped in my mom's assisted living facility by someone whose brother was several years behind me in high school and who reported to her that my looks—Heinz 57 of Europe—were thought exotic. Only in Southwest Virginia. I enjoyed books and writing, acting, music, and art. My intellectualism and artsy-ness (introverts, watch your back!) branded me precocious in other ways, but I was not. I had decided that my happiness lay in getting out of town for college, not in getting laid. I idealized college as a haven for bookworm bohemians, so I made a project to avoid any untoward contact with anything that might slow me down, such as teenaged guys and their equipment. Around me high school girls were dropping out as their bellies swelled. This was better tolerated by most of the townsfolk than a teen girl's reading of existentialist novels. After *A Happy Death*, I checked out *The Stranger*.

Frankenstein mirrors the alienation of its writer, Mary Wollstonecraft Godwin Shelley, a teenaged home wrecker, mother and wife. Her mother, a champion of women's rights, died giving birth to her. Her husband's abandoned first wife jumped in the river. Sin and redemption, high drama, life and death wound together. Into this atmosphere a reconstructed brainchild of a scientist was given life from lightning on the page and named *vile, hideous, murderous, monster*. No creature on earth was ever as lonely, the monster rants to his depressed maker.

The monster, reviled of men, seeks knowledge through observation of humans. Autodidact once he learns to read, the monster educates himself with *Paradise Lost* and thereby glimpses the mercy of God, who supported his creation, Adam, generously and made no creature without a mate. Obviously rejected by this God, the monster comes to identify more with Milton's Satan. Once "evil...become[s] [his] good," he unleashes his scourge upon his maker and all human representatives who would exclude and doom him to an alienation even worse than Satan's, for even Satan had friends, "fellow-devils." The monster also studies *The Sorrow of Young Werther* but does not choose Werther's suicide exit from the love triangle, instead pledging that he will be with the scientist who made him on his wedding night. (Hmmm.)

All of this havoc clearly stems from the monster's rejection at birth on the basis of his looks. Victor Frankenstein turned in horror from his creation once it breathed: he had made an ugly baby and blamed the baby. Baby turned bad, lashing out at dad who would neither love him nor make another to love him, a female monster who might lend him comfort. A race of monsters? Victor considers his options but decides he cannot be responsible for more evil than he's already authored. One wonders why he cannot design a spayed mate or neuter his monster. Maybe it was impossible for the author of *Frankenstein* to imagine a marriage without issue, even when her own birth had meant her mother's death, or perhaps especially when that fact lay at the center of her existence. Author Mary, having pushed her readers' suspension of disbelief so far as to reanimate corpses, could not imagine providing the monster companionship and also birth control or sterility. Mary had stolen someone else's husband through a pregnancy, perhaps feeling her powerful fate in progeny. How fitting that this monster *Frankenstein* would be the issue for which she is known.

Robotic penguin undercover agents, penguin imposters, live among the real flock, filming them from within their society in *Waddle All the Way*. How many of us are faking a waddle while collecting data on *real* humans? We have penetrated human society with our robotic simulacrum hearts and at the same time we live apart, isolated, closeted, or defeated. "Charm school dropout" reads the T-shirt my colleague dons periodically. But about charm I'm not speaking; I'm talking instead about the ties that bind us one to another. What is it that relaxes us into ourselves, making us really real, as in authentic? Do we need to have the fur nearly rubbed off of us first, like the Velveteen Rabbit? What if we're not lovable enough to become really real, and our lack of reality or authenticity hinders our feeling loved? Catch 22 me. Twist me in the wind.

I take a moment to sign in to Facebook and scroll through what is called "home." I see a picture post of an eighteen-wheeler bearing a giant image of Jesus in flowing hair and robes: *The Lord's Closet*. Well, Lord, come on *Out! Live proud!*

Incident with Gorilla Glue: The shiny, twirling door hook dumps the pajamas onto the floor. This happens without ceremony when no one is looking. It doesn't matter that these here designer hooks were expensive and their assemblage involved an interior piece of plastic held by one screw onto which the fancy chrome hook snapped. By installing three of these hooks, A. and I learned that the solid doors we ordered actually were not; the screws found something like cardboard to connect with inside the doors. At any rate, the designer hooks snapped into place, and I forgot that we had reframed the hooks as merely decorative until many months later when a guest found a lump of pajamas on the bathroom floor below a hook turned upside down, captured by gravity.

What to do? Cry, of course, after the guests have gone. Cry now, more than three years after my aunt Glade died. The day it happened, though, I couldn't cry because I was too stunned to be back in her nursing home room, standing beside her bed only twenty-five minutes after having left her there alive. I couldn't cry then, with her body before me, so there, and she so not. Instead I gathered up a few things I thought might disappear if I left them for even a day: her cell phone, glasses, a few books, her watch, loose change, and the M&M dispenser she kept for her helpers to help themselves.

I pried apart the weak hook assembly and pondered my predicament for a few days. The interior plastic piece didn't fit flush to the door but beveled up on little ledges. It befuddled me, a maintenance crew of one: what a wonderful opportunity to cast blame. In *When Things Fall Apart*, Pema Chödrön retells the story of the Buddha's assault by the forces of Mara. As Buddha sat under a tree "on the night on which he was to attain enlightenment...the story goes that they shot swords and arrows at him, and that their weapons turned into flowers." But Chödrön's explanation of this story kills me: "Whether we experience what happens to us as obstacle and enemy or as teacher and friend depends entirely on our perception of reality. It depends on our relationship with ourselves." Of course I am no Buddha. At first I despaired, but I grew in determination that I could or ought to be able to fix all broken things by myself, alone. After all, I have Gorilla Glue. I decided that I ought to be able to surmount my difficulty with a few refined drops, careful realignment of the plastic part onto the door, and a stiffly pressured thirty-second hold of chrome over plastic. I dried my hot tears. This I could do. For good measure, I screwed in the old useless screw and spun it around and around with the Phillips head screwdriver. I left the scene for twenty-four hours while the glue did its thing, and then with mustered confidence I snapped the fancy hook over its plastic base now flush and tight, better than new. Bring it on, hang a wet towel: I am the guru of glue.

The oldest DNA in North America comes from a baby buried more than 12,000 years ago in Montana who is related to a culture in Clovis, New Mexico. The baby was honored in death with many relics and a coating of red ocher. There's delicacy and dignity in the manner of burial. This Moses has come a long way, floating down river to tell us something about being a blessed son or daughter and then to confirm the ancestry of tribal peoples, tracing them back across the vanished land bridge. First peoples were probably already of mixed descent, East Asian and Eurasian. History conquers space. Displacement, though tragic, brings us the God of justice and redemption, while the gods of space wage endless wars. This baby has found a way around to point toward home.

Snow day extraordinaire and with it a suspension of schedules and expectations, Olympics on the tube, glowing blue from Sochi. As workers struggle to keep the snow hard packed for tricks, throwing down salt and water for Olympic skiers, I settle beneath a local blizzard in Roanoke, Virginia. Out the windows there is nothing but a whiteout, blowing layer upon layer. In my pantry, one dose left of designer hot chocolate. *Lucky, lucky, lucky,* like Sigourney Weaver in *Alien.* I also have a cinnamon stick and one remaining orange for zest. The movement of driving flurries against a dull backdrop of no visibility brings the tallest building in downtown Roanoke into an odd close-up through weather distortion. I can just see the pyramid peak of the twenty-some-story bank building as it takes on a layer of snow. Soon the copper roof will be coated solid white. With a lightning-rod antenna sticking out its pyramid top and nothing but snow swirling the air between here and there, it looks like the triangle crowning the building is dangling from a taut rope, a magic rope that has nothing holding it from above. Whole triangles of snow have been known to break from this roof and cascade after sun heats the metal. The avalanche could kill someone.

I woke in the night to the train hauling double-decker containers, and on the street a snow blower, as faithful workers tried their strength against the blizzard-blocked sidewalks of the government building across the way. With shovels and blower, they cleared a footpath that steadily filled up behind them, and then they gave up. A great quiet dropped over the city, and I fell back asleep as the storm socked us in.

This morning, I can hardly squeeze out the door sideways. Attacking the ice with my shovel brings me awareness of my aching ribcage and hip. I've torqued up my running routine to half-marathon training. The goal race is still months away, but no heroics—I'm just making sure the front door will open against the accumulating ice, making sure I can get back inside after my mission across the bridge to check on Mother. I stow the shovel and walk into a weird white world, unable to discern any edges, my footing unsure and glasses stung with fierce frozen bees.

Mother looks up from her book. "Gosh, I didn't expect to see you to-day! You didn't drive, did you?"

"I walked. How are you?"

Trudge, trudge, retracing. I could really use some snowshoes, but I make it back across the bridge. Another day winds to an end with nearly constant snow until, at dusk, it drizzles to a half-hearted stop. Then out of gray mist the yolk of the moon breaks open the clouds, and my heart opens wide, resonating, falling through the sky.

Invisible Cities

After stepping into harnesses and belay clips, we drop through a square manhole, and descend a wobbly well-rusted service ladder in Piazza del Popolo, to slog around beneath the center of Todi, a hill town in Umbria. We are heading in the direction of the bowels of the Basilica San Fortunato. Our few scattered LED headlamps blip limestone walls of the Etruscan, Roman, and Medieval-improved cistern system, five kilometers of passages, tunnels, and five hundred wells, drained now but still sucking our shoes into thick cold mud. Here, stuck in mud, the historical narrative begins in Italian and ends in English, passing quickly voice to ear, voice to ear, echoing so that I miss half of what we're learning. As usual, it's hard to tell what the lesson is.

Furnaces stoked by servants fearing for their lives provided hot water and piped in floor heating to those living in splendor above. It's an old story. When we rip below strata to the subconscious layers, we arrive where we departed—in a structure of haves and have-nots. Living in proximity to del Duomo, the highest point, still provides a measure of wealth or clout. I'm not claustrophobic, exactly, but when presented with an opportunity to descend lower into this damp anthill, after we've crept through a couple of dank chambers, I decide I'd rather not slither feet first with ragged rock clawing my back. Instead, I wait with Alison and one of her reluctant students in the intermediary muck while the rest of her brave band explores with our spirited guide Frederico, or Berro as he says to call him.

Sitting in self-imposed timeout, I feel like a child with the large plastic hardhat seeking equilibrium on my head, strapped tighter than a toothache with the interior sizing strip. Some miner I'd make. More like the fragile canary we hope is chirping in its cage. I haven't worn one of these plastic hardhats since inspecting the loft while it was under construction. And going farther back in time, it's been quite a few years since I tried rappelling into Southwest Virginia saltpeter caves. The thought of gunpowder components lends no comfort at this precise underground juncture, nor does remembrance of belly-crawling through the tunnels of my youth. Our guide Berro bellows in a voice from the grave, taunting Alison about her refusal to venture deeper into his slime hole. I'm not sure what he is saying, but in their comedic back and forth Alison sounds somewhat amused when not feigning horror; I am certain I understand the drift when she shouts back to him in Italian perfecto that there is no chance in hell she's going to slither through the sluice. It is difficult if not impossible not to think of Dante's *Inferno*.

Before I came over, I got a note from Alison in which she called Todi "home." Surely she did not mean this exact spot. She's been before, she says; she crawled through the mouth of hell on her belly last year and feels no need for a repeat. Admirable, I think, but I am not going. I will never know what lies beyond this room, in the labyrinth of manmade burrows beneath the hillside that cleverly follows the topography. I don't care. Calling this dungeon a *room* is more than generous. It's like a crypt straight out of Poe's "The Pit and the Pendulum": "I was sick—sick unto death with that long agony; and when they at length unbound me, and I was permitted to sit, I felt that my senses were leaving me." The tight interior band of my hardhat puts the squeeze on my brainpan. I feel queasy, blood pressure alert. What kind of a silly word is that? *Queasy*, I think, and then my headlamp goes out.

"Kublai Khan does not believe everything Marco Polo says when he describes the cities visited on his expeditions, but the Emperor of the Tartars does continue listening...." Thus opens *Invisible Cities* by Italo Calvino. "Only in Marco Polo's accounts was Kublai Khan able to discern, through the walls and towers destined to crumble, the tracery of a pattern so subtle it could escape the termites' gnawing." This "tracery of a pattern" must be the stuff of language itself and the structures that underpin it. This nonmaterial, perhaps numinal yet enduring pattern escapes the termites' destruction.

The physicist David Bohm has theorized that there is a visible and an invisible universe, an enfolded or invisible realm running parallel to the unfolded or visible one. The enfolded universe gives rise to what is unfolded or visible, lending it form; ideas and values must precede what is manifest and finally hold more true power than things seen.

Calvino typically states contradictions with authority. In *Invisible Cities*, he writes that "[t]here is no language without deceit," and also "[f]alsehood is never in words; it is in things"; each statement offers a truth, the first about language and the second about things. Side by side, these statements coexist on different planes of understanding, only false in relation to each other; both are true.

❧

I am invisible...because people refuse to see me. For whom are lesbian writers invisible, or, as Kay Ryan wrote of poems, where does the work of lesbian writers experience "the brief visibility of the invisible"? For whom is lesbian writing visible? Why should it matter? *How, beginning in absence, erasure or negation, do we raise this alienated writing to an art?*

A friend of mine laughs, remembering having ordered the book *Eye to Eye: Portraits of Lesbians* by JEB in the early1980s "just to see what they looked like." To see what we looked like; I, too, remember the importance of that book. A lesbian writer and lesbian writing can reflect, change, perhaps save lives. Mid-twentieth-century lesbian pulp, despite its dubious target audience and sometimes authorship, contributed positively to the formation of lesbian identity and culture. As Yvonne Keller writes,

> The 1950s were a time when most lesbians could not access any stories about themselves, much less positive ones, since lesbianism was mostly invisible in popular culture. When it was conceptualized at all in the 1950s, homosexuality was a crime, sin, or illness; many homosexuals thought of themselves as "flawed individuals" or people with "a homosexual problem." In this difficult context, lesbian pulps were in the phrase of Joan Nestle, "crucial 'survival literature.'"

Almost seventy years later, literature depicting heterosexual romantic relationships is still considered universal, but literature that depicts romance between two men or two women or any other fluid two is narrowly specific, presumed for an audience of same-oriented readers. Gay and lesbian writers often become the subject themselves, instead of their work. *In any discussion of art and the artist, heterosexuality is backgrounded, whilst homosexuality is fore-grounded. What you fuck is more important than how you write.* It's not only the literature that must survive; it's also the writers who must survive outside of the mainstream privilege of being heard: *whatever words come out of the lesbian's mouth, whatever ideas sprout from her head—certain listeners hear only one thing: lesbian, lesbian, lesbian.*

In my Valletta apartment up five flights of stairs above the historic Maltese theater, I flip through pages, looking for a way to entertain myself past nine o'clock at night in this ninety-nine percent Catholic country fraught with competing church bells. In Lord Byron's "A Farewell to Malta," which could as easily have been titled a good riddance to the same, he characterizes Valletta as a city of "stairs, smells and bells." Keeping in mind his clubfoot, I imagine the steps probably were a giant hassle. I cheerfully extend Byron's salutary list to snares, yells, and drills, as the charming historic theater where my apartment and two others occupy the top floor constantly erupts with construction noise, except on Sundays when the proximate bell towers ring like canon fire dawn to dusk. I tell myself it's only for a month.

Hermes has been quite active on this journey, erasing flights and causing interminable layovers. I find little to quell boredom once I reach Malta, outside of ruins, cups of espresso, the flickering Internet, olive oil-soaked bread, and roasted or raw vegetables covered with chopped garlic and again lots of olive oil. I visit the nearby Internet café to consult Wiki on Hermes and learn his familiars are turtles, a favorite of mine, and cocks, decidedly not. Hermes, god of travelers and all who cross borders, including writers and artists: now we're getting to the heart of the matter. Promises of introduction to Maltese artists and poets never materialize, so I spend the better part of most days on long bus rides bouncing toward or away from various sites I must see. Some days I have a companion, an experimental filmmaker, preoccupied and moody, who breathes through his camera as if it were a ski mask. I can't complain. It is interesting to roam among stones and slabs overcome with scents of purple blooming thyme and feel past and present energies converge on promontories overlooking the sea. On other days there are catacombs. An audio guide at St. Paul's catacombs asks the question, "Am I buried here?" The female voice posits this question every time I descend stone steps to yet another chamber. The recording finally concludes that *she*, of course, cannot be buried here because her station is too lowly.

The settings of most temple ruins, Hagar Qim and Mnajdra, as well as Ggantija on Gozo, claim the best views of surrounding land and ocean. From Mnajdra's perch I gaze out into frightening deep blue water to the tiny isle of Filfla, which appears serene until I learn that it was used for target practice during WWI and is still pitted with unexploded munitions. While the filmmaker darts here and there with his camera shielding his face, crone that I am, I make my way silently to Mnajdra's oracle room, bend down to the blowhole to hear a pronouncement from the chamber. But nothing reaches me. The longish days unravel and pass. When Italian-dubbed episodes of *The Simpsons* stop rerunning at the restaurant where I take my evening meal and my daily dose of wine, sometimes with the moody filmmaker who vaguely reminds me of my father, I retreat to my apartment up the many flights of hideous stairs into American mass-market fiction. The filmmaker eventually becomes friendlier and lends me some Carl Hiaasen paperbacks. It occurs to me that it is oddly true that paper can last longer than people, and perhaps it is even better to write on stone. For a bilingual country, there is precious little English-scrawled paper available. I open yet another Hiaasen thriller set in the wilds of the Florida Everglades and wish I had splurged and packed a reading device for some variety.

Beneath Todi's old butcher shop a pile of discarded bones grew for a hundred years, filling the dark stagnant cistern until a party of scuba divers startled upon them as onto a crime scene. Gradually these chambers were drained of water, cleared of butchered bones, and archaeologists began to map them. We can hear laughter echoing from beyond the pizza-oven-shaped opening five feet below us that connects to another room, and beyond it to still others. In Alison's absence, Berro has forgone his native tongue for Spanish, and his Spanish turns into English through one of the student's quick translations. Then a silence of concentration ensues. Reborn to us, each student scoots through the opening that's barely wider than her shoulders, barely taller than a head with a large Roman nose. And lastly returns our Berro, who notices my equipment failure and easily switches my headlamp back on.

With slime and mud slathered over bare summer legs and a smattering of oozing scratches where rocks ensnared flesh, our reconfigured group files back to the first chamber, acclimated now to slurping mud. One by one we climb the rickety ladder to street level to blink in sunlight. Tourists and their fidgeting children overtake us, keen to journey into the dark. We explain that these guides in red jumpsuits, one stationed above ground with a safety rope tied to a tiny car bumper and our Berro below, both friends of Alison's, are not for general hire.

From the top of our street with my land legs wavering, walking steeply down toward the Port of Perugia, one of four entry/exit points through the encircling Todi walls, I stop to consider the ancient well I've been passing without a thought. I lean to peer into its depths, to tap a divination, but bright reflection blocks my eyes from penetrating the surface. Long ago I could have drawn up water, tapped from the table and softened by rains. Today I drop Euro coins through the bolted iron grate with a wish to return to Todi, sending ripples across my own image.

≈

Emperor Kublai Khan and his highly favored explorer Marco Polo enact the complex relationship of reader and writer as they recreate language and the world, moving their conversation from gesture and pantomime to emblematic object, then into words and finally into story, in order to capture the cities of the world that signal Kublai Khan's vast empire. The empire, like the chess game with which they gradually become obsessed, exists between them as imaginary territory. Their fates intertwine with that of the empire as first one and then the other tries to capture it with description. Eventually, as the novel's opening paragraph states, their attempts to describe the empire are what render it real. By their words they lend the empire substance. Neither emperor nor explorer—reader nor writer—can render reality without the aid of the other. Every teller needs a listener, but this is not a simple active/passive binary.

When I lived for a time in the granary near Lexington, I witnessed swarmers flying out of the eight-by-eight support beams. What were these flying things? I had my suspicions but assumed that termites only wriggled around unseen inside wood, secretly gnawing the interior life, leaving only a semblance, a shell waiting to collapse. I had seen what termites could do, hidden behind thin scrims of seemingly perfect wood in a paneled room in my aunts' house. Perhaps it took years, but termites were thorough fanatics; they would leave nothing in their wake even if the project took them generations and eliminated all of their housing and food stocks in the process. By comparison, these clouds of weird bi-winged fliers buzzing the air, helicopter pilots lacking precision, seemed somewhat flippant. But indeed, I learned they were termite children seeking the light. With large double wings of equal length and bodies shaped like belted capsules, they were as icky as any flying ant. Though unlike flying ants they didn't have tripartite bodies.

In the middle of winter on a warm sunny day, they woke up spontaneously and swam en masse into the air toward the large row of kitchen windows. I had covered all of these windows with plastic, tightened with the heat of a hair dryer, to make cheap interior storm windows. The glass had been recycled from a Victorian house in Richmond's Fan district, leaving a few historic gaps. The thousands of released wings made a sound like loudly beating hearts as they drummed the plastic sheeting and failed to find purchase. Just enough give in the plastic created waves that pitched and pissed the critters off when they all tried to sucker their feet and grip at once. Watching them, I felt sorry for myself and then speed-dialed my lady of the lands to inform her that flying insects were invading her rental house.

Nonplussed, my landlady appeared with a spray can that drove me, and my cat, into the back bedroom. It felt as though the landlady were actually spraying me, not the bugs. Admittedly, I could be considered a demanding tenant. After a few hours the swarmers' great release and migration ceased, and even their great dying had peaked and trickled. I swept them up in piles. Yet nothing about it felt truly over. I stood vigil, waiting for the next infestation. Vigilance is always rewarded, I've found, but it ruins the time between onslaughts. I didn't have long to wait before a wave of copperheads arrived, and when they did the spray can was of little use.

The long winding stairs into the St. James Center from Valletta street level are spaced wide so that horses could gallop up and down. I can imagine this place, a fortress to deter invaders, filled with the sound of clanging armor and deafening hooves as I spill out and grab hold of the banister after watching a film. Beneath the castle and beneath these streets, I've heard there is another city mirroring this one, into which the ingenious Knights of St. John could vanish completely, confounding enemies, usually Turks or versions of the Turks. After the last Grand Master was double-crossed and beheaded in France would have been such a time. I am not sure whether this city beneath the city, invisible city with miles of passages, is myth or fact. The Knights of St. John, cast to this isle south of Sicily by a pope, built Valletta and, if it exists, the city below it.

The Turks, whose passing ships the Knights could not seem to stop raiding, tried to stop the Knights' plunder by conquering them, finally winning a horrendous battle in which the Knights rained St. Elmo's fire down on them, boiling the invaders ablaze in oil as they scaled port ladders into the fortressed capital city. Hundreds of Turks fell like meteorites and sizzled, screaming, into the salty sea. The Turks won by human sacrifice and yet abandoned Malta afterward, demoralized by the number of their casualties and the viciousness of the Knights, who incidentally had begun as a nursing order—thus the Red Cross on their flag—but evidently had discarded their compassion entirely for the might of the sword and boiling oil. The Knights did not cease pirating for long, either. They broke the terms of their surrender in a few short seasons to resume plundering the Turks' passing ships.

What does the sexual orientation of a character or of a writer serve to indicate? What is lesbian writing? Was Alice Walker's *The Color Purple* (1992) more or less lesbian than Dorothy Alison's *Bastard Out of Carolina* (1992), which contains no explicitly lesbian material but whose writer identifies as such? Is it lesbian because the author is or because the content is? How I wish I could skirt this issue by saying we are all beyond it.

The editors of the reference *Gay, Lesbian, Bisexual, and Transgendered Literature: A Genre Guide* describe the situation this way:

> Much debate surrounds the question of what constitutes GLBT literature. Is a work considered GLBT literature simply because the author identifies as a member of the queer community? ...GLBT literature exhibits the same characteristics that all other literature does, but what distinguishes it are sexual and gender orientation or identity and voice. The authors assert that this identity is so central to the literature that it qualifies these works as a genre.

Stephanie Foote concurs:

> Authorship's relationship to the lived identity of the writer has a special intensity for almost all writing by minority subjects who recognize themselves in a marginal relationship to major literary traditions. This is not simply because they are who they are but because for them the literary sphere is not a disinterested sphere of communication. Rather it is a sphere in which interested social actors make claims against and for normativity.

There is, however, often a defining characteristic of this literature, which begins with the word "unfortunately": "Unfortunately, the myth that gay or lesbian content renders a work obscene persists. Books with homosexual content consistently top the American Library Association's (ALA) list of most challenged works...including a children's book, based on a true story, about gay penguins—clearly neither obscene nor pornographic." What is literary or mainstream writing and what is obscenity? Many gay modern writers have tried to pass by disguising the gender of characters or recasting their longings as heterosexual cisnormal. How can mainstream writing contain protagonists of non-normative sexual orientations and identities for an audience of all orientations without being labeled obscene? Is this possible only if the material is kept light and amusing, as in TV sitcoms?

If wishes were horses, writers of various identities would ride equal acclaim. How I wish I didn't have to proclaim what I am. Here's what I am: ally to every outsider. Does knowing the sexual identity and the ethnicity of the writer change the way you read what's written and change what you think of what you read? I am not really asking. Pop quiz: Name as many lesbian characters as you can in literary fiction or mainstream fiction of the past twenty years. Name as many American lesbian writers of mainstream fiction that incorporates unmistakable lesbian characters as you can. Hint: YA literature is miles ahead.

Must the marginalized judge success by the extent of our literary products' assimilation into commodity culture, evinced by literary prize culture and thus visibility? Do the measures of success attained by a few representatives render them blind to the general case? It seemed so when I moderated a panel on lesbian writing a few years ago and the most conventionally successful queer writer in the room defended the system. Does the success of a few render the rest unacknowledged by default, as in, we have our two gays and lesbians at the trough? Do we therefore need other means to assess the impact of our art? Evidence of non-assimilation: we have our own prizes to hand out. Can the writing survive assimilation? Will the writing survive without assimilation? How do invisible writers survive? How do writers survive invisibility? This should not be a competition among those who are regularly excluded, nor should it be another area of pale-skinned masculinist control.

Memo issued by straight male reviewers: please send me an artistic work by a no-more-than-thirty-year-old available woman with long hair.

How can we in good conscience assign lesbians to the ranks of the post-queer, tripping from unmentionable (buried, invisible, silent) to irrelevant (re-buried, invisible, silenced), without ever having acknowledged the works? How can the problem be summarily over? What a relief! We never had to look at all. (Oh, even greater relief—a new section starts after the break. Stop your sobbing.)

Long before the apostle Paul's shipwreck hit the rock of Malta, by best calculations between 5200–4000 BC, primitive Sicilian farmers strapped together wooden rafts and floated over to a string of three teeny islands, the largest of which was only a fraction of Sicily's size. Malta also offered only a fraction of the amount of inland fresh water and rainfall they'd left behind, but we're told that they rafted over in order to build megalithic structures dating from the Temple period, 4000–2500 BC. Some of these structures they hand carved into living rock several stories below the surface using only obsidian blades. If you can accept this, you probably do not subscribe to alien architectural theories. Then, like the Chacoans, these ancient folks migrated away in time for the Bronze Age (2500), leaving behind more than two dozen temples and burial sites that would last into the twenty-first century. The next group of Maltese shipped in from ancient Phoenicia.

Beneath a neighborhood outside the center of Valletta, Malta, an underground cave structure known as the Hal Saflieni Hypogeum, carved out from 3300–3000 BC, was discovered at the turn of the twentieth century because of suburban expansion. Built over three hundred years, it's as if someone in a tri-cornered hat (1776), brocaded cutaway coat, white hose and buckled shoes began a building project that someone dating a lady in bustles, ruffles, and drapery continued (1876) and handed down to someone in bell-bottoms (1976), who then made a few adjustments to the plan verbally, since nothing had ever been written down, before leaving the work to be completed by robots (2076). To say the least, it is now hard if not impossible to imagine anything like a society consistent enough in aims and goals to bring such a project to completion over as many generations.

In 1902 a number of new cisterns damaged the subterranean structure of the Hypogeum, whose entrance was probably cleared by heavy earth-moving equipment before the historical site was reported to authorities and came under curatorial government protection. Though caverns are an extensive and common geological feature of Malta, these particular caves showed human activity in a beautiful and purposeful way: coordinated, aesthetic construction over hundreds of years. Carved out in a series of rounded alcoves, the Hypogeum replicates the design of above-ground temples, complete with columns, archways, and painted plaster walls. The subterranean Hypogeum is like an invisible root system, a branching reflection beneath the visible portion of a great tree. Its purpose was probably for burials, but it looks more like an underground theater set with giant lintels carved into living rock along with intricately spiral-painted walls decorated with murals of delicate ochre designs. Light funnels into these underground rooms through a series of strategic portals, ancient light tubes, to illuminate various stage-like spaces.

The limestone walls seep moisture, as a few visitors a day who have made a reservation weeks in advance tread a solemn path through the designated interior rooms several stories below the sidewalks. I feel the air go not exactly stale but tinny and thin with cold, close to the brittle taste of blood's iron on the tongue when fear sets you running. Mold threatens to slowly destroy the marvels. Breath, my breath and the breathing of others, who like me want to see, causes slicks of green to spread on the walls. I sign the waiver that says I won't make a claustrophobic scene while walking single file along the damp dirt trail winding through contours of bowl-shaped rooms. But do I really know myself well enough to promise I won't have a panic attack? I've already jotted my name. I step forward, fall in line with people from every point on the globe.

The most famous Maltese artifact, known as The Sleeping Lady and synonymous with the country itself, was unearthed here from a wall alcove burial site. Before visiting the Hypogeum I'd already seen her and fallen deeply in love. She resides under glass at the National Museum illumined by reverentially dim light in a room of other glass cases, none containing anything as important. Her compact reclined figure, less than a foot long, is intricately carved. This sleeping goddess with a styled head of hair lies upon a pillow, plump sleeping arms supporting her side slumber, with the fringe of her dress modestly draped over the mounds of her thighs.

For twenty-five years give or take in northern New Mexico, Ra Paulette has been busy digging out dwellings or sacred spaces in sandstone hills. "Sometimes I feel more like an archaeologist," he says, "uncovering something that's already there." Alone with his dog, he estimates he's dug the sandstone about 900 hours and counting. Dug it with hand tools only—shovels, a mattock, and scrapers capable of smoothing sandstone into a surface that looks like marble. In juxtapositions of columns, soaring arches, skylights, and smallish rooms with curved walls covered in relief patterns that look as if they have been molded and then released, he is hoping to "open up people's feelings" with something he calls "the cave effect." Paulette's intimate cathedrals of intricately designed surfaces recall the imagination of Antoni Gaudí's Sagrada Familia. Like Gaudí, he's making "wonder," and then he's moving on.

～

"One path goes into the mental space of...abstract forms, vectors of force. The other path goes through a space crammed with objects and attempts to create a verbal equivalent of that space...," Calvino writes of two divergent paths in language in "Exactitude." Perhaps this can be more simply stated: There are words to approximate the world of ideas and words to approximate the world of things. Where do these word-worlds converge? *Invisible Cities* contains interpolated passages of abstract conversation and passages describing the cities themselves, but neither sort of section is purely one thing or the other: both owe their existence to words. One might say that through things ideas are realized and through readers texts are completed, but Calvino delves further. In the course of bringing the emperor stories or news of his empire, Marco Polo learns to speak the Khan's native Tartar language. This would seem essential for their communication; however, once this occurs their relationship becomes strained and "words fail." Their communication, which at first appeared limited by the exchange of gestures and emblematic objects, expands into word pictures, but when it does Marco Polo cautions Kublai Khan that possession of the emblems of his empire will mean death: "On that day you will be an emblem among emblems." The Khan's grasping, acquisitive nature has the capacity to render him unreal.

An enduring truth, that the shaping of individual experience takes place in the corridors of power, was driven home to me a few years ago when I managed to wreck my car at dusk on a Black Angus cow. The hindquarters of the cow blended perfectly with the color of the asphalt, thus I never saw it until too late: a cow innocently munching grass with its ass in the road. My first thought was that I'd hit the monolith featured in *2001: A Space Odyssey*. This really was my first thought.

The "farmer," a recent suburban transplant, owned only two decorative cows. When I was upset at the fate of car and cow, he told me, "That's what insurance is for." Roughly translated, I suppose he meant that an insurance policy was capable of enacting a double resurrection. As it turned out, it would be my insurance not his; my agent informed me with a sigh that taking the cow's owner to court in Virginia would be futile. Gentlemen farmers had written the laws quite a while back with generous exceptions for wandering livestock, which was to be treated like an act of god under what was well known to my agent as the "cows will get out once in a while" clause, which remained in effect even if farmers neglected to mend their fences. The poor cow was going to stay dead, but the legal interpretation of events shaped the rest of the outcome: the non-collision side of my coverage was invoked; I paid the $500 deductible and accepted the insurance company's compensation for my totaled car, which had just been in the shop for major service at 60,000 miles and shod with four new tires. With borrowed thousands added to my insurance bundle, I could buy a new car, lucky me.

Despite this drama's unfolding as I recovered from having a bad patch of skin scooped out of my leg, and as my father lay dying in the hospital following a car wreck, I did feel somewhat lucky. The monolith had not fallen. The day after I picked up my new car, I drove it to my dad's funeral.

My father in the role of lieutenant commander and chief communication's officer was on the other side of the world in 1944–45, in the South Pacific Theater, dodging the Japanese fleet around obscure islands, choppy seas. After this chapter, he maintained little use for the British Isles and Europe, never taking my mother to Paris or London, either of which she would have liked to visit. He always sailed west or south and stopped short of a full rotation. During WWII Malta was especially well placed for misery and nearly bombed back to the Stone Age by Germans fighting the English, who had occupied the island since around 1800 when the French claim folded with a mighty whimper. Malta, a tiny target of only seven by nineteen miles, was devastated by bombs.

"We don't bomb/We don't bomb," Allen Ginsberg chanted from "Hum Bom!" during the first Gulf War. A solitary figure seated upstage with the New Market Battle mural behind him in Virginia Military Institute's War Chapel, Ginsberg pressed on: "Don't bomb! Don't bomb!" Flags of many battles lined the aisles of the War Chapel. The poet worked his way through another stanza of his poem as waves of cadets awoke from their slumbers in the balcony, rose to their feet, fists pumping, and chorused back, "Bomb, bomb, bomb!"

"Human humidity," a somewhat ambiguous phrase from Nabokov, signals both escape from the bondage of nostalgic sentimentality and embrace of true compassion. A more prosaic sort of human humidity causes condensation in the Hypogeum. In our hunger to see the beautiful designs ingenious ancients carved and painted, we install lights that encourage algae to creep across the patterns they left behind. Our body temperatures will someday break these walls down to dust. The frescoes are deteriorating from the moisture of our best intentions.

Every stone ledge I see looks like a slab meant to receive a body, and there are some unambiguous crypts, burial alcoves, and freestanding hollow graves of rock that have yielded up bones. The more we observe and study the Hypogeum the more it degrades. I feel guilty because I want to see this palatial rock sculpture that thousands of hands carved. I rationalize my footsteps on the spiral path and the emissions of my breath as such small disturbances they hardly matter in the scheme of thousands of years, but the fact remains that since 1960 a thousand years of damage has occurred in an eye blink. While still buried in dry heaps, this underground trove was protected from us as well as from rain and modern plumbing pipes. My entry fee helps preserve this treasure and pay government employees, but I cannot visit without causing more damage.

An underground creek runs beneath Campbell Avenue in Roanoke, Virginia. Basements across from my building require conduits the size of small cars to channel the old stream. Several modest-sized buildings with crumbling foundations and creeping mold await renovations that may never happen because of the cost of bringing them up to code. I imagine the creek someday will reclaim the street. Someday the creek will rise.

Marco Polo's warning to the great Khan about the consequences of acquisition touches off a more pronounced power struggle between them for ownership and control through knowledge and comprehension of the empire. While Marco Polo was formerly an active explorer and the Khan a passive receptor of news of his empire, now both will participate in description. The Khan demands more influence on Marco Polo's stories by "dreaming" them first: "From now on, I'll describe the cities to you. ...in your journeys you will see if they exist." But since Kublai Khan imagines a "norm" city and Marco Polo "an exception," their cities can never match. This leads to a confrontation in the walled garden when the Khan accuses Polo, his greatest explorer, of never really having left the garden at all, of making up all his adventures, all the cities, and only journeying through his own memory. What's worse, the emperor accuses him of smuggling "moods, states of grace, elegies!" from the empire. The Khan asserts his authorship by accusing Polo of dishonesty, theft, and plagiarism.

This crisis between them, we learn, is "perhaps only imagined." The two remain suspended, "silent and motionless." Stuck without a story for a time, they begin to suspect that the world they inhabit is really a ruin, that only their eyelids separate the hanging garden from the wasteland beyond, and they "cannot know which is inside and which is outside." This breakdown of the Platonic Ideal into subjectivity leads them to sad speculation about which world, the outside or the inside, is real. They only succeed in comically disproving their own existence, yet they stubbornly remain in the garden, and the emperor becomes obsessed with the chess game, wherein mastery of the rules, he hopes, will produce mastery of his empire.

Kublai Khan clearly falls into existential despair, deciding that "nothingness," or no meaning, is at the heart of the chess game that has come to symbolize his empire. Just at that moment, though, Marco Polo teaches the emperor to go deeper into the surface information, to "read" even the game board itself for meaningful signs of the world beyond. The substance of the game board is the living tree whose whorls can still be seen.

Somewhere in Tuscany at another world heritage site, researchers in 2013 disturb the bones of a presumed Etruscan prince. They announce their findings before completing the carbon dating but eventually conclude that these bones, buried with spear and nearby bling, are those of an adult female of high station, aged into her forties.

If, as Oscar Wilde wrote in *The Picture of Dorian Gray,* "The true mystery of the world is the visible, not the invisible," I wonder how we can hope to understand much more about the visible world without our enthusiasm's erasing its mysteries, as my breath in the Hypogeum serves to destroy it. I'm drawn to sites called ruins not merely because entertainment remains scarce on the three tiny isles of Malta but also because I'm pulled to points that serve as passageways, portals into the sacred. I may be walking a labyrinth of devotion mapped out for me step by step. If so, I am blind to it, an amnesiac of any grand scheme. And yet, three years after spending my month of Maltese exile courtesy of the St. James Center for Creativity, with my mind drifting to New Mexico, I open an article on Chaco Culture written by a noted archaeologist who serves up a comparison photo of the Temple of Mnajdra, the coastal Maltese site I visited twice. Double take. I remember standing among gigantic slabs of stone reflecting on the question of why I was occupying that particular space at that time, standing *there,* as in alive. A second trip to the oracle's chamber yielded no further clarification. Time's layers intersect with me in these places. I feel empty in the edifice, baffled and silenced by the scale of the construction and its age relative to the human body. I run through all my words and want to find more technical expressions to extend the vocabulary of reverence, of hot sun, cool light, and the deep gorgeous blue Mediterranean sparkling below this high cliff temple. Connections are all I have and am.

Beneath Perugia there's a network of cisterns like the one beneath Todi, every Italian hill town touched by ancient industry is much the same. We drive the twisty road to Perugia to eat high cuisine near the city's gates, then walk from there, winding up and up to the old square after dinner, blending in with throngs from a music festival. I'm feeling the twenty years I have on everyone by the time we've milled around half an hour, my drink quotient already drunk, feet tired, and conviviality wearing as thin as fresh air with everyone puffing strong Euro-cigs. No matter, Italy is nothing if not friendly. It's difficult to stay a wallflower, on the edges of things in Italy, impossible not to be pulled into conversation with quick touches for emphasis that become easy access portals.

Marco Polo's new way of reading "overwhelms" Kublai Khan and rescues him from despair. Polo points out through his reading of the wooden chessboard the deep involvement of the world in every idea—that what we can know of the world matters, that the world is implicated in what and how we know ourselves. We can begin our search for meaning from any point, because the center is everywhere. *God is a center whose circle is everywhere.* Move anywhere you like on the chessboard; start from any square. *Act so that there is no sense in a center.* (Nelson, Carson, Stein, Cézanne, Jesus, etc.)

The relationship between writer and reader, teller/listener, subject/object gains further definition when Marco Polo tells Kublai Khan, "It is not the voice that commands the story: it is the ear." In other words, it is the listener who controls the story; the explorer reminds the emperor that he indeed holds power over the fabled cities and thus the cities themselves, yet the Khan responds by partially abdicating his power of listening: "At times I feel your voice is reaching me from far away, while I am prisoner of a gaudy and unlivable present.... And I hear, from your voice, the invisible reasons which make cities live, through which perhaps, once dead, they will come to life again." Even if our empire crumbles we can find reasons to live. The same relativism that launched despair can create meaning again; reader and writer can co-create rather than be rivals lost in an antique power struggle over one true meaning. But will they?

"Do-not-let-me-forget-my-pillow," Alison implores me and her painter-amico Chris. Anger underpins her will, and her voice carries the force of heart's injury. It's the day before we leave Todi. Chris and I lock eyes; we will not let her forget. We all know about the pillow, plucked from the cold marriage bed, house and former things passed away—all except the pillow. There's no way she will forget it. As we leave before dawn with our bags, bound for the Rome airport and the Blue Ridge Mountains beyond, Alison carries her sacred relic, her talisman. Home is something she is learning to live without, lost by hard choices. She's traveling back to her studio space, a place she can drop her bags, then on to a friend's house for a few days before launching herself into the next chapter. She boards the plane and lays her head upon the blessed pillow for the long journey into her future. But Hermes has already reared, delaying our transatlantic flight. We've spent several extra hours in Rome, long enough to feel seat-tired before boarding. Alison rebooked our connecting flight, slipping us ahead of the chain reaction that will combust thousands of travel plans when the morning sun strikes the East Coast.

A world and hours later we line up to scan everything through customs and our last security check. We run through the Charlotte airport half asleep, determined to make our Roanoke flight, and arrive winded at our gate to learn of yet another delay; our rebooked seats have mysteriously been given away. Alison arrives at the gate with tears streaming down her face.

"My pillow," she says. Her arms are open and bare.

"Go back to the checkpoint," I tell her. "You have time."

She runs back. After some long minutes she returns, trudging. *Oh, Persephone, home's not where I / thought it was. / Home is where the heart gives out and we arouse / the grass.* She cannot stop crying, explaining between gulps to the one student who's still travelling with us, headed back as are we to the hills of Virginia from the hill towns of Italy, "I don't really have a home right now. My pillow was my place."

☙

Just when their power appears almost equal, and therefore resolved, Emperor Kublai Khan reasserts himself over his explorer, and the primacy of reading over experience, by holding the atlas: "I think you recognize cities better on the atlas than when you visit them in person." Unpredictably, the greatest explorer concurs: "Traveling, you realize the differences are lost.... Your atlas preserves the differences intact: that assortment of qualities which are like the letters in a name." The atlas holds the form of cities "that don't yet have a name" alongside many cities that exist in myth and legend as well as in fact. The "invisible reasons" Kublai Khan hears in Marco Polo's stories provide him with possibilities of symbolic and metaphorical meanings imbued with moral value in "a gaudy and unlivable present," not with possession of objective truth or reality. Nevertheless, the atlas keeps the emperor and his empire intact.

At the end of *Invisible Cities* we learn that the inferno is in the visible, in what exists, not in the multiple possibilities of the invisible, and yet we know that any truth we find in Calvino's work always contains its mirror. We can find that which is *not inferno* also in the visible, if we can recognize it and give it space.

Hole through which the Power Could Come

"Anywhere is the center of the world."
—*Black Elk Speaks*

Red twine binding stale bales of hay. I want to tie it up with meaning, make it stay. Bales lining the old flatbed aren't going anywhere. I run tractor paths until they end in tall grass or hay shelters. Stop. Turn. Run back. Dodge cow patties, a scatter shot of deer droppings, and piles of dark scat studded with rich red berries, possibly from a bear. Why not just step in it, entangle my feet with what meets the earth raw, wet, and steaming? Still I dodge, almost twist an ankle, wobbling in my orbit. My eyes follow plump red hoses wound at the farm vehicle gas tanks back to the red twine. A huge bundle of twine, coiled cobra in the shed beneath the canoes. Nothing to do but follow the Yampa River, follow the string as it unravels. Box elders turn, in echo of the last strong rays of summer sun. Wind flicks their leaves, shaking out the gold.

"The wind went down and it grew very cold, so we had to keep the fire going all night. During the night I heard a whimpering outside the shelter, and when I looked, there was a party of porcupines huddled up as close as they thought they dared to be, and they were crying because they were so cold. We did not chase them away, because we felt sorry for them."

Beneath the huge spruce tree beside the Carpenter Ranch house, Outreach Manager Betsy, artist Tom, and I are scouting porcupine poop. The tree has dropped a lot of light-colored cones, which in this context we might mistake since we are looking for woody scat chunks. Like horse and cow manure, porcupine poop bears immediate witness to what the critter has consumed. I thought porcupines lived in holes, but these rodents forage for food in trees and eat bark in winter when they can't find a berry. Trees surrounding the house have been wrapped with metal sheeting to prevent porcupines from climbing and eating their bark, making these firs into upside-down antennas, conducting what's carried from the roots into the air; or maybe the trees receive some strange channel only porcupines watch. Male porcupines have the peculiar habit of peeing at high velocity on prospective mates. Okay, Cupid! The only porcupine I see in Colorado amounts to a mound of wind-ruffled quills in the center of the double yellow lines on Route 14 between Fort Collins and Steamboat Springs.

We're searching hard beneath the branches, but last winter's woody pellets must have softened back to earth in summer rains. Twelve straight days of rain fell at the end of August just before I arrived at the ranch. The three of us walk around heads bowed to the ground, as Tom and I ask of a distant god, "Is this it? Is this it?" and "How about this?" Each time, Betsy says, "No," "No, not it," and "Sorry, no."

Rain, I write as it pours, cascading gutters and spouts from gray metal roofs all over the ranch. I scramble toward our guesthouse and some grub. A small figure in hooded red raincoat dashes in the corner of my eye and then ducks into the lean-to sunroom. I can't help thinking of *Don't Look Now*, a film by Nicolas Roeg adapted from a short story by Daphne du Maurier, in which a red-hooded figure leads a bereaved father into danger down a Venice side street. A red-hooded figure opens the door to the guesthouse, not expecting anyone. "Oh," she says. She's sharing patty-pan squash she's just picked; she drives out from Steamboat to garden. The power went out this morning early, before Betsy and Geoff left for a Nature Conservancy meeting in Boulder. I was reading Farrington Carpenter's autobiography between 3:00 and 4:00 A.M. when my bedside light blinked three times.

Aside from several copies of the Carpenter autobiography, stocked here for our edification concerning the ranch and providing us a certain slant on the history of the surrounding territory, there aren't a lot of books on the small bookshelf in the living room of our cottage. I cycle between two. Without hesitation my hand also falls on *Black Elk Speaks*, a book I read in college forty years ago, yet I feel differently about it now as I reread John Neihardt's words, which are neither a translation nor a whole-cloth creation. I feel drawn to the difficulty instead of repelled by it, simultaneously longing to read the exact words of Black Elk, a longing that this book has ignited, and also knowing that I cannot read his lost words. These words of Neihardt's are their replacement, and I begin to feel even more uncomfortable as I am once again mesmerized by the writer's language, unable to stop reading even as I am torn. Last night, I had to find my bookmark in the dark, close my book, and close my eyes. The power plant's glow from across the highway warmed the bedroom's darkness, an eerie recompense.

&

"The boys tried to hit the swallows with stones and it hurt me to see them doing this, but I could not tell them. I got a stone and acted as though I were going to throw, but I did not. The swallows seemed holy."

Waiting for cranes at the viewing station at the end of county road 69A, Tom and I scan the sky in all directions for twenty minutes or so. Layered in green fields speckled with marsh and cattails, four horses graze, two dappled or paint, a sorrel, maybe, and one Tom calls chestnut. Their four tails of different colors continually sweep and switch. In the farther distance a small number of stocky elk snort and erupt. Even from here their bunched musculature is clearly not that of skittish deer. Grayish-brown deer edge closer to us; we can almost see light through their pert mule ears. Three of the deer bound away, mounting tall grass on springs. I think of watching dolphins hurtle surf. Emerging from brush and bushes, doves like warm-up pitches. dart diagonals overhead. Waves of swallows push up and crest, then soar in spirals.

John, who owns this property, comes out and tells us the cranes will roost together in the shallow Yampa tonight. Standing in groups in the middle of the river on their big feet, heads tucked, they will be well situated to hear splashing predators: coyotes, from the howl of things. Sandhill crane threesomes dot and dash the sky, encoded in families. The young ones' heads remain gray-brown without the red patch adults wear on their faces. Not red feathers but bare red skin. Cranes lay a couple of eggs, and if chicks hatch maybe one survives. Both parents raise the young, working in concert. By migration time the offspring have grown nearly as large as their parents, up to five feet high for these greater sandhill cranes, with wingspans of six feet. Cranes can live twenty years and mate for life, staying with each other around the seasons. "So what do they do when one dies?" Tom asks. "Do they find another mate?" I have no idea. We'll have to look that up.

Sandhill cranes swoop in of a sudden in groups of five, signaling a family plus a pair, then multiples of three, or groupings of five and three. I study the sky for groups of youthful bachelors. Cranes don't mate until age four or five. Occasionally there's a group of four flying together; these lucky parents have two surviving chicks in tow. Cranes will famously eat anything and have a knack for survival, present in some variety in the fossil record for ten million years. These old souls arrive with a certain throaty blurt as they converge on the river from west and east. Close over our heads, too. John starts his count out loud, committing it to memory, saying his wife has entrusted him with the tally tonight and dashing out of sight for his clipboard. And then it is happening all around us, a rain of cranes too many to follow. Some fiercer shrieking blurts over our heads. "Cranes?" I exclaim, excited at another rush of wings, a large, close grouping. I point my camera and shoot as Tom says, "Geese." The difference is their size, neck carriage, and feet. I get a good shot of the geese.

The gray cranes fly low, necks and feet outstretched, to the Yampa, flashing white between the trees as they lower to the river and disappear. Earlier today it threatened rain. In the distance streaks of water issued from a cloud in that meteorological event called virga, when precipitation never reaches the ground. By the time tonight's crane arrivals are nearly complete and their bugles settling down in the air, the risen full moon sharpens its edges to hover and pierce. So close this *lune* could burst, each surface feature magnified. Supermoon doesn't fly like a plane or a bird but seems to float in place. Old oculus: it sees us, as a straggling pair of cranes crosses it in silhouette. This moon spies Sandhill cranes in the river and covers them with glisten.

"Every little thing is sent for something, and in that thing there should be happiness and the power to make happy. Like the grasses showing tender faces to each other, thus we should do, for this was the wish of the Grandfathers of the World."

Yesterday I found an amazing piece of bird artwork blown from a tree, constructed with bits of the red twine along with blue plastic strips, tumbleweed fiber, Easter grass from a child's basket, shreds of darker twine, and strands of hair. It was lined with dull white fur, or maybe thistle fuzz or dandelion fluff, and softly withering orange-colored leaves. Not a bad place to hail from. A robin might have built this nest. I've seen them here though they are duller than the Eastern sort. This deep oval pocket holds neither babies nor eggs but holds my attention. The intricacy and strength of its weave, even the small twigs still attached at its perimeters, snapped from the tree in this afternoon's gusting, are things from which I cannot look away, and things I can never thoroughly see. I touch the nest, its textures intact though fallen. I take it into my bedroom, my own nest, and keep studying the details: red twine, white fibers, blue strips of plastic, surely an American robin's nest, a mix of detritus that makes a haven, a home.

In the shadow of the power plant, we are observing cattle, hearing cattle moan and sometimes roar; we watch dogs scramble and tussle for belly rubs, and men moving calves and cows from lower to middle pasture; we watch horses in their stalls crunching alfalfa, dogs meandering purposefully after something only they can track by scent, barn cats pouncing on prey. Somewhere behind us perking up: Bears Ears and Hahn's Peak in the Elkhead Range. In front, the Union Pacific tracks cut the width of Carpenter Ranch, Highway 40 streams east-west with cars and trucks, and on the knoll above the highway rise the sullied stacks of the coal-fired power plant. Just to the west lies the airport, in concentric layers of what progress means to this pastureland along the riverbank. The first thing Farrington Carpenter did in 1926 upon leasing the John B. Dawson Ranch for his enlarging herd of Performance beef was install electric lights and indoor plumbing in the house, a cluster of five conjoined homestead cabins, and then he moved his wife and three children here from Oak Point.

Living in the shadow of the power plant, our electricity still blinks and wavers. When it went out we could see the plant blowing steam and sense the invisible particle pollution it produces. The scaffolding of a tall crane looms to one side of the plant, towering over the smoke stacks. The crane is good news, bringing 160 million dollars worth of emission reduction upgrades by the end of this year. In 2006, public emissions data showed that this plant spewed more than four million tons of CO_2 that together with other pollutants equaled six deaths and ten heart attacks by the reckoning of the Clean Air Task Force. The valuation on lost human life from this power plant's emissions equaled forty-six million dollars that same year.

Sometimes coal cars stop moving on the tracks, and the train switches engines and backs all the way to the plant while we wait at the crossing. At night, swirling trails of steam and soot shoot out of the plant's huge stacks into the sky, illuminated by orange lights. I think of that early German expressionist dystopian film, *Metropolis* by Fritz Lang, as I try to photograph the power plant at dusk. In my pictures, the plant always appears farther away. *Metropolis* represented mechanized life in the city—with human beings dwarfed by industry and underlings forever controlled by rich barons—in a way many take for granted these days when corporate entities have been extended the same legal protections as citizens. I cannot photograph the layers of pasture behind the ranch house towards the river and the power plant together; the power plant is far away from what I want to remember, removed from the howls of coyotes and the honking migration of cranes. I try to edit it out of my pictures, but most people mark the ranch and the nearby town of Hayden by its proximity. If you fly in to ski at Steamboat, you can't miss the plant on your way into town.

Scanning pastures behind the house with the power plant at my back, I see, on a ridge just over the river, something I don't want to see there or anywhere: a platform, a drilling rig for a fracking operation. And now there's no place I can look to avoid our hunger for energy and the metal that makes us crazy. I do a computer search of "fracking" and the first entry reads, "Fracking supports 110,000 Colorado jobs." I find no notice of the New Mexico or Oklahoma towns that are reporting a series of odd earthquakes, no mention of the science that confirms fracking caused them. I refine my search strategically and still the first header reads, "Fracking, a safe way to extract energy: the truth about fracking." This is not the whole truth about fracking. Just down the road is a coal ghost ranch. Land "reclaimed." But there's nothing there. The mining has continued, just moved farther out. Energy still drives the local economy. Coal comes out over there, fires up here, and the ski resort down the road experiences none of the grit in its eye.

Tourists come to the Yampa Valley Crane Festival in September to see the migration. Questing cranes, do these visitors also note the smokestacks and the fracking rig? Once nearly extinct, cranes have been hunted west of the Mississippi since 1961. I thought I could blot the power plant from view and from mind if I turned my back, while still wanting the Internet to run faster, the DVD to play smoothly; I want to keep track of correspondence, upload photographs from my phone, stay in the swim of things while I'm far from home. This splitting is who we are. This morning Tom points to the sky, to a low squat rainbow. We have to look toward the power plant side of things, into the particulates ruled "safe" for us to breathe, to see the spectrum fade.

"You have noticed that the truth comes into the world with two faces. One is sad with suffering, and the other laughs; but it is the same face, laughing or weeping."

ৎ

These days the shape of the riverbank has been changing fast. After the siphoning of irrigation ditches by multiple ranches and a subsequent rearrangement and dumping of silt, a fifty-foot stretch of this bank bordering the ranch has been undercut and eroded, and the river has grown a new island. The Yampa split around the island, wider and shallower than when fish slipped like slick messengers. Heavy equipment and engineers swarm; dump trucks and earthmovers roll through the river on tires the size of my car, shoring up and reshaping the bank with rock and earth from the now-vanished island, the river's momentum restored. A berm and repositioned rocks redirect the heavy current. An artist at the controls of the earthmover, the driver paints the new bank with transplanted grasses and shrubs removed from the island before it was scooped away. This soil and natural growth moved to the new bank with ginger swipes of the mechanical bucket will give the river a buffer zone. In little more than a week the river moves swifter and deeper in this place. Maybe roundtail chub will favor the waters here and leopard frogs again hop along the bank. There might even be a proper swimming hole for two-leggeds.

A scene of slaughter in the laundry room: three sprung traps filled with fat mice. I debate emptying the traditional wooden traps; I know how it's done but don't know where to dump the corpses. Something was mentioned about a shovel, but I'm not sure where to dig the hole. I close the laundry room door. Last night I finally turned on the heat in my room. In the kitchen of our cottage we hang our fruit and veggies high, stuff the refrigerator's door and shelves. Jim has posted traps around the perimeters of the kitchen and living room. This morning he hands me the assignment of reading "Undressing the Grizzly" by Terry Tempest Williams. In the titular scene a grizzly sow kills an elk calf in front of its mother, gorges herself and her two cubs with it, buries what's left for a later meal, and goes to sleep on the mound of slaughter. The elk mother watches all of this, vainly stomping her forelegs, only leaving after the burial. Williams interprets the wildness of the feminine in terms I recognize as shadow material for the unconscious male energies among us. The lone woman here in the guesthouse, with Tom and Jim, I leave the book on the kitchen table and slink back to my den without registering a kill.

☙

"It was the power from the outer world, and the visions and ceremonies had only made me like a hole through which the power could come to the two-leggeds. If I thought I was doing it myself, the hole would close up and no power could come through."

Crane count (unofficial): 301 and falling by the day. The young birds practice riding thermals in widening circles. Flocks fly slower in the fall to accommodate the ones just stretching their wings. Every day they get better at it. One of these days they will disappear and head on south and forget about the Yampa River until this time next year. A few birding couples straggle into Nature Conservancy headquarters to ask about the cranes. I direct them west to Route 69A. The heavy equipment for the restoration work near the ranch has discouraged the cranes from roosting, or perhaps they've always preferred the stretch of the river two doors down. I've only seen one crane pair flying over Carpenter Ranch, and those two usually arrive midday, skirting the trees and landing just to the west.

At the A1 Alcohol stop the clerk swiping my plastic says, "Virginia, you're far from home." I walk out with two representatives of Kentucky, two of California, one of Chile. This liquor store's a crossroads: the clerk just returned from a South Carolina camping trip.

An accidental chunk of stacked paper laser cut from the local newspaper falls onto the kitchen table in the shape of a cloud, scattering a mosaic of news in many thin layers. Cloud says, "House Bill 1398, the pot finance"; cloud says, "what is happening"; cloud says, "without first knowing"; cloud says, "Challenges for the next 100 years"; cloud says, "community, community, community"; cloud says, "75 acres of hops"; cloud says, "need to know"; cloud says, "resale market for iPhones"; cloud says, "strategists at Goldman Sachs"; cloud says, "loaded leather"; cloud says, "Time to sell?"; cloud says, "Must be able to lift 50 lbs."; cloud says, "lackluster performance"; cloud says, "Highlands Ranch $324,900" (pictured: a ranch house not an actual ranch).

Somewhere there's a newspaper with a doughnut hole in it, a space for something to fall through, an opening for a little light.

≈

Blackbirds and beavers at the sluice. *Chupping*, stuttering Brewer's black-birds, and Tom's squeaking brown shoe. "Show yourselves, beavers," commands Tom, and they do. We count four altogether after we trace one, then two, and another making wakes of wide V's swimming to their lodge. The sluice shines glassy, reflective, until the beavers tread through in diagonals, folding the water with waves of competing patterns. In the field, a small herd of elk with distinctive dark heads on thick necks moves toward us as we walk closer to the sluice gate. The elk seem to be converging upon us in an uncomfortable way, but then they redirect their energies to hurtle fences and train tracks to the front field nearer the highway. Each elk takes a turn, bounding fence then tracks and another fence. On the far side of the tracks, one by one they congregate, awaiting the last elk's leap before the herd turns its attention to grazing.

Observed by us, a beaver dives leaving concentric waves. Surfacing twenty yards farther along, only the prow of the beaver's head crowns the water that holds reflections of a darkening sky at day's end. Blackbirds fan out, landing on every barbed and taut electrical wire, even on train tracks. Dead tree limbs naturally receive the roosting blackbirds like dark leaves sprouting. The blackbirds weave into flight, taking off as one impulse running one body; a group is called a murder. What they're doing is almost a murmuration. Tom and I are still watching, not talking. Meanwhile beavers locate their lodge, a lump of sticks, a small knoll in the water, and a few geese flap toward the Yampa.

"Then I was standing on the highest mountain of them all, and round about beneath me was the whole hoop of the world. And while I stood there I saw more than I can tell and I understood more than I saw; for I was seeing in a sacred manner the shapes of all things in the spirit, and the shape of all shapes as they must live together like one being."

Hahn's Peak. Not the ghost town gold fever left behind but the mountain itself, a wimp of a peak for Colorado at under 11,000 feet. Nearly to its summit—an exaggerated rock pile in the shape of a cone, or more precisely a laccolith formed from the uplift of magma, cooled and splintered, sheltering a core of igneous rock—we scramble scree above the timberline. I lower my center of gravity, nearly squatting, and lighten my load by abandoning my pack after almost tipping backward from the incline. My head swims a bit. I am a creature come from the east, from living at only 1,000 feet. I'm sucking wind, which chills and whips us. There's nothing blocking the gusts up here but our shirts. The white and yellowish rock with iron striations varies from the size of a footstool to riprap and turns whiter and smaller, gravelly toward the top. Avoiding an ankle twist is the trick, and not looking down or out. I don't mention Hitchcock's *Vertigo*, but I'm thinking about the signature scene in which Jimmy Stewart spirals up the bell tower. There's nothing between us and the edge of this sky. Nicole calls it quits at just over 10,000 feet and backs down the trail to wait for the two old mountain goats to ascend another 839 feet. Rewarded with views of lakes and distant ranges, including Nipple Peak worth a giggle, Chris and I mug for each other's cameras and take video panoramas before crawling down.

Aspen coinage showers us as soon as we descend below the timberline. Romping downhill it's hard to stop one's knees with every step, hard to lean forward just enough and not lean backward too much, hard to stay steady. Loose soil and gravel soon connect with my worn soles like black ice, and I go skidding. Balancing the fall with a hip roll, I land on palms and one knee. Not much of a problem—a scatter of small rock brings a little seep of blood to my knee—but for the rest of our descent my shoes slip-slide. The walking stick Nicole hands me after giving me a hand up catches me more than twice.

Eight days later, Nicole and Chris are back home in Leadville, and I'm digging four little pieces of Hahn out of my palm with a needle: three form a constellation and one's a stubborn orb buried off by itself on the mound beneath my thumb. The removed black specks leave four shallow holes in my flesh.

Early October, about the time I'll be gone from here, sandhill crane hunting season begins east of the Continental Divide (and in Jackson County) in Colorado. For a couple of months you can bag three a day of this species brought back from the verge of extinction in the last sixty or so years. I'm wondering what one does with the carnage of three dead cranes—every single day.

James Brown Center of the Universe Bridge in Steamboat Springs. I feel good, and I demand to go there, while suspecting some kind of a scam. At the Depot art center I see a photograph from the bridge dedication ceremony in the 1990s. James Brown is there, climbing into or out of a vehicle in his signature tight pants, his car like a parade float. I ask the volunteer docent, "Where's the bridge? Is it far from here?"

Paint peeling, the bridge spans the Yampa. Beside the walkway, two dead garter snakes flattened by traffic have been churned to the side. Snake count—living: 4, dead: 2. Sleek garters all. "*Thamnophis elegans* occurs in a wide variety of habitats…populations in the Great Basin and Rocky Mountains are semiaquatic."

Below the James Brown Center of the Universe Bridge, a hand-drawn sign directs "ALL TUBERS to Exit" before the rocks. Is this the center of the universe? Is it? Is it? If it isn't, why not?

"Crazy Horse dreamed and went into the world where there is nothing but the spirits of all things. That is the real world that is behind this one, and everything we see here is something like a shadow from that world…. It was this vision that gave him his great power."

Mountain Time. Scrambling up from behind. After nearly two weeks I'm finally waking at eight instead of six in the morning. This morning Jim's offering on the kitchen table consists of a copied title page: "THE UTE WAR: A HISTORY OF THE WHITE RIVER MASSACRE AND THE PRIVATION AND HARDSHIPS OF THE CAPTIVE WHITE WOMEN AMONG THE HOSTILES ON GRAND RIVER—ILLUSTRATED."

I'm still rubbing sleep from my eyes, dealing with a new wrinkle in my flesh from the pillowcase that traces my right cheek. Such rancor before a cup of coffee. I reconsider my position among the savages—CAPTIVE WHITE WOMAN—as I make my breakfast, breaking two brown eggs into the skillet. My hardships and privations are few, yet I'm invited on this morn to consider the grand scheme of things in which men and unsubjugated women dare not share quarters without gendering the experience.

You with the bright male plumage have obviously confused my pale breasts for harmless. Here sleeps Artemis, no one's squaw: don't wake her. I might have to summon my inner Apache and scalp someone—or stomp and devour a baby elk in front of its mother. Only if I must.

I give up. You're going to have to two-step this one without me, lock your big ole horns with a shadow creature, perhaps an alien from New Mexico. I have too little time here in this life to engage with further shenanigans of the white man.

Reclaiming squaw. "Squaw is NOT an English word. It IS a phonetic rendering of an Algonkian word that does NOT translate to 'a woman's private parts.' The word 'squaw'—as 'esqua,' 'squa,' 'skwa,' 'skwe' and other variants—traditionally means the totality of being female, not just the female anatomy." If giving voice to the voiceless is all the morality a writer can hope to muster, let it start with reclaiming one word, and then another.

"Everything the Power of the World does is done in a circle. The sky is round, and I have heard that the earth is round like a ball, and so are all the stars. The wind, in its greatest power, whirls. Birds make their nests in circles, for theirs is the same religion as ours."

Birding at Yampa River Preserve with expert Ted Floyd, we begin modestly with an unspecified raptor too distant to name and a magpie. A Wilson's warbler says "blink"; it's a small yellow bird with a black head that cocks its tail like a wren. Then Audubon's warbler; orange-crown warbler *pshissing* when a predator's near; yellow-rumped warbler and sharp-shinned hawk, a small five-ounce raptor with a short squared-off tail, appear. Falcons enter in, which are not raptors but related to songbirds, and someone says, "Is that really true?" as in, doubtful. "You must have an old bird book," replies Ted, who's written a new one covering Colorado. Enter jays, blue and Steller's; and western scrub with the long tail; and sparrow, whose "disjointed song indicates a young male learning how to sing." Red-shafted flicker zings into the picture, a salmon-colored flash; and evening grosbeak, "flying pigs," noted for eating everything at the winter feeder; then American robin, four together of the sort that probably made the nest I found. Red-naped sapsucker, common here in summer months, tails a red-winged blackbird. Cedar waxwing dives into the sun with a "high shrill buzz"; no song has this bird, only a call. Black-capped chickadee comes hither, while belted kingfisher flies low toward the Yampa River. An American kestrel perches high, orangey with erect posture, "just at the right-hand side of that left dead clump," Ted says and points. "If you see a dead tree, leave it for the birds," he instructs.

One hour of immersion in the songs and names of birds, flashes and field glasses, just after and just before, and a sudden close-up ending as a warbler strikes a pose. The sun has climbed and the temperature risen from the thirties into the high forties during our birding. Over us, the gibbous moon does not fade from the morning sky.

A billboard in the shape of an American bison or buffalo crests a hill between Cheyenne and Fort Collins on I-25. Out of scale, this 2-D creature looms. I can't read any writing on the dark shape, don't know what the billboard's advertising or why it's there. I try not to survey the painted billboard too long, pulling my eyes back to the road; seventy-five miles per hour feels pretty fast in my old Forester. Every time we get a Republican governor in Virginia the speed limit goes up, but not this high. Out here it's a free-for-all since the federal fifty-five, imposed during the 1970s oil crisis, has long expired.

Where did all the buffalo go? Confronted with this silhouette/replica, I want a real American bison with a hump and a shaggy head. I wish I could get off this road and find a horse trail, even if my riding skill is suspect.

"The Wasichus [whites] did not kill them to eat; they killed them for the metal that makes them crazy, and they only took the hides to sell. Sometimes they did not even take the hides, only the tongues; and I have heard that fire-boats came down the Missouri River loaded with dried Bison tongues. You can see that the men who did this were crazy. ...they just killed and killed because they liked to do that. When we hunted bison, we killed only what we needed. And when there was nothing left but heaps of bones, the Wasichus came and gathered up even the bones and sold them."

Near the sign at the Congregationalist Church in Hayden, "Truth is Lived not Taught," I turn. At Wild Goose Coffee in the granary, Yuri, whose family emigrated from Macedonia, roasts the perfect macchiato though it's not on the menu (coffee, *black medicine*). Yuri reads my license tag out the window; "Virginia is a long way from here." I sip perfection, munch the breakfast burrito with salsa, listening to the same conversation churn over and over, its basic unit of measurement being the date when one's family crossed the Front Range and landed on the Western Slope: English, Swedes, Vermonters, Midwesterners, and someone's grandmother at two years of age traveled by covered wagon in 1909. We're all sitting here together, with our medicine.

On another day at the coffee shop a group of elk hunters takes all the chairs. As the hunters leave donning blaze-range vests, Yuri tells them the elk can't see very well and not to sneak up on them. "They aren't like the deer," he says. "Go ahead, call and make noise. The elk think it's more elk."

On the way out the door I shake hands with Yuri, wish him luck with the film he's making about shepherds west of Craig, and I finally meet a local character named Leigh, who wears dark glasses guarding her eyes. The former rancher turned artist-philosopher, dancer, and writer had a brain injury that rebooted her life. "Late-breaking savant," say the doctors. Jim has interviewed her and told me her talk is profound, like jazz, and once the words are said she can't repeat them; you have to listen quick, Jim says, catch the drift as it rolls by.

In his final years, Black Elk went on healing the sick of his people with his medicine power but regretted not having been able to use his great early vision to heal his nation. When he was still a young man he fought at Wounded Knee and witnessed the murder of women and children who had done nothing wrong but try to escape the massacre. Their bodies piled up in the gulch where they ran to hide, and the snow fell on them at the end of the battle. Only about a hundred braves of the four hundred Native peoples were able to fight the encircled soldiers with their cannon. The rest of the people were old and sick, women, children, and babies in arms. Black Elk saw a baby still sucking its dead mother's breast. He was able to scoop up another swaddled infant and rescue it.

"I did not know then how much was ended. When I look back now from this high hill of my old age, I can still see the butchered women and children lying heaped and scattered all along the crooked gulch as plain as when I saw them with eyes still young. And I can see that something else died there in the bloody mud, and was buried in the blizzard. A people's dream died there. It was a beautiful dream."

The Indispensable Condition

"This must be the place...."
—Talking Heads

In my teens and twenties I spent a lot of time making photographs and short films, which meant I spent a lot of time in the dark or staring into chemistry baths in red-lit rooms waiting for images to transform from invisible to visible, to rise up from stinking waters—of developer, stop bath, and fix. I stood in tiny, completely blacked-out rooms or closets unloading the canister from my camera by feel, cracking open other canisters and spooling that slinky of single lens reflex black and white 35mm film onto a reel, then sealing it against light so it could be developed. During this process, I seemed to take for granted that something would become visible, that I would finally be able to print from the negative, produce a positive image, dodge and burn it into being. Sometimes I wonder where all that faith came from.

Filmmaking in college required that I spend many hours in a small attic room of the theatre formerly occupied by pigeons, festooned with 16mm film. I wore white cotton gloves and used a hot splicer to edit pieces of raw footage into short films, which I had first drawn shot by shot on 3x5 notecards. Like prayer flags, pieces of film waved in loose coils from every ledge and surface in the attic room. It was a far cry from a dust-free environment but useful enough for college experiments. Most of my films involved soulful acting by friends under my direction, except for a few animation projects I shot from drawings or from images made using the sort of plump colorful felt I hadn't handled since grade school. One of my efforts was in the claymation vein of the Canadian Film Board I worshipped, my actor a clay elephant sculpted by hand and animated by shooting the elephant frame by frame as I poked and prodded. Floodlights melted my elephant into a sad blob as I shot it....

The whole painstaking process of filmmaking in those days prior to digital—before immediate access to video on one's phone in almost any light condition—from drawing storyboards to directing, shooting with balky hand-cranked cameras, and editing mechanically with a device called a Moviola, which I still own, was seemingly boring to anyone but me. It was also fairly expensive to buy and have a lab develop 16mm film, and hard to predict the quality of the outcome. I used my light meter like a Bible, but conditions were always uncertain. Reshooting for any reason raised the cost and labor considerably.

While editing in the attic room above the theatre balcony, it was necessary for me to kiss raw footage to identify the sticky emulsion side before connecting the shots with the hot splicer. When you think you have found a potsherd in the dirt you can identify it by taste. If you bring the shard to your lips and your kiss meets stickiness, you have really found part of a pot not a rock or a clump of soil. Beyond the age of three, how many portions of the world find our lips, I wonder. Mostly, it's food, drink, or smokes we taste, utilitarian up to a point. Occasionally our lips might meet surfaces like clay pots or film. If our lips meet other lips, we can know a lot of things quickly, like whether the stomach sinks and knees quake as gravity falls briefly away—or, if impatience sets in, we know we're not that into whomever. If we close our eyes and lose ourselves in a kiss, we know something about what's possible; we enter an inner landscape without words or logic, sensing what we might find by being with another in more ways than a kiss. Part of what we know will stay inarticulate, in the sensory, nonverbal realm. The most concrete of experience can lend itself to the ethereal. Kissing is a meeting place, a map, a shifting Mobius strip.

After kissing the film, I scraped the emulsion and painted a thin stripe of asphyxiating glue on the pieces to be joined before pressing down the splicer arm to seal the deal. Only an introvert could spend large chunks of college like this without any beer. I awoke in the attic room, stowed away after all-nighters slaving over the hot splicer, with pigeons scuttling the ledge, their cooing amplified against the window glass.

Mothlight by Stan Brakhage: an experimental film about all brokenness, all broken things, like pasted wings passing in quick succession as light blasts through, raising them from the dead. The projector light re-animates the dried, severed wings; they flicker and fly. While almost X-rayed, they arise. And they break—disintegrate, stuttered and torn, running through the projector, turning to dust, re-dying.

The first time I saw *Mothlight*, I didn't know how the film was made, that Brakhage attached real moth wings directly onto a strip of clear acetate:

a live thing—moving—made from dead wings. *Things have causes and not ends.* As I said, it was a way to see dead wings fly, but seeing them at first I couldn't know that they had died. It took my breath away. I was crying in film class that this art could reach into the dark, find and collect broken places, and shoot them through with light.

I wrote to Stan Brakhage some years later after publishing my first collection of poems, *Phenomena*, which contained a poem inspired by *Mothlight*. I think Brakhage was teaching in Boulder at the time, later commuting to Chicago to teach at the Art Institute. Just when I was sure my poetry had never reached him, I received a letter dated mid-August 1986, forwarded from my press as he had lost my address, and a book by him, *Metaphors on Vision*, filled with insights:

> To see is to retain—to behold. Elimination of all fear is in sight— which must be aimed for. Once vision may have been given—that which seems inherent in the infant's eye, an eye which reflects the loss of innocence more eloquently than any other human feature, an eye which soon learns to classify sights, an eye which mirrors the movement of the individual towards death by its increasing ability to see. But one can never go back, not even in imagination. After the loss of innocence, only the ultimate of knowledge can balance the wobbling pivot. Yet I suggest that there is a pursuit of knowledge foreign to language and founded upon visual communication, demanding a development of the optical mind, and dependent upon perception in the original and deepest sense of the word.

I can still open this hand-stapled book bound in cardboard covers and read any paragraph for inspiration, for affirmation of the power of art, for immersion in the reality and metaphor of sight.

In the accompanying letter, Brakhage wrote that he had had "one of the most difficult summers" of his life, and then he said, "I have endured a long period (about a decade) of worse-than-neglect—i.e. of active antagonism not only to my films but to the very idea of films-as-poetry, even to the continuance of Film itself. But you bring me close to the original impulse to making the film ('insists itself to be')." Seeing this small quotation from my poem transcribed in his handwriting, parenthetically enclosed, thrilled me, of course, because my art had spoken to his, even re-inspired the one who had inspired me. We kept in touch a bit, and thankfully, despite many illnesses physical and mental, he lived long enough to see his work appreciated again, studied, revived. At a celebration of his work, when he was frail from arthritis and strokes, I read several poems in tribute. I finally shook Stan's hand, but it was the light pouring through his work that had shaken and grounded me more than twenty years earlier, the work that continued, that insistence on being.

Luna moth attached to a branch outside the studio door in Bath County, Virginia, Nimrod Hall. In the cedar tree, hanging dead, a single luna moth with a torn scalloped wing clings to a twig (July 30, 2014). I remember dozens of lime luna moths pressed to the plate glass of my father's drugstore in Richlands, Virginia (circa 1967), in early fall. This vision of the surreal real will never leave me. I remember. I remember.

As I pack up the items stashed in my desk drawer, I stop to open my baby book, which appears to have been written all at once in my mother's hand, as though one day she finally filled in the blanks in one guilty rush. I stare at my light reddish-brown hair from my first haircut, a coil of hair preserved from 1958. I read a jotted note: "Brushed own teeth at a year and a half."

"Cast your bread upon the waters: thou shalt find it after many days" (Ecclesiastes 11:1). This concept is something like the slang understanding of karma: what goes around comes around. Good works and money given away will come back to you—eventually. I uncovered this phrase in Farrington Carpenter's autobiography, a lesson that had stuck with him from his mother's Bible, but I had jotted the idea for this section ("cast your bread..."), months before stepping foot on the Carpenter Ranch and reading his autobiography.

Is it right or wrong to work as hard as you can and simultaneously believe God will provide? I've never mastered the light touch in preparation, the full embrace of trust in Thee, who watches over the sparrow and surely over me. I heard "Be prepared" at a Girl Scout meeting. It stuck. On a bright sunny day, I might head into the woods carrying a flint and steel for fire starting, water tablets, a plastic poncho, a first-aid kit, and a signal mirror just in case I get lost. Is it wrong to obsess over stories of people struck by lightning? When someone very close tells you her father died by lightning strike on the beach where you both played as children, it says something about what it means to be prepared: preparation's not enough. But I can't believe we're supposed to give up on it, either.

The US Air Force has a program called SERE (Survival, Evasion, Resistance, Escape). There's no mistaking that the acronym evokes a quick cauterization of meat over a blazing fire. I feel like a graduate of the force because I survived my childhood. I neither take this for granted nor give myself much credit. Clearly supernatural powers were at work, at the very least a fiercely protective angel. Still, I wish the achievement of survival offered more than cold comfort. We're always supposed to be accomplishing more and more, something productive on the other side of survival, as though to be alive were not miracle enough. As my father took the curves ever faster on the Wilderness Road, I am here to testify to the miraculous.

I see a little trailer, classic teardrop tow camper, turquoise and white in the backyard of everyone's favorite cottage on Walnut Avenue. Mary, my realtor, says, "Did I ever tell you about moving into one of those with my mother and brother when I was four years old? Did I dream that? I asked my brother. A tornado came down the street one day and wiped out every trailer in the opposite row. Did I dream that? 'No,' my brother said. 'It happened. I was there, too.' That was the day we almost died."

"That was the day you lived," I say.

Over the summer, two of Mom's acquaintances in assisted living turn 100. Her highest form of praise is the outburst, "She can *walk!*" Mom elaborates, "She can't hear much unless you get right up in her face, but she can walk on her own." Walking is just about everything, as every elderly person knows. Falling (i.e., not walking) will land you in a facility faster than not remembering where you are. It's exactly what brought Mom here. Her most arthritic knee got infected, and she had to have surgery. A long recovery ensued with six weeks of intravenous antibiotics and rehab, which succeeded in getting her back on her feet but a lot more slowly than before and without the stamina to stand and cook her meals. All of that happened more than two years ago. These days she still walks daily in a use it or lose it campaign, but she uses a wheelchair to navigate distances.

Mom and I both know she doesn't want to live to be 100. I know it because in her next breath she tells me again, "I hope I don't live that long." I don't know how to respond to this except to take it into my gut. I get it. But in my gut still lives a little child hoping her parents will always be there. And one is already long gone. I went through a phase in young adolescence in which I was convinced my parents would die before morning. I never told them about my anxiety, just checked on them when they were sleeping to see if they were still breathing, as they must have done when I was a baby. After a few nights of watching their chests rise and fall my fear faded. Sleep overruled my fixation on their imminent deaths. I do love to sleep.

I nod back at Mom, thinking, "Don't go." How utterly selfish it is of me not to want her to leave, not to believe enough in life or afterlife to let her go. My faith could rest inside the mustard seed, even smaller than that seed, a fleck at its center, a microscopic, bitter whisper of faith. I hold Mom's hand, so warm in my hand, give a squeeze to her shoulders, say, "I love you." "And I love you so, so much," she replies. "You'll never know how much," she says, in a way that humbles me to the core.

The hardest thing about getting older (and older) appears to be that it becomes more (and more) difficult to hope for anything other than heaven. You hope you will keep what you have as far as functioning goes while you're alive, but you are surrounded by the alternative. You learn to live by losses. The people around you are slipping, and so are you. My mom often listens to TV sermons and reports that it was nice but "not for her." These sermons usually involve embedded or blatant messages about bucking up, changing your life for the better, using your talents to the fullest, or waiting on the Lord to deliver on His promises for your amazing destiny. Tom Magliozzi of "Car Talk" fame, who died from Alzheimer's disease, proclaimed, "It's better to travel in hope than arrive in despair." Mom stays faithful, prayerful, but hope, she thinks, demands more of a future. I note that she seems to agree with Simone Weil that hope "is faith in so far as it is oriented in Time towards the future. It is the supernatural equivalent of the resolve to persevere in the path of virtue." Mom perseveres in her virtue, chastises herself for faulting her maker's wisdom. "We just don't know why," Mom concedes. I say, "You got that right."

Jeremy Bernstein's *A Palette of Particles* reminds me that the dozens of elementary particles we predicate the universe upon—electrons, neutrons, protons, neutrinos, anti-particles, strange acting sub-particles, and quarks—are abstractions, and none can be seen with the eye or microscope. When CERN confirmed they'd found the building block, the Higgs boson, they depended on the Hadron Collider for evidence. Most of us will have to take their word for it. What physicists see are merely the microscopic tracks or trails of even the largest of the universe's smallest parts: "Only after a chain of theoretical arguments are we persuaded that what we are observing has been made by an invisible object." We have been through this before with the atom as it evolved from symbol to reality at the end of the nineteenth century. Its existence was hotly debated, and now we can serve up photographs: Say *cheese*, atom. This is unlikely to happen with the smaller particles. With smaller and smaller particulates, we must "accept their existence because it explains what we *do* see." What we can see: the limited world itself. And still we know that far more than half of the universe remains unaccounted for. This living is mostly unaccounted for, yet we persist in inhabiting its edges, edge habitation, transitional space where the seen meets the unseen. We seem to gravitate toward the borderlands within our small slice. It appears unlikely that God does not exist, for seldom can we find anything as unlikely as the world itself.

At the John Herron School of Art and Design in Indianapolis, late 1950s to early '60s, my brother-in-law, Jack, tells the story of a life model who bicycled through the snow trailing a cross as large as a person. The bottom of his wooden cross cut a line through the powder as he pedaled in a black full-length wool coat with high collar. When he modeled nude playing Easter Jesus, he held the cross behind him hitched to his arms, entangled in it. One day he crashed into the mercury lights with his cross and gas exploded into the studio, sending all of the students flying, fearing the cold war and alien invasion. But it was just their art school model Jesus banging his cross into the lights.

Get outta the boat, Peter. This parable has always bothered me. Let's just say I share a lot of sympathy for Peter, who sized up the churning waters, the waves licking his tiny wooden boat during the fourth watch of the night, and decided not to venture out in his sandals. Why wouldn't Jesus leave him alone? Why does Jesus always seem to choose the most unlikely folks, the ones afraid and, well, stuck in their logical minds, like Peter, like Thomas, like Nicodemus? Like Zacchaeus, the tax collector up a tree? Jesus was out there in the ocean, in the stormy night, walking toward the disciples' boat, and when they saw him they thought he must be a ghost. Not even close.

Peter called out in his excitement, "Lord, if it is you, command me to come to you on the water. And he said, 'Come!'" (Matthew 14:28). I figure Jesus could have asked for a volunteer but instead he answered Peter. I bet Peter was immediately sorry he had impulsively called out. There's no place to hide with this Jesus; he calls us just as we are. Peter stepped out into the water. He did fine until he lost his shit and started sinking. "Lord, save me!" Peter cried. Then Jesus told him, "If you can believe, all things are possible..." (Mark 9:23). I think this means that Peter's faith had to save him, not Jesus exactly. "[F]aith is the state of being grasped by an ultimate concern, and God is the name for the content of the concern," writes Paul Tillich. Jesus did not reach over and grab Peter to prevent him from drowning. He threw him faith, a flotation device. It did not inflate on its own; Peter had to hug his seat cushion and blow in the air.

All the sweet green icing.... Homeless in too much house no longer a home, I am beset in my small way, suffering from the elemental tussle over turf, waiting for the Lord of time to rescue me. "The gods of space who are strong in every human soul, in every race and nation, are afraid of the Lord of time, history, and justice, are afraid of His prophets and followers, and try to make them powerless and homeless," Tillich writes. If being brought close was the reason, here I am, Lord. This condo needs to sell, Lord; release me from my last life. Lead me out of Egypt. I'm ready, since I must go from here, to start over. I've got little St. Joe buried in the biggest ceramic pot. I'm ready to call in the Christian witch doctor to bless my four corners and lift the curse off this loft.

Throw down your crutches and walk. There was an old joke my aunt Glade loved to tell. Oh, how I miss the jokes she brought home from her career among hard-smoking men at the railroad, especially the one about a holiness-styled preacher and his healing powers. We'd all fall down and wet our pants when she started to tell the joke at our request. Yes, I said at the beginning. We'd heard it so many times her movements and intonations bore the semiotics of humor, cuing our laughter. That joke stayed almost as funny as the one about the tailored suit that didn't fit, a physical joke that required her to rise from the table and mimic the contortions of the main character, conned by the tailor to hitch one sleeve by his elbow, arch his back to straighten the hem, grasp one sleeve by the hand to shorten it, then scrunch his head into the collar, while the tailor assured him the suit was a perfect fit. "Look at that poor crippled man," someone said when the duped customer walked out of the store. And then the punch line: "But isn't he wearing a good-looking suit!"

This is what families used to do together before staring into individual illuminated screens was an option. We sat around the table stuffing our faces with non-organic food composed of gluten, meat, and dairy products, our vegetables drenched in butter, slightly sedated but fully present in the moment, and then someone told a family story plucked from previous generations, usually a story we'd heard many times before. Even the blessings were legendary. Uncle Kirt, champion of blessings, chanted one as long as a hymn in five verses passed down from his father, a white-bearded Brethren minister. Kirt had survived shrapnel in WWI, recovering in a French hospital and eventually winning a belated Purple Heart, but children all over the world could starve waiting for his blessing to resolve: "And as we partake of this food, give unto us the Bread of Life, go with us into the evening and through the night. This we ask in the name of Jesus, Amen." *Amen.*

What's faith got to do with it when there's a dose of morning stardom in the Internet teacup? There's no need for real effort or accomplishments, just a narcissistic rush of "likes" on shares from reciprocal fans and followers. "Home" means a stream of postings, random bits of data, personal photos intercut with news and ads and kittens. Cue old-fogey: it actually took me months to realize why I kept seeing postings from the same group of folks. I remember when you had to build a spaceship and fly to the moon, fight in a war, protest by marching in the streets, or get arrested to get your mug broadcast on a screen. Of course, some of what we saw was no doubt staged and all of it was highly selected and edited for the news, but hell, didn't we know that was part of the game?

The Ray-Ban Wayfarers I'm currently wearing in my Facebook portrait are more than thirty years old. I never threw them out after the Blues Brothers made them popular in the first of many revivals. Up until very recently I still owned every pair of glasses I'd worn since eighth grade algebra when I sat on the front row to see the problems the teacher wrote on the blackboard with actual white chalk. Dusting erasers for teachers meant you were teacher's pet. After being hit in the head with a basketball I never saw coming, I was refracted for nearsightedness and picked out my oval wire grannies. I wanted the round John Lennon signature frames, but it was the seventies by then and ovals were in. Circles would be back, of course, as would the giant frames I wore in the eighties, Ray-Bans among them. Upcycling. Each of these passing fads and trends, new-fangled things, came with the bright feeling of being cutting edge, of pushing aside the old folks who inevitably were out of style. How odd it has been for me to witness seventies parties with shag rugs and haircuts, polyester leisure suits, and John Denver taking us all home again. I have to wonder if I've ever moved at all. Galileo: *and still, it moves.*

Believe it to see it: seeing's believing. Frederick Buechner's entry on faith separates "Evil" from "Feet." Ever since I picked up *Wishful Thinking: A Theological ABC* in 1976, I've been smitten with this abecedarian. Under "Faith" I find a longish discussion for this little book of two whole pages, so I know I'm going to find everything I need. At any rate, I'm betting I will want to rip up my chapter on faith or at least retitle it after seeing what Buechner brings to the table. This probably holds true for any subject he's tackled. I dip into *Wishful Thinking* and wait for his rush of wisdom to wash over me. He writes about Abraham laughing in the face of God when God said his wife Sarah, aged one hundred, would be having a baby. "Abraham came close to knocking himself out—'fell on his face and laughed' (Genesis 17:17)." Sarah laughs, too, and God seems to share their gales when he tells them to name the baby Isaac. "Isaac in Hebrew means *laughter.*" Buechner follows this with "Faith is 'the assurance of things hoped for, the conviction of things not seen' (Hebrews 11:1). Faith is laughter at the promise of a child called laughter.... Faith dies, as it lives, laughing." Buechner imagines Jesus on the cross: it only hurts when I laugh. "Faith is not being sure where you're going but going anyway. A journey without maps." The opposite of faith is proof not doubt.

Let us proceed on faith, then, full of doubts. Laughing all the way. Doubt suits me; it's becoming. Busting a gut in anticipation of being caught in foolish happiness, in God's fool's paradise. I know I can try this, at least for a day, embracing doubt, abstaining from proof.

I escaped but too late...until the lights of Paris burn bright again (*The Third Man*, 1949). A love letter, a scrap of paper hidden in a clock and too easily found by an enemy. Scraps beneath love's table, let me gather them. All I thought I had is now scrapped, replaced by glimpses into the past when I was loved, I thought, but maybe not. Did I love enough? I ached. I said the words and meant them, yet what power did they ultimately hold? Love's spell is not permanent. Am I good enough even though love has cast me out, said "be gone"? *The Third Man*, Carol Reed's noir classic, haunted me as a film student. I flip on my TV and am surprised to see an iconic scene playing out. Shadows lengthen in the back streets and alleyways of Allied-occupied Vienna. Men are no more than shadow figures here; layers of betrayal cast larger hulking shapes that dwarf individual lives as they scurry from each other's grasp. A man eludes capture in a steam room where he must confront an assassin by roasting him, turning up the heat. They have to sweat it out together until one passes out or flees.

Post WWII, love's aspiration is not borderless, and time will tell: "until." The lights will return. Love, turf-ensnared, waiting for the Lord of time.

Home is where we tussle over chairs and rugs and dishes. I've been to this lost island before and said, "Never again." Home is where you bought the barrel lamps and white dinner plates and I the rugs and yet you want them, take them. Home is where the cat lives now because you brought her inside only to leave her in my care. Home is where I forgot the details and let my guard down. Home is where, ten years later, all receipts have gone missing.

The texts we studied in "Ideas of God" were authored by spiritual doctors and philosophers I've continued to read, Simone Weil a giant among them. To gain entry as a first-year college student I had to pass an interview with Dr. Gordh: "Are you troubled by different ideas of God?"

"No," I said, "I'm a Methodist."

Dr. Gordh laughed and said he knew just what I meant. I did not know why he was laughing.

Weil's pithy writings revel in contradictions not in reconciling them; she was a Jewish Christian thinker who refused to convert, contemporary of Sartre and Camus. Weil takes faith further into metaphysics and away from matter. She may have taken us even further into humility than Jesus: "We possess nothing in this world other than the power to say I. This is what we should yield up to God, and that is what we should destroy." Or this is what Jesus taught from the cross. Weil's ascetic, political life makes her words ring true: "All that man vainly desires here below is perfectly realized in God....

They alone will see God who prefer to recognize the truth and die, instead of living a long and happy existence in a state of illusion." Rough stuff, Weil. I open the index to "faith," lodged between "factory work" and "fascism": *To die for God is not a proof of faith in God. To die for an unknown and repulsive convict who is a victim of injustice, that is a proof of God.*

We have to die every day of our lives at the hands of Flannery O'Connor's misfit, knowing we are misfit to this world in trying to find or to be the good. O'Connor had it so right in her vision of heaven, "the last shall be first." Who am I without my discerning mind, my judgments and predicaments? I am finally overcome with a toothache so enormous I want my head to shatter, want someone to shuck it from my crawfish body: pinch da tail, suck da head. Head in the clouds sounds so serene. Take my head away, suck out this pain. One day past Claudia Emerson's funeral, great poet, friend, and colleague from years ago, and number eighteen has to be extracted, says the root canal doc, after she says what I already know: "I don't pull teeth." After all of this hullabaloo: root canal, three crown preps, each more painful than the last before finally getting the gold crown, and nearly constant pain from July to December. Beneath the surface lay a festering. As I drove to Richmond and back for Claudia's funeral, the tooth was brewing up a storm, and now it is my Vesuvius. Red and blistered, as if they have been burned up in a fire are my gums. Is it because I had so little faith in root canals to begin with? Have I jinxed my tooth?

Iktsuarpok—Inuit word for "the frustration of waiting for someone or something to show up." Iktsuarpok Godot. Iktsuarpok love. Ditto sex. Ditto companionship. Ditto. Ditto. Ditto. Pity party: ditto. So saccharin, that Tom Cruise movie and yet: Ditto. You had me at goodbye. Your goodbye has undone me.

In the eighteenth century tract, *A Key* to the Narragansett Indians, "Williams notes that one of the natives' most important gods resides in the Southwest. 'At the Southwest are their forefather's souls,' he writes. 'To the Southwest they go themselves when they die; from the Southwest came their corn and beans.' For these beliefs, Williams concludes that '[the Indians] are lost.'" Roger Williams means, arrogantly of course, that Native Americans are lost to his God.

About three hundred years later, speaking of depleted soils in New Mexico, Aldo Leopold wrote, "The same landscape was 'developed' once before, but with quite different results. The Pueblo Indians settled the Southwest in pre-Colombian times, but they happened *not* to be equipped with range livestock. Their civilization expired, but not because their land expired." If the Indians had worked livestock instead of only taking what they needed to survive, they could have depleted their land before first contact. Instead, their early culture regenerated without ending, overwritten in the same place, juxtaposing past with present. Gradually, they spread and rebuilt, following water after drought cycles, going with the promptings of shamans. The Southwest is one of the few places where I am found. An early experience of feeling unexpectedly at home in an alien environment sealed this into being as I sat, perched cliffside in 1975, scribbling in my journal above the Virgin River in Utah. Mystical events of dropping back into our skins cannot easily be explained. Where were we to begin with? We are so split and splintered, creatures beside ourselves, unused to unity even with ourselves. Only once in a while do we pull it all together, in moments other than sex, and feel whole through our bodies as a landscape dissolves into us and the electric pricking of the world becomes transparent.

Williams later expressed no enthusiasm for converting the Narragansett, as he believed only the elect were saved by the tenant of predestination. And of course he thought he knew the mind of God! God's select: All others pay cash and hope. Faith alone cannot save you. Try works, our pilgrim inheritance. By good works you demonstrate your godliness before others and exhibit the qualities that might stow you away in God's ship for the final crossing. Yet you toil always with the knowledge that good works in themselves are doomed; your name isn't necessarily on the manifest of the elect just because you are knocking yourself out. The road to heaven, how is it paved? Feelings of emptiness, I suspect, come from too much expectation about what our works can accomplish, but I'm not sure what else we should be doing here besides working and trying to get along with each other. Informed by a strong work ethic, thank you pilgrim hats, I try my best. At the same time, I try not to deplete the soil from which I sprang.

Driving home from the hospital I hear Depak Chopra on the radio talking with a religion professor from Rice University: "Faith is belief in what is unseen." A certainty without proof, I think. Mom's come down with the flu and took a spill in her room two days ago. I opened her door to bring something as mundane as toilet paper, and she was talking up at me from the floor. "Been here two hours," she said. "I'm so disgusted with myself. I can't get up. Couldn't reach the pull cords."

Next day she said from her ER bed, reflecting on her spill, "The world looks weird upside down." Yes it does, I think. Yes it does. Not much right side up these days, though. This morning at the hospital Mom tells me she has to stay another day. I say, "Good. They can take better care of you here."

"I'm so much trouble," Mom says. "Why am I still *here*? I can't do anything for anyone."

"Maybe you are doing something by being here," I say. "It's all a mystery."

"I know that," she says.

"Maybe a chaplain could talk with you better about this," I say, wriggling under the thumb of it all.

"Right," she says. "They don't know anything more than I do. I read the Bible. Nobody has any answers."

"You're probably right," I say. I open the Sunday paper. "Would you like to read *Parade*?"

"Yes," she says, "I would. The coffee was stone cold this morning."

"I'm sorry," I say.

"The eggs were hot."

"Good," I say. "At least that's something."

"That is my expectation. I may not be around to see it, but it will happen," Ruth Bader Ginsburg said when interviewed by Katie Couric about her thirty-five-page dissent in the Hobby Lobby case. All but one of her male colleagues ruled in favor of companies seeking to limit or deny medical coverage of contraception for women employees based on the religious beliefs of company owners, who are of course mostly men. But Ginsburg believes that in the future her dissent will become the law. For now, "The court, I fear, has ventured into a minefield." Let us wait on the Lord.

Georgia O'Keeffe was sixty-two when she moved to New Mexico full time. She described it as her spiritual home. In her garage on Ghost Ranch she painted her giant cloud paintings, climbing ladders and scaffolding when she was sixty-three. She lived another lifetime in red dirt and came to be identified with that place over every other.

Carol, fellow poet and friend, and I take the bus tour out into the landscape. Guides hold up pint-sized reproductions of iconic O'Keeffe paintings in front of the landscape features she interpreted and insist there was no abstraction, only a series of more closely cropped views. O'Keeffe refined reality, enlarged its details through successive reframing. A small band of us travels by bus to O'Keeffe's winter home in nearby Abiquiú. We skirt the perimeter of the garden, observing the irrigation furrows that made the garden possible, old water rights conveyed. In the west you cannot talk about land without talking about water rights, mineral rights. Rounding the walls outside O'Keeffe's living room, we peer in through protective glass, but we do not walk across the sensitive dirt floor. We take in O'Keeffe's stopped-in-time stock of dusty cans and utensils in pantry and kitchen, stand near the varnished plywood kitchen table. Her narrow bookcase stuffed with organic gardening and cookbooks was removed to the O'Keeffe museum in Santa Fe. When I visit there I take a picture of the bookcase, such a homely item to place in a museum, but we sometimes forget that her paintings were also made by hand.

Our last Abiquiú tour stop is O'Keeffe's studio. I have seen so many images of this space that it looks familiar and slightly unreal, as if we have stepped into a photograph of the studio not the studio itself. Parts of it function as a time capsule; its very starkness belies any messy process that might have taken place here. Adjacent to the studio is a small bedroom. O'Keeffe's last stand was in Santa Fe, but before that a nurse attended her here.

Querencia is both a physical place and the feeling or emotion that ties a person or people to that place. It is almost impossible for me not to think in binaries, like phenomenon and noumenon, and yet "*Querencia* is the place of return, the central space of desire, the root and urge to belong, life's destination and the most propitious place for death, the neighborhood where we first encounter light" (Enrique Lamadrid).

Home as belonging: Amelia says at breakfast on the last day of writer's camp, "I feel like I'm home." Knowledge in opposites: I did not feel at home when I tried going back to a denominational church; instead I felt oddly at sea with the mono-focus on Christ, the father God's punishing Old Testament admonishments, and the minister's condescending attitude, especially toward outlaws like me. What would it be like not to live under constant judgment, to rest easy in conformity, to pass? What does it feel like to pass but to feel un-synched with what you are passing as? After the service I was caught in a downpour so strong, lightning and thunder so jarring, that I parked beneath a bank drive-through as my car shook in the storm with giant radiating streaks cracking the sky. Dial forward twenty years: the same minister developed a whole ministry around resisting progressive measures in his denomination, his message being that homosexuality is the greatest sin. I want to say, kill me now, but I have trouble resting in the irony.

"This is a story I told myself about home and how I would find it." Home as self-portrait: *Tiny: A Story about Living Small* by Merete Mueller and Christopher Smith. The tiny house started as a summer project between jobs, but it took Chris and Merete more than a year to complete. The materials cost more than expected. Construction with a limited set of hands proved difficult. At the end of the documentary, Chris pulls his tiny house up to a plot of land he's bought and installs it with a portable solar-powered generator— a contemporary revision of western homesteading.

Farrington Carpenter and a friend applied to homestead stakes of 160 acres each and went into partnership in the Hereford business before Carpenter graduated Princeton. Carpenter was prompted into this strategy by observing the presence of a strong spring, necessary for irrigation and watering cattle in high desert land. Six months of tumbleweeds and six months of snow with little in northwestern Colorado between extremes. I turn a page of his memoir and see a photograph of Carpenter and his friend holding up wolf pelts as large as themselves, wolf tails trailing down, wolf heads at the level of the young men's smiles. In "Thinking Like a Mountain," Aldo Leopold describes his encounter with *green fire* as a young man; it happened at the moment he locked eyes with a dying wolf he'd eagerly taken down with a plural of wide sloppy shots. He arrived at the wolf in time to see wisdom flare in the old wolf's eyes, and many years later came to understand much more about the balance of predators and prey, the pyramid of creatures that's required to keep a mountain healthy. "In human history, we have learned (I hope) that the conqueror role is eventually self-defeating. ...implicit in such a role [is] that the conqueror know...what and who is valuable, and what and who is worthless, in community life. It always turns out that he knows neither." Leopold examines his own naïve dream of wildlife abundance minus predation to find that it was the wolves that kept the deer in check and were crucial to the health of the forest; without the wolves, hungry deer stripped the trees, overpopulated, and eventually died of starvation. Deer skulls littered the mountain and the soil eroded.

As a young man, Leopold, like Carpenter, grinned while holding up a wolf pelt. As a wiser man, he wept remembering *green fire*, the moment when his eyes met those of dying wolf wisdom.

Most people lost in the mountains will walk downhill, try to follow water, but in doing so they remove themselves from the long view that might save them. If they walk up to the top of the ridge instead, they'll have a better chance of rescue. In a misguided attempt to dial in profits without risk and bide time against losses, naïve investors will take a small guaranteed profit. Caught in riptides, many swimmers, especially if they are strong, will fight the currents, gulping seawater and perhaps drowning, rather than tack to safety. What's wrong with us?

Doing what feels good often leads to bankruptcy. Statistically speaking, a monkey can randomly select a group of stocks from the newspaper and do better than someone handpicking and selling on impulse. What makes us so stupid? Impatience, emotion, stubbornness against change, avoidance of discomfort, the very things we think will lead us to the prize. We think we have found love when we have found comfort, but love has other plans, lessons to lend. If love is my teacher, I've been no better than an average student. I have been loved raw at times. I'm hopeful that I've not yet failed love's final, and that I will, at least, recognize the exam when it comes.

The brown bull in the field here at Carpenter Ranch has begun to hold its ground against the larger, older black bull. We discuss this in the kitchen and ponder. Tom, a sculptor, seems to know more about cattle than I, which doesn't need to be much, since I know next to nothing but have a hunch that their gestation period is probably longer than a human's. It is slightly longer, from 270 to 295 days, and calves will pop out around the calendar, in winter barns as readily as in summer fields; let's say that when a pregnancy hits 285 days, the farmer might start pacing. On a drive back from Hayden, I passed a field of cows and saw a black calf in a face-plant, butt in the air. I thought it might be dead, but no, it was sleeping. Calves tire out and sleep where consciousness stops them.

There are so many things to know about cattle. At night when the silence of the ranch or the night coal train wakes me, I keep dipping into the autobiography of Farrington Carpenter, the man from Illinois who took over this land and developed the original "performance" Herford herd. I walk out to the nature trail along the Yampa River and snap a few pictures of slow-moving cattle below the Flat Tops to the south and an impossibly blue sky painted with clouds—clouds with ballooning edges of the sort children draw, clouds that equal clouds in a way that not all clouds do. Not even scratching the surface of things, I shoot frames of this picturesque late afternoon in a pause before the farmer arrives in his white truck, as he does every day, to open the green gate into the field. Wind shakes the cottonwood leaves, a silver rattle. As any picture will, my pictures turn the dimensional world into a flat plane meant to trick the eye. Limits are clearer here; my limits are quite clear, like the sky after a storm.

I stick a fork in my cold quartered potatoes, a dish I eat no matter where I am, drench them with homemade salad dressing, and cut some thyme into the bowl from the plant I've been tending on the balcony of the sixth floor loft. I've done my part; the thyme cuts green and tender with my scissors. I have an odd thought that maybe things are always exactly the way they are supposed to be. Before I can protest and cling to my agnostic position on glimpsing any form of certainty, I consider that this minute is my only home, nothing more or less. If I could only embrace it, as seconds tick by, and the next minute and the next. Isn't that what every guru says for us to do before breakfast? Such insipid advice has to be wrong, doesn't it? Dive into space without tether, one thoroughly conscious breath at a time. But there's a part of me so contrary I want to spit in the eye of Mindfulness. We make place by memory and story, so how can we ever wrap ourselves around life moment by moment without erasing everything that matters to us and losing who we are? Take one look at the tragedy of dementia or Alzheimer's and tell me what's so sacred about living in the moment? Do we not mourn the mind's unmooring?

Maybe places, like people, are better understood in their absence, the way some say we have to know God. Experiments in displacement taught Galileo how to measure volumes of water. He dropped a lot of bricks into his bathtub. And this absent life I've built for myself is still an authentic relationship to place if it at least proves the theory of displacement. In other words, this space is still a place, this house a home, even with only me in it, even with bricks in my bath. I can measure my love by the absence of my ex. I can tell you stories. In recollection, all of my lost places appear to be simultaneous, interwoven—childhood homes, family homeplace, marital ranch, granary west of Lexington, little red house in Catawba, transitional Victorian, love's condo—and all of their lessons learned only to be learned again. After nearly twenty years apart, Jonna and Gary will be married. "Where were you all this time?" she asks him. "Lying dormant," he says. Sometimes we must wait and wait before springing forward like a seedpod opening. Our living makes meaning of time even while time eludes us and collapses.

In memory and story we give meaning to places, but maybe we would be better off receiving meaning in the unmoored moment. I give myself a case of the chills because my phrase about how maybe this is just how it's supposed to be echoes something my father said before he died: "Things turn out the way they're supposed to." I think his version was more of the long view on disorder into form, the "all things work together for good" approach, but it takes faith to get to either place of meaning.

If my mother were a Mojave woman, she could look forward to an afterlife in the place of the spirits in the desert of Needles, her soul written "as charcoal strewn across the desert." She wouldn't have to fear being lost in something as vast as eternity, nor would she be having that recurring dream of slogging, never finding home. She'd be encouraged to check out her eternal stomping grounds before dying and get comfortable in the thought of where she'd be next. She could visit the property before buying the farm, so to speak. And when she bought the farm, she would introduce herself to the spirits there based on where she came from, because that would be so much more important than where she was or where she was going. She would still be herself and unafraid. Tell me a real story. Make reality with me.

From my loft, I can see the Norfolk Southern tracks extend in two directions. To the west the tracks bend out of the city along multiple bands of steel that sparkle at sundown like a river. Coal trains roll east and everything else chugs west. Eventually these sections of track connect with the Union Pacific rails I run beside on the Carpenter Ranch in northwestern Colorado. Tracks that enable iron horses to move, trains that finally removed the last Ute in Colorado to a thin strip of land. These tracks speak to me about lateral connections, as well as what's above and below. They draw a dividing line in my vision and make me consider what they connect—and what they separate, remove.

"I don't believe in God," my friend tells me with trepidation, awaiting judgment, as we sit beneath stars like white-hot matches at her home in Colorado. I don't protest. I don't know why, but I think believing is easier for some than others. I take no credit for the feeling in myself. My indispensable God is for others a cultural burden that can kick them out of their social circle if they are truthful about their disaffection or plain confusion. Still, this faith I'm going with is not in the gentle Jesus my childhood sensibilities embraced. I remember an oft-reproduced portrait of Jesus in my early childhood Sunday school classroom. Jesus the Shepherd: white male with curling brown hair and beard. I'm surprised they didn't shave him for the picture. "Jesus loves the little children" is all I could comprehend of what they said. Back then, like VBS (Vacation Bible School) every summer, it was enough. Now, I think it still sums up our childlike relationship to God, but is it enough?

"Life itself," says my friend who still prays for her children, "I have faith in life." I think that's enough to understand, more than enough to go on. The life force that has sent us to this orbiting speck, the contradictory force that makes us feel like things stand still as we know they are moving. The meaning is that we are here.

I look around and take in this loft as an amazing architectural space, which has become my solitary confinement cell. I try to lean back and really see this space, which was of course designed for another sort of life entirely. A life with two people in it, sharing the making of a home and sharing a home was the design-build plan, and what I must wrap my arms around is the fact of being alone here. Hug this new territory to my chest, this new unplanned reality, press it to myself, kiss it like a sister, and breathe it in and out, in and out. Every moment is turning out, every moment enough, and so I am lost, and so I am home.

I think I've lost my faith, the kind I had when I marched myself to church as a grade-schooler while singing a rousing hymn in my head—"For the Beauty of the Earth"—but maybe not the practical kind I had when I waited for photographs to swim up from the murk. My Jesus pen has run dry, but my

Mickey Mouse pencil has plenty of leads. I comb back and forth over my words like a metal detector. When you drive across Kansas twice, forward and backward, you'll know what I mean. The prairie grasses sway, the sky is ever evolving in shades of blue with clouds boiling up and wheeling, and all you have to do is keep driving, keep driving, keep rowing your car forward and adjusting your back, lumbar spine, in various, slightly torqued, ever subtly shifting positions. For part of the trip you might listen to Dawn Upshaw's *Angels Hide Their Faces*, as she sings Bach's Cantata BWV 199 and selections from Purcell, composed between 1659–1759. Especially Purcell's "I Attempt from Love's Sickness to Fly." And when you sleep, if you can, you'll still feel the road for the days and nights it takes to cross Kansas.

When my friend Joe tells me he's going home to Kansas to revisit the stark, solitary landscape, the fallow fields where he had his first church assignment, I know a little of what he means, though Kansas is not home to me. I've written and revised until I sweated so much I stuck to my chair and had to stick my head under the shower to revive from the fog of words. I act as if the writing matters enormously; fault me as a fanatic, a Looney Tune of the vibrant interior life. You can see all of my brush marks, my struggle to bring up the goods. This flawed surface is a confluence, a place where the invisible comes to light in a squint, shrinking back from the glare. When one chases tumbling words, one also finds rocks in the rapids, irksomeness in the foam and fluff. Like walls to live within, one can fully inhabit one's limits and know, "The beauty of this world is the mouth of a labyrinth. The unwary individual who on entering takes a few steps is soon unable to find the opening. Worn out, with nothing to eat or drink, in the dark...he walks on without knowing anything or hoping anything. ...For if he does not lose courage, if he goes on walking, it is absolutely certain that he will finally arrive at the center of the labyrinth. And there, God is waiting to eat him" (Weil and wail again). We must be eaten, and we must change. I must lose my life to find it. But leave me a red thread.

"Surrender Dorothy!" written in the sky, beneath which I cringe as I keep trying to click my heels home. I surrender. I don't know anything; I have nothing more. I fall on my knobby, scarred knees in surrender. This is where I've always belonged, on my knees. My condo homeland is being sold out from under me. This is what I hoped for, isn't it? Off the market, it has sold at last! I am released, to be homeless again. Filled with pain medicine, I sign on the line to sell the loft two days before the oral surgeon puts me out of my misery. My tooth, number eighteen, comes out in two large pieces, gold crown first and then what's left of the tooth. Twelve-year molar, last in line along my jawbone, crowned in gold just a couple of months ago, and gone pecan. This world is crazy, upside down, and feels as strange as Mother said. I make offers on various houses that are rejected, and after I've given up hope one contract is accepted. And so I am moving a few blocks west, back to my old neighborhood, back to the hood where I cut my community teeth, to a different block of the very same street, but this time I'm going alone. Soon my ex will follow, sort of, circling back to our old neighborhood, to a house we first looked at together more than ten years ago.

Western Virginia, how I revel in your twists and turns, your Wilderness Road of inscrutable head-scratching history of contradictory divided loyalties, a place where the Democratic party was the party of massive resistance and the Republican party decidedly that of Lincoln; a contested place where my old/new street is proudly named for a veteran of The Grand Army of the Republic, Robert Day, a union soldier who dug his way out of Libby prison in Richmond in 1865. And when he died at ninety-four after fifty years in Roanoke, he was one of its oldest residents.

The giant hole in my mouth heals as I pack and pack, as various friends help pack boxes and boxes of books and all my earthly possessions. In the midst of too much stuff, why does it feel like I have nothing? I have almost a mouthful of perfectly straight, white, unfilled original teeth. I did nothing wrong; still I search myself for blame. What I wouldn't give to get that one part of myself back, but there is nowhere to roll but forward and hope the raw hole heals.

On the last day before closing, my ex and I return to clean the final shreds of our lives from the loft. I realize she has inadvertently moved my little St. Joseph, buried in one of her heavy ceramic pots. He has definitely done his work here in bringing us a buyer, but I want him out of the dirt. We take a load of stuff to her warehouse studio, and barehanded she digs up St. Joe, her nails black and broken. Hands careful and rough. I watch her motions, wonder at all her hands can do. At my new house, a workman's Victorian, I immerse my saint in dishwater and wipe potting soil from his eyes. He sits drying on the kitchen windowsill only a few days before Rick, my former downtown neighbor, comes over for a scotch and leaves with St. Joseph sticking out of his shirt pocket. My little saint waves farewell, off on a new assignment, but I know he'll be back someday. We make brief eye contact. *It's okay, you can go*, my stare tells him. I'm already here.

Chapter Notes and Sources

1. *The Final Frontier*

The Incredible Shrinking Man (1957), directed by Jack Arnold, adapted from the Richard Matheson novel, *The Shrinking Man.*

Invasion of the Body Snatchers (1956), directed by Don Siegel, adapted from the Jack Finney sequel and novel, *The Body Snatchers.*

Star Trek (1966–69), original TV series created by Gene Roddenberry.

Nikki Giovanni, *Artemis* journal celebration, Taubman Museum of Art, Roanoke, Virginia, May 6, 2016. Giovanni discussed the untold stories of Appalachians who aided escaped slaves and suffered punishment from the state for their actions. Giovanni said several times, "These stories need to be told."

Tia Ghose, "Big Bang, Deflated? Universe May Have Had No Beginning," *Live Science*, 26 February 2015, http://www.livescience.com/49958-theory-no-big-bang.html.

Stephen W Hawking, *The Theory of Everything: the origin and fate of the universe* (Beverly Hills CA: Jaico Publishing House, 2006).

2. *Cleaning Out the House*

Sarah Susanka, *The Not So Big Life: Making Room for What Really Matters* (New York: Random House, 2007) 30.

Edgar Allan Poe, "The Fall of the House of Usher," first published in 1839.

Joshua Foer, *Moonwalking with Einstein* (New York: The Penguin Press, 2011).

Edward S. Casey, "How to Get from Space to Place in a Fairly Short Stretch of Time: Phenomenological Prolegomena," in *Senses of Place*, ed. Steven Feld and Keith Ha Basso (Santa Fe NM: School of American Research Advanced Seminar Series, 1996) 13–52: "A place is more an *event* than a *thing* to be assimilated to known categories. As an event, it is unique, idiolocal" (26); "…places not only *are*, they *happen*" (27).

Stewart Brand, *How Buildings Learn: What Happens after They're Built* (New York: Viking, 1994) 23.

James Elkins, *What Painting Is* (London: Routledge, 1999) 72: "Artists cannot begin in antiseptic abstraction, like philosophers with their notepads, or theoretical physicists at their blackboards. They have to begin *in medias res*, literally in the middle of things: oil, canvas, squalor. So it is the artist's task to discern somehow what is worth saving, and what can be transformed, and finally to crawl out of the morass."

Paula Gunn Allen, "She Is Us: Thought Woman and the Sustainability of Worship," in *Original Instructions: Indigenous Teachings for a Sustainable Future*, ed. Melissa K. Nelson (Rochester VT: Bear & Company, 2008) 138–44: "You always have to have a subject, you have to have a verb, and you have to have an object. That's the way language works. And you have to have a main theme. You have to have a single thread of thought. The minute I start doing that with native systems I start telling it wrong. Then I start creating misunderstandings" (139).

Jeannette Armstrong, "An Okanagan Worldview of Society," in *Original Instructions*, ed. Nelson, 66–74: "In our language, the word for our bodies contains the word for land, so when I say that word, it means that not only is my ability to think and to dream present in that word but the last part of that word also means 'the land.' ...I'm saying that I'm from the land and that my body is the land" (67).

3. *My Life in Snakes*
Max O'Rell, "My First Snake," *The Ladies' Home Journal* 11/9 (August 1894): 1.

4. *Neighborhood of Desire*
Elkins, *What Painting Is*, 147–67.

5. *Spirit House*
W. E. Trout, ed., *The Upper James Atlas* (Lexington VA: Virginia Canals and Navigation Society, 2001).
Allen, "She Is Us," 138.
Philip Sheldrake, *Spaces for the Sacred: Place, Memory, and Identity* (Baltimore MD: The Johns Hopkins University Press, 2001).
Jay Shafer, *The Small House Book* (Boyes Hot Springs CA: Tumbleweed Tiny House Company, 2009–10).

Alec Wilkinson, "Let's Get Small: The Rise of the Tiny-house Movement," *New Yorker Magazine*, 25 July 2011, 28–34.

6. *Dream House*
Sheldrake, *Spaces*, 3.
Anne Carson, *Autobiography of Red: A Novel in Verse* (New York: Vintage, 1999) 90: "…*Time isn't made of anything. It is an abstraction. / Just a meaning that we / impose upon motion. But I see*—he looked at his watch—*what you mean.*"
Susanka, *Not So Big Life*.
Marshall B. Davidson, ed., *Notable American Houses* (New York: American Heritage Publishing Co., Inc., 1971).
Mat Johnson, *Pym* (New York: Random House, 2011) 30.
Witold Rybczynski, *The Perfect House: A Journey with the Renaissance Master Andrea Palladio* (New York: Simon & Schuster, 2002).
Plato, *The Republic*, 380 BCE.
Richard Florida, *The Rise of the Creative Class* (New York: Basic Books, 2002).
Thomas Frank, *Listen, Liberal* (New York: Henry Holt and Company, 2016) 134–38.
"Too Many Books," Monticello website, https://www.monticello.org/site/research-and-collections/featured-letter-too-many-books.
Christopher Alexander et al., *A Pattern Language: Towns, Buildings, Construction* (New York: Oxford University Press, 1977).
Rina Swentzell, "A Pueblo Woman's Perspective on Chaco Canyon," in *In Search of Chaco: New Approaches to an Archeological Enigma*, ed. David Grant Noble (Santa Fe NM: School of American Research Press, 2004) 50.
Edgar Allan Poe, "The Cask of Amontillado," first published 1846.
Monticello's curatorial staff, website text, with reference to Kimball's *Jefferson Architect* and Jefferson's letters as noted, https://www.monticello.org.
John Brinckerhoff Jackson, "Jefferson, Thoreau, and After," in *Landscape in Sight: Looking at America*, ed. Helen Lefkowitz Horowitz (New Haven: Yale University Press, 1997) 175–82. See this essay for an engaging discussion of Thoreau and Jefferson as authors of our "distinct anti-urban tradition."
Brand, *Buildings*, 38–43.

Italo Calvino, "Lightness" in *Six Memos for the Next Millennium* (New York: Vintage Books, 1993). Calvino wrote similarly of Lucretius, *The Nature of Things*.

Italo Calvino, "Why Read the Classics?" in *The Uses of Literature* (New York: Harcourt Brace and Company, 1986) 125-134.

8. *Place as Language*

Reginald Gibbons, interview with William Goyen, *TriQuarterly* 56 (Winter 1983): 97–125.

Patricia L. Price, *Dry Place: Landscapes of Belonging and Exclusion* (Minneapolis: University of Minnesota Press, 2004).

Eudora Welty, "Place in Fiction," 1956, http://xroads.virginia.edu/%7EDRBR/welty.txt.

William Goyen, "Ghost and Flesh, Water and Dirt," in *Ghost and Flesh: Stories and Tales* (New York: Random House, 1952).

Goyen, "Precious Door," in *Had I a Hundred Mouths: New & Selected Stories, 1947–1983*, ed. Reginald Gibbons (New York: Clarkson N. Potter, 1985) 256, 271: "An artist transforms" (256). Goyen embraced gender fluidity most directly in his last novel, *Arcadio*, titled for an inter-sexed character.

David Rivard, "If You See Something, Say Something," *The American Poetry Review* 44/6 (November/December 1915): 13–17.

Martin Heidegger, *Poetry, Language, Thought* (New York: Harper Collins Publishers, Inc., 1971): "Poetic creation, which lets us dwell, is a kind of building."

10. *Natural Disasters*

George Plimpton, interview with Ernest Hemingway, *Paris Review* (May 1954).

Maggie Scarf, *Unfinished Business: Pressure Points in the Lives of Women* (New York: Ballantine Books, 1980).

Gurney Norman, *An American Vein: Critical Readings in Appalachian Literature* with Danny Miller and Sharon Hatfield (Athens, Ohio: Ohio University Press) 2005.

Alice Fulton, *Barely Composed: Poems* (New York and London: W.W. Norton & Company) 2015.

Paul C. Adams et al., eds, *Textures of Place* (Minneapolis: University of Minnesota Press, 2001).

Pete Spotts, "East Coast Earthquake: How Does a 5.9 tremblor happen in Virginia?" *The Christian Science Monitor*, 23 August 2011, http://www.csmonitor.com/USA/2011/0823/East-Coast-earthquake-How-does-a-5.9-temblor-happen-in-Virginia.

11. *Lost Places*

Martin Heidegger, "An Ontological Consideration of Place," quoted in Philip Sheldrake, *Spaces for the Sacred: Place, Memory, and Identity* (Baltimore: The Johns Hopkins University Press, 2001) 7.

Franz Kafka: "You do not need to leave your room. Remain sitting at your table and listen. Do not even listen, simply wait. Do not even wait, be quite still and solitary. The world will freely offer itself to you to be unmasked, it has no choice, it will roll in ecstasy at your feet." BrainyQuote.com, Xplore Inc, 2015, http://www.brainyquote.com/quotes/quotes/f/franzkafka134853.html.

Attributed to Goethe: "Until one is committed, there is hesitancy, the chance to draw back. Concerning all acts of initiative (and creation), there is one elementary truth, the ignorance of which kills countless ideas and splendid plans: that the moment one definitely commits oneself, then Providence moves too. All sorts of things occur to help one that would never otherwise have occurred. A whole stream of events issues from the decision, raising in one's favor all manner of unforeseen incidents and meetings and material assistance, which no man could have dreamed would have come his way. Whatever you can do, or dream you can do, begin it. Boldness has genius, power, and magic in it. Begin it now." For a full discussion of why this quotation is probably not from Goethe, see German Myth12, http://german.about.com/library/blgermyth12.htm.

Gertrude Stein, "What Are Masterpieces and Why There Are so Few of Them," 1936, http://www.sackett.net/SteinMasterpieces.pdf.

Casey Claybough, *Confederado: A Novel of the Americas* (Banner Elk NC: Ingalls Publishing Group, Inc., 2012) 209: "I gather you know the old army legend, that when the moon is up the restless souls of dead fighting men drift up out of the earth on moonbeams and wander the land. I never glimpsed such specters, though I knew there were far older bones beneath those of the dead we would bury the next day."

Simone Weil, *The Simone Weil Reader*, ed. George A. Panichas (New York: David McKay Company, Inc., 1977) xxxi.

J. N. McDonald and C. S. Bartlett, "An Associated Musk Ox Skeleton from Saltville, Virginia," *Journal of Vertebrate Paleontology* 2/45 (1983), https://en.wikipedia.org/wiki/Saltville_(archaeological_site).

Walter Brueggemann, in Sheldrake, *Spaces*, 7.

Nicole Gonzales and Monica Garske, "Man Finds 100-Year-Old Photos inside Antique Camera," NBC San Diego, 16 January 2013, http://www.nbcsandiego.com/news/local/Man-Finds-100-Year-Old-WWII-Photos-Inside-Antique-Camera-186569991.html.

Belden C. Lane, "Seeking a Sacred Center: Places and Themes in Native American Spirituality," in *Landscapes of the Sacred: Geography and Narrative in American Spirituality*, expanded ed. (Baltimore and London: The Johns Hopkins University Press, 2002) 73–93.

Paul C. Adams, "Peripatetic Imagery and Peripatetic Sense of Place," in *Textures of Place: Exploring Humanist Geographies* (Minneapolis and London: University of Minnesota Press, 2001) 186–206.

"Canyonlands: Geology," National Park Service, US Department of the Interior, Canyonlands Natural History Association, 2012, https://www.nps.gov/cany/learn/scienceresearch.htm.

Callimachus, Hymn 4 to Delos 311ff. (trans. Mair).

John Brinckerhoff Jackson, *A Sense of Place, A Sense of Time* (New Haven and London: Yale University Press, 1994).

Simone Weil, *Waiting for God* (New York: Harper & Row, 1951) 134–35: "It is only necessary to know that love is a direction and not a state of the soul. If one is unaware of this, one falls into despair at the first onslaught of affliction."

Colin Renfrew, "Chaco Canyon: A View from the Outside," in *In Search of Chaco: New Approaches to an Archaeological Enigma*, ed. David Grant Noble (Santa Fe NM: School of American Research Press, 2004) 101–06.

The National Historic Preservation Act of 1966, sec. 106.

Ruth Van Dyke, *The Chaco Experience: Landscape and Ideology at the Center Place* (Santa Fe NM: School for Advanced Research Press, 2007) 15, 17, 25.

W. James Judge, "Chaco's Golden Century," in *In Search of Chaco*, ed. Noble, 1–6.

Craig Childs, *House of Rain* (New York: Back Bay Books, Little Brown and Company, 2006). Childs follows the Anasazi trail down to the Mogollon Rim and the Rio Grande, all the way to Paquimé, Mexico, pointing even further into the Sierra Madre. He traces their movements to the forceful drip of natural springs that could predict the corn crop. This work also references Malta's (3000 BCE) Tarxien temples (44). For research concerning the mounds and alignments of Fajada Butte and the roads, see 34–36. For reference to unprecedented astronomical and geologic events during the 1054 supernova, Halley's comet, a volcanic eruption in Arizona, and a black spotted sun, see 40.

R. Gwinn Vivian and Bruce Hilpert, *The Chaco Handbook: An Encyclopedic Guide, Second Edition* (Salt Lake City: University of Utah Press, 2012).

Carrie C. Heitman and Stephen Plog, eds., *Chaco Revisited: New Research on the Prehistory of Chaco Canyon, New Mexico* (Tucson: University of Arizona Press, 2015).

For everything Chaco, see The Chaco Research Archive, http://www.chacoarchive.org/cra/.

12. *The Gorilla*

Paul Tillich, "The Struggle Between Time and Space," in *Theology of Culture*, ed. Robert C. Kimball (New York: Oxford UP, 1959) 30–39.

Ellen Meloy, *The Anthropology of Turquoise: Reflections on Desert, Sea, Stone, and Sky* (New York: Pantheon, 2002) 84–91.

Patricia L. Price, *Dry Place: Landscapes of Belonging and Exclusion* (Minneapolis: University of Minnesota Press, 2004) 53.

Albert Camus, *A Happy Death*, trans. Richard Howard (New York: Alfred A. Knopf, 1972).

Meg Grant, "A Fearless, Funny Finale," *AARP The Magazine* (Oct/Nov 2013): 60.

Mark 8:34-35 (NIV): "Then he called the crowd to him along with his disciples and said, 'If anyone would come after me, he must deny himself and take up his cross and follow me. For whoever wants to save his life will lose it, but whoever loses his life for me and for the gospel will save it.'"

Wm Moeck, "The Monster Reads Milton: *Paradise Lost*." exhibitions.nypl.org/biblion/outsiders/creation-remix/essay/essaymoeck.

"Claire Messud Discusses Albert Camus," National Public Radio, aired 7 November 2013.

Mary Wollstonecraft Shelley, *Frankenstein: or The Modern Prometheus*, 1818; 1831 ed.

Pema Chödrön, *When Things Fall Apart: Heart Advice for Difficult Times* (Boston: Shambhala, 1997) 65.

Meeri Kim, "Fossil Study: Native American's Ancestry Looked More Eurasian than East Asian," *The Washington Post*, 20 November 2013, https://www.washingtonpost.com/national/health-science/fossil-indicates-eurasian-roots-for-native-americans/2013/11/20/2777ac24-51fa-11e3-a7f0-b790929232e1_story.html?utm_term=.f415f20378f0.

13. *Invisible Cities*

Italo Calvino, *Invisible Cities* (New York: Harcourt Brace and Company, 1974) 48, 62.

Ralph Ellison, *Invisible Man* (New York: Random House 1952) 3: "I am invisible, understand, simply because people refuse to see me."

Kay Ryan, "Specks," *Poetry Foundation*, 3 September 2013, https://www.poetryfoundation.org/poetrymagazine/articles/detail/70041: "The poem is a space capsule in which impossible combinations feel casual. The body of the capsule is of necessity very strong to have broken out of gravity. It is the hard case for the frail experiments inside. Not frail in the wasted sense, but frail in the opposite sense: the brief visibility of the invisible."

Elizabeth A. Meese, *(Sem)erotics: Theorizing Lesbian: Writing* (New York: New York University Press 1992): "How, beginning in absence, erasure or negation, do we raise this alienated writing to an art?"

Joan E. Biren, *Eye to Eye: Portraits of Lesbians* by JEB (Tallahassee FL: Glad Hag Books, Naiad Press, 1979).

Yvonne Keller, *"Was It Right to Love Her Brother's Wife So Passionately?"* Lesbian Pulp Novels and U.S. Lesbian Identity, 1950–1965," *American Quarterly* 57/2 (2005): 385–410.

Jeanette Winterson, "The Semiotics of Sex," in *Art Objects: Essays on Ecstasy and Effrontery* (New York: Random House, Vintage International, 1997) 103–104.

Maggie Nelson, *The Argonauts* (Minneapolis: Graywolf Press, 2015) 49, 54.

Ellen Bosman, John P. Bradford, and Robert Ridinger, eds., *Gay, Lesbian, Bisexual, and Transgendered Literature: A Genre Guide* (Santa Barbara CA: Libraries Unlimited, 2008).

Anthony Pace, ed., *The Hal Saflieni Hypogeum, 4000BC–2000AD* (Malta: National Museum of Archaeology Museums Department, 2000).

Jeffrey Karloff, *Cavedigger*, documentary film, 2014.

Calvino, "Exactitude," in *Six Memos*, 74.

David Grant Noble, ed., *In Search of Chaco: New Approaches to an Archaeological Enigma* (Santa Fe NM: School of American Research Press, 2004).

Tia Ghose, "Oops Etruscan Warrior Prince Really a Princess," Yahoo News, 19 October 2013, http://news.yahoo.com/oops-etruscan-warrior-prince-really-princess-112810200.html.

Oscar Wilde, *The Picture of Dorian Gray*, 1890 edition (Brooklyn NY: Millenniem Publications, 2014) 16.

James Galvin, "Leap Year," in *X* (Port Townsend: Copper Canyon, 2003) 40.

Krista Humphrey, "GLBTQ Protagonists and the Mainstream Market," in *The Writer's Chronicle* 47/5 (2015): 106–18.

For readings in lesbian fiction and criticism, aside from the mainstream market concerns I have raised here, see "Women in Literature: Lesbian Fictions," a course designed by Professor Suzanne Raitt at University of Michigan, for a classic example: http://www.umich.edu/~womenstd/courses/315/readinglist.html.

14. *Hole through which the Power Could Come*

John G. Neihardt, *Black Elk Speaks: Being the Life Story of a Holy Man of the Oglala Sioux*, as told through John Neihardt (Lincoln and London: University of Nebraska Press, 1961) 43. Neihardt's *Black Elk Speaks* was originally published by William Morrow & Company in 1932. When I first read this text as a college student, I was persuaded by the poetry of the text to accept it as a container of certain truths worth saving. While my reading is no longer naïve, I still appreciate the book's message and music. The book has been celebrated by Black Elk's descendants and also derided as cultural appropriation.

Neihardt, 154.

D. H. Lawrence, "Reflections on the Death of a Porcupine," in *Reflections on the Death of a Porcupine* (Bloomington: Indiana University Press, 1963) 193–219. The best of this essay gives us wonderful close observations of porcupines. I found the essay after writing mine, and among other smart things you'll find this: "Logic is far too coarse to make the subtle distinctions life demands" (207). The essay ends, "We are losing vitality, owing to money and money standards. The torch in the hands of the moneyless will set our house on fire, and burn us to death, like sheep in a flaming corral." As for the objectionable prejudices also expressed in this essay, it is by Lawrence.

Neihardt, 77.

Colorado Cranes, http://coloradocranes.net/crane-facts/crane-faqs-and-facts/.

Neihardt, 193.

Farrington R. Carpenter, *Confessions of a Maverick: An Autobiography* (State Historical Society of Colorado, 1984) 206.

Neihardt, 189.

Terry Tempest Williams, "Undressing the Grizzly," in *An Unspoken Hunger: Stories from the Field* (New York: Pantheon, 1994).

Neihardt, 205.

Neihardt, 43.

Western garter snakes, https://en.wikipedia.org/wiki/Western_terrestrial_garter_snake.

Neihardt, 85.

Thomas F. Dawson and F. J. V. Skiff, *The Ute War: A History of the White River Massacre and the Privation and Hardships of Captive White Women Among the Hostiles on Grand River* (Denver: Tribune Publishing House, 1879).

Marge Bruchac, "Reclaiming the Word 'Squaw' in the Name of the Ancestors," November 1999, http://www.nativeweb.org/pages/legal/squaw.html. Bruchac continues, "During the contact period, northeastern American Indian people taught the colonists the word 'squaw,' and whites incorporated it into their speech. English observers described women's medicinal plants such as 'squaw vine' and 'squaw root,' among many others. There are rumors about the word's usage as an insult by French fur traders among western tribes who were not Algonkian speakers. But the insult was in the usage, not in the original word."

Neihardt, 195.

My notes from a bird walk with Ted Floyd, 8:30–9:30 A.M., September 13, 2014, near the Carpenter Ranch, Hayden CO.

Neihardt, 213.

Neihardt, 83: Coffee, "black medicine."

Neihardt, 270.

15. *The Indispensable Condition*
Simone Weil, *The Simone Weil Reader*, ed. George A. Panichas (New York: David McKay Company, Inc., 1977) 7: "Faith is the indispensable condition."

Mothlight, directed by Stan Brakhage, *By Brakhage: An Anthology*, DVD (1958; New York: The Criterion Collection, 2003).

Weil, *Reader*, xxxi: "The absence of finality is the reign of necessity. Things have causes and not ends."

Stan Brakhage, "Metaphors on Visions," in *Metaphors on Vision*, second edition, ed. P. Adams Sitney (New York: Film Culture, 1963, 1976) unnumbered pages.

Weil, *Reader*, 421.

Jeremy Bernstein, *A Palette of Particles* (London and Cambridge MA: The Belknap Press of Harvard University Press, 2013) 3–4.

Paul Tillich, "Time and Judaism," in *Theology of Culture*, ed. Robert C. Kimball (New York: Oxford, 1959) 39–40.

Frederick Buechner, *Wishful Thinking: A Theological ABC* (New York: Harper & Row, 1973) 24–26.

Weil, *Reader*, 428.

Meloy, *Anthropology*, 94.

Sarah Vowell, *The Wordy Shipmates* (New York: Riverhead Book, 2008) 159–60.

Aldo Leopold, "Thinking Like a Mountain" and "The Land Ethic," in *A Sand County Almanac* (New York: Ballantine Books, 1986) 137–40; 237–63. This book was originally published posthumously in 1949. Aldo Leopold died in 1948.

Natalie Diaz, "How to Sacrifice Your Brother Even when He Is an Aztec," *Pen America: A Journal for Writers and Readers* 18 (2015): 171–77.

Weil, *Reader*, 473–74.

Acknowledgments

Several of these chapters were published in earlier or different versions. My thanks to the editors of *Desire: Women Write about Wanting*, Seal Press, "Neighborhood of Desire"; *Shenandoah*, "My Life in Snakes"; *James Dickey Review*, "The Final Frontier"; *Still: The Journal*, "Natural Disasters"; and *Scoundrel Time*, "Dream House," an excerpt.

My thanks also to The Jackson Center for Creative Writing at Hollins University, the Virginia Center for the Creative Arts, Colorado Art Ranch, The Carpenter Ranch, Luke Vilelle for citation assistance, and to the following folks who read and reacted to drafts: Carrie Brown, Jonathan Callard, Douglas Jackson, Susan Jamison, Karen Osborn, and Rick and Kelly Sheridan.

Love and Scotties to Jonna McGraw.

About the Author

Born in the Appalachian Mountains of Virginia, Cathryn Hankla has authored more than a dozen books in multiple genres, including *Great Bear*, *Galaxies*, and *Fortune Teller Miracle Fish*. She is a professor in the Jackson Center for Creative Writing at Hollins University and Poetry editor of *The Hollins Critic*.

Learn more about her at www.cathrynhankla.com.